MW0061484

"This series promises to be spiritually and ʋ careful, solid biblical exegesis. The method and content of this work wiʟ ʋ helpful to teachers of the faith at different levels and will provide a reliable guide to people seeking to deepen their knowledge and thereby nourish their faith. I strongly recommend the Catholic Commentary on Sacred Scripture."

—**Cormac Cardinal Murphy-O'Connor**, Archbishop of Westminster

"This series richly provides what has for so long been lacking among contemporary scriptural commentaries. Its goal is to assist Catholic preachers and teachers, lay and ordained, in their ministry of the word. Moreover, it offers ordinary Catholics a scriptural resource that will enhance their understanding of God's word and thereby deepen their faith. Thus these commentaries, nourished on the faith of the Church and guided by scholarly wisdom, are both exegetically sound and spiritually nourishing."

—**Thomas G. Weinandy, OFM Cap**, United States Conference of Catholic Bishops

"This new Bible commentary series is based on solid scholarship and enriched by the church's long tradition of study and reflection. Enhanced by an attractive format, it provides an excellent resource for all who are serving in pastoral ministry and for the individual reader who searches the Scriptures for guidance in the Christian life."

—**Emil A. Wcela**, Auxiliary Bishop (retired), Diocese of Rockville Centre; past president, Catholic Biblical Association

"The CCSS is a long-awaited addition to Catholic books on the Bible. It is clearly written, sticks to the facts, treats the Bible as true history, and does not get lost in idle speculation and guesswork about the sources of the Gospels and the other books. Homilists will find here the pearl of great price and the treasure hidden in a field. Laypersons who are looking for a truly Catholic interpretation of the Bible will find it here. Those who want to know more about God's holy word in the Bible will want to purchase the whole set."

—**Kenneth Baker, SJ**, editor, *Homiletics and Pastoral Review*

"This new commentary series appears to me to be a gift of the Holy Spirit to Catholic clergy, religious, and laity at this historic moment. Pope Benedict has effectively announced the rebirth of Catholic biblical theology, bringing together

Scripture, tradition, and the teachings of the Church. This commentary reflects not only biblical criticism but also the unity of the Word of God as it applies to our lives. This is a marvelous and timely introduction."

—**Benedict J. Groeschel, CFR**, author and preacher

"This new commentary series should meet a need that has long been pointed out: a guide to Scripture that will be both historically responsible and shaped by the mind of the Church's tradition. It promises to be a milestone in the recovery of a distinctively Catholic approach to exegesis."

—**Aidan Nichols, OP**, University of Oxford; Fellow of Greyfriars, Oxford

"The Catholic Commentary on Sacred Scripture employs the Church's methodology of studying Sacred Scripture in a faithful, dynamic, and fruitful way. It is now the go-to resource that I can enthusiastically recommend to all my students."

—**Jeff Cavins**, founder, The Great Adventure Catholic Bible Study System

"Mary Healy and Peter S. Williamson, with Kevin Perrotta, have launched an exciting and most promising Catholic Commentary on Sacred Scripture. I plan to read and use it as a basis for preaching and am already profiting from the advanced segments."

—**Michael Scanlan, TOR**, Franciscan University of Steubenville

"The Catholic Commentary on Sacred Scripture fills a great void by giving us a serious, scholarly, and orthodox commentary series. These volumes are deep and profound yet lucid, easy to read, and rich with detail. This set will fill a great void for Scripture students of all ages, levels of education, and experience."

—**Steve Ray**, lecturer; author of the Bible Study Guides for Genesis and Acts; and writer, producer, and host of the ten-part documentary series *Footprints of God: The Story of Salvation from Abraham to Augustine*

"The Catholic Commentary on Sacred Scripture affords its readers a helpful guide for encountering the books of the Bible in a way that respects both the whole of Scripture and the givens of Catholic faith. Many will discover in the volumes of this collection wellsprings of spiritual refreshment."

—**Romanus Cessario, OP**, St John's Seminary

Ephesians

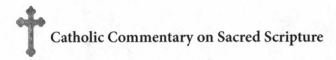 Catholic Commentary on Sacred Scripture

Ephesians

Peter S. Williamson

Baker Academic
a division of Baker Publishing Group
Grand Rapids, Michigan

Published by Baker Academic
a division of Baker Publishing Group
P.O. Box 6287, Grand Rapids, MI 49516-6287
www.bakeracademic.com

Printed in the United States of America

Library of Congress Cataloging-in-Publication Data

Williamson, Peter S.
    Ephesians / Peter S. Williamson ; Peter S. Williamson and Mary Healy, general editors.
      p.   cm. — (Catholic commentary on sacred scripture)
    Includes bibliographical references and index.
    ISBN 978-0-8010-3584-5 (pbk.)
     1. Bible. N. T. Ephesians—Commentaries. 2. Catholic Church—Doctrines. I. Healy, Mary,
  1964– II. Title.
  BS2695.53.W55 2009
  227'.5077—dc22   2009029385

Contents

Illustrations

Editors' Preface

The Church has always venerated the divine Scriptures just as she venerates the body of the Lord. . . . All the preaching of the Church should be nourished and governed by Sacred Scripture. For in the sacred books, the Father who is in heaven meets His children with great love and speaks with them; and the power and goodness in the word of God is so great that it stands as the support and energy of the Church, the strength of faith for her sons and daughters, the food of the soul, a pure and perennial fountain of spiritual life.

Second Vatican Council, Dei Verbum 21

Were not our hearts burning while he spoke to us on the way and opened the scriptures to us?

Luke 24:32

The Catholic Commentary on Sacred Scripture aims to serve the ministry of the Word of God in the life and mission of the Church. Since Vatican Council II, there has been an increasing hunger among Catholics to study Scripture in depth and in a way that reveals its relationship to liturgy, evangelization, catechesis, theology, and personal and communal life. This series responds to that desire by providing accessible yet substantive commentary on each book of the New Testament, drawn from the best of contemporary biblical scholarship as well as the rich treasury of the Church's tradition. These volumes seek to offer scholarship illumined by faith, in the conviction that the ultimate aim of biblical interpretation is to discover what God has revealed and is still speaking through the sacred text. Central to our approach are the principles taught by Vatican II: first, the use of historical and literary methods to discern what the biblical authors intended to express; second, prayerful theological reflection to understand the sacred text "in accord with the same Spirit by whom it was written"—that is, in light of the content and unity of the whole Scripture, the living tradition of the Church, and the analogy of faith (*Dei Verbum* 12).

The Catholic Commentary on Sacred Scripture is written for those engaged in or training for pastoral ministry and others interested in studying Scripture to understand their faith more deeply, to nourish their spiritual life, or to share the good news with others. With this in mind, the authors focus on the meaning of the text for faith and life rather than on the technical questions that occupy scholars, and they explain the Bible in ordinary language that does not require translation for preaching and catechesis. Although this series is written from the perspective of Catholic faith, its authors draw on the interpretation of Protestant and Orthodox scholars and hope these volumes will serve Christians of other traditions as well.

A variety of features are designed to make the commentary as useful as possible. Each volume includes the biblical text of the New American Bible (NAB), the translation approved for liturgical use in the United States. In order to serve readers who use other translations, the most important differences between the NAB and other widely used translations (RSV, NRSV, JB, NJB, and NIV) are noted and explained. Each unit of the biblical text is followed by a list of references to relevant Scripture passages, Catechism sections, and uses in the Roman Lectionary. The exegesis that follows aims to explain in a clear and engaging way the meaning of the text in its original historical context as well as its perennial meaning for Christians. Reflection and Application sections help readers apply Scripture to Christian life today by responding to questions that the text raises, offering spiritual interpretations drawn from Christian tradition or providing suggestions for the use of the biblical text in catechesis, preaching, or other forms of pastoral ministry.

Interspersed throughout the commentary are Biblical Background sidebars that present historical, literary, or theological information and Living Tradition sidebars that offer pertinent material from the postbiblical Christian tradition, including quotations from Church documents and from the writings of saints and Church Fathers. The Biblical Background sidebars are indicated by a photo of urns that were excavated in Jerusalem, signifying the importance of historical study in understanding the sacred text. The Living Tradition sidebars are indicated by an image of Eadwine, a twelfth-century monk and scribe, signifying the growth in the Church's understanding that comes by the grace of the Holy Spirit as believers study and ponder the word of God in their hearts (see *Dei Verbum* 8).

Maps and a Glossary are located in the back of each volume for easy reference. The glossary explains key terms from the biblical text as well as theological or exegetical terms, which are marked in the commentary with a cross (†). A list of Suggested Resources, an Index of Pastoral Topics, and an Index of Sidebars are included to enhance the usefulness of these volumes. Further resources, including questions for reflection or discussion, can be found at the series web site, www.CatholicScriptureCommentary.com.

It is our desire and prayer that these volumes be of service so that more and more "the word of the Lord may speed forward and be glorified" (2 Thess 3:1) in the Church and throughout the world.

Peter S. Williamson
Mary Healy
Kevin Perrotta

Note to Readers

The New American Bible differs slightly from most English translations in its verse numbering of the Psalms and certain other parts of the Old Testament. For instance, Ps 51:4 in the NAB is Ps 51:2 in other translations; Mal 3:19 in the NAB is Mal 4:1 in other translations. Readers who use different translations are advised to keep this in mind when looking up Old Testament cross-references given in the commentary.

Abbreviations

†	indicates that the definition of a term appears in the glossary
ACCS	Ancient Christian Commentary on Scripture
Catechism	*Catechism of the Catholic Church* (2nd Edition)
CCSS	Catholic Commentary on Sacred Scripture
DS	Denzinger-Schönmetzer, *Enchiridion Symbolorum, definitionum et declarationum de rebus fidei et morum* (1965)
ESV	English Standard Version
JB	Jerusalem Bible
Lectionary	*The Lectionary for Mass* (1998/2002 USA Edition)
LXX	†Septuagint
NAB	New American Bible
NIV	New International Version
NJB	New Jerusalem Bible
NRSV	New Revised Standard Version
NT	New Testament
OT	Old Testament
RSV	Revised Standard Version
TOB	John Paul II, *Man and Woman He Created Them: A Theology of the Body*, trans. Michael Waldstein (Boston: Pauline Books, 2006). The pope's distinctive use of quotation marks and italics is followed in every citation.

Books of the Old Testament

Gen	Genesis	Tob	Tobit	Ezek	Ezekiel
Exod	Exodus	Jdt	Judith	Dan	Daniel
Lev	Leviticus	Esther	Esther	Hosea	Hosea
Num	Numbers	1 Macc	1 Maccabees	Joel	Joel
Deut	Deuteronomy	2 Macc	2 Maccabees	Amos	Amos
Josh	Joshua	Job	Job	Obad	Obadiah
Judg	Judges	Ps	Psalms	Jon	Jonah
Ruth	Ruth	Prov	Proverbs	Mic	Micah
1 Sam	1 Samuel	Eccles	Ecclesiastes	Nah	Nahum
2 Sam	2 Samuel	Song	Song of Songs	Hab	Habakkuk
1 Kings	1 Kings	Wis	Wisdom	Zeph	Zephaniah
2 Kings	2 Kings	Sir	Sirach	Hag	Haggai
1 Chron	1 Chronicles	Isa	Isaiah	Zech	Zechariah
2 Chron	2 Chronicles	Jer	Jeremiah	Mal	Malachi
Ezra	Ezra	Lam	Lamentations		
Neh	Nehemiah	Bar	Baruch		

Books of the New Testament

Matt	Matthew	1 Tim	1 Timothy
Mark	Mark	2 Tim	2 Timothy
Luke	Luke	Titus	Titus
John	John	Philem	Philemon
Acts	Acts of the Apostles	Heb	Hebrews
Rom	Romans	James	James
1 Cor	1 Corinthians	1 Pet	1 Peter
2 Cor	2 Corinthians	2 Pet	2 Peter
Gal	Galatians	1 John	1 John
Eph	Ephesians	2 John	2 John
Phil	Philippians	3 John	3 John
Col	Colossians	Jude	Jude
1 Thess	1 Thessalonians	Rev	Revelation
2 Thess	2 Thessalonians		

Introduction

The Epistle to the Ephesians is the most eloquent of the letters attributed to St. Paul and contains some of the richest theological writing in the Christian tradition. For nearly two thousand years Christians have thrilled to read its inspiring prayers, its awesome depiction of Christ as the head of creation and the Church, its narrative of grace and salvation through Jesus' death and resurrection, its proclamation of the oneness in Christ of †Gentile and Jew in the sevenfold unity of the Church, its lofty ethical invitation to "be imitators of God, as beloved children" (5:1), and its lyrical comparison of marriage to the spousal relationship between Christ and the Church. Many of the themes from Paul's earlier writings are recapitulated in Ephesians and expressed in a highly polished manner, in contrast to the rough and ready style that characterizes the earlier Galatian and Corinthian letters. The impact of Ephesians has been immense. According to Raymond Brown, "Among the Pauline writings only Romans can match Ephesians as a candidate for exercising the most influence on Christian thought and spirituality."[1]

The Author and His Circumstances

Although no writer of the early Church expressed any doubt that the apostle Paul wrote Ephesians, during the last two centuries scholars have raised reasonable questions about whether Ephesians came directly from Paul.[2] They point

---

1. Raymond E. Brown, *Introduction to the New Testament* (New York: Doubleday, 1997), 620.
2. Similar questions have been raised about other letters attributed to Paul. The current status of the discussion is that the authorship of seven Pauline letters—Romans, 1–2 Corinthians, Galatians, Philippians, 1 Thessalonians, and Philemon—is †undisputed (see undisputed letters). The authorship

to differences in vocabulary, style, and theology between Ephesians and earlier letters and to similarities with Colossians that suggest a later author may have imitated and adapted that letter. These scholars suggest that an anonymous disciple wrote Ephesians fifteen to twenty-five years after Paul's death in order to recall his teaching and apply it to new circumstances. If that is the case, all we know about the author is that he knew Paul's writings very well, especially Colossians, Romans, and 1 Corinthians, and that he was a brilliant theologian who did not hesitate to develop Paul's ideas in bold new ways.

Other scholars, however, do not regard these considerations as sufficient to overturn the judgment of the early Church. The distinctive vocabulary and style of Ephesians can be accounted for by Paul's literary versatility or by his use of an amanuensis, a skilled secretary, to put his thoughts in writing—a common practice in Paul's day. Several of the letters attributed to Paul show the work of a secretary (Rom 16:22; 1 Cor 16:21; Gal 6:11; 2 Thess 3:17), although it is not clear whether this role was confined to receiving dictation or was more extensive. The theological development of Ephesians can be credited as easily to Paul himself as to a later disciple. The similarities and differences to Colossians could well be due to Paul writing both letters around the same time but for different purposes. The arguments for and against Paul's authorship of Ephesians are complex. A summary of the discussion and the reasons I am persuaded that the apostle Paul is the author is available on our series website at www.CatholicScriptureCommentary.com under "Reader Resources."

From the perspective of Christian faith, whether or not Paul wrote Ephesians does not change its status as inspired Scripture or make a great difference in how it is interpreted, provided one accepts the underlying unity of Sacred Scripture. According to Catholic exegete Frank Matera, "Whether or not Ephesians was written by Paul, the fundamental task of New Testament theologians in regard to this letter remains essentially the same: to identify and clarify the letter's theology, noting and explaining, when possible, its theological development in comparison with other Pauline writings."[3] Following the convention of the Catholic Commentary on Sacred Scripture, this volume will refer to Paul as the author of Ephesians since this is the way the letter presents its author and the way the lectionary introduces readings from Ephesians. This volume will also draw freely on what we know about the life and ministry of Paul from the Acts of the Apostles, since our goal is to understand Paul as the New Testament

---

of six letters—Ephesians, Colossians, 2 Thessalonians, 1–2 Timothy, and Titus—remains a matter of scholarly debate.

3. Frank J. Matera, *New Testament Theology: Exploring Unity and Diversity* (Louisville: Westminster John Knox, 2007), 228.

presents him to us. It is clear that the author of Ephesians intends his readers to understand themselves as addressed by the apostle Paul, so we will not err if we attend to Paul as he is depicted in the letter, as "a prisoner for the Lord" (4:1).

During his imprisonments Paul fulfilled his mission both by speaking (e.g., Acts 28:30–31) and by writing (Philippians, Colossians, Philemon, and 2 Timothy were also written from prison). As a prisoner Paul had the opportunity to preach to the soldiers who guarded him (Phil 1:13), to the judges who heard his case (Acts 24–26; 2 Tim 4:17), and to visitors who came to see him (Acts 28:23–31). Acts reports two extended periods Paul spent in legal confinement, first in jail in Caesarea (Acts 23:33–26:32) and then under house arrest in Rome (Acts 28:11–31). In contrast to 2 Tim 4:6 and Phil 1:20 and 2:17, Ephesians does not indicate that Paul feels he is in imminent mortal danger. Rather, the tone is tranquil, which fits both periods of imprisonment reported in Acts, perhaps especially the two years of house arrest in Rome mentioned in Acts 28:30–31, commonly dated between AD 61 and 63. Ephesians 6:20 depicts Paul as chained, probably handcuffed to a Roman soldier, the customary treatment of a prisoner in military custody. Even though prisoners could experience a greater freedom of activity when in military custody than in other forms of Roman imprisonment,[4] they were real prisoners, bearing the shame of being under criminal prosecution. This entailed real suffering and restriction, and everyone knew it. Rather than pass over the matter in embarrassed silence, Paul calls attention to his imprisonment for Christ, inviting his readers to pay close attention to his word on account of what he is suffering: "I, then, a prisoner for the Lord, urge you to live in a manner worthy of the call you have received" (4:1). Indeed, Paul is imprisoned not only on behalf of Christ but also on behalf of his Gentile readers (3:1, 13), a fact that would have lent his words a particular poignancy.

Paul in Ephesus

The Acts of the Apostles recounts that Paul's mission in Ephesus lasted about three years (20:31), longer than anywhere else. The investment in Ephesus was strategic, as it was the fourth largest city in the Roman Empire, numbering about two hundred thousand, and was a center of commerce. It was the capital of the Roman province of Asia (the western part of modern-day Turkey) and was famous for its large and beautiful temple to the goddess Artemis, an edifice

---

4. A helpful description of the categories of Roman prisoners and their conditions is available in Richard J. Cassidy, *Paul in Chains* (New York: Crossroad, 2001), 36–54.

considered one of the seven wonders of the ancient world. Besides worshiping Artemis, the Ephesians had temples to the goddess Roma, to the divine Caesar, and to an assortment of other deities, and they were known for the practice of magic.

Jews also had a significant presence in the city. According to the first-century Jewish historian Josephus, a Jewish community had existed in Ephesus for more than three hundred years, and many Jews enjoyed the status of citizens of the city. They were allowed to practice their religion and to send offerings to the temple in Jerusalem and were exempt from military service because the religious and dietary practices of army life conflicted with Jewish law. It is quite likely that Jews comprised 10 percent of the population of Ephesus, which would put their number at around twenty thousand.

Acts tells us quite a bit about Paul's apostolic ministry in Ephesus (18:19–20:1; 20:17–38), even though the account is necessarily brief and selective.[5] Paul began his preaching in Ephesus at a Jewish synagogue, as was his custom. Although some Jews accepted the †gospel and were baptized, three months later, when the opposition became fierce, he withdrew with those who had become believers to the lecture hall of Tyrannus (Acts 19:9), where he continued his preaching and teaching ministry for two more years. Acts reports an extraordinarily successful ministry "with the result that all the inhabitants of the province of Asia heard the word of the Lord, Jews and Greeks alike" (Acts 19:10). So successful was Paul's ministry that believers who had previously practiced magic burned their books, which, we are told, had a value of fifty thousand silver drachmas (Acts 19:19). The silver drachma was the typical daily wage of a laborer, so this amount suggests the conversion either of a large number of practitioners of magic or of some very wealthy ones. The effects of the church's growth began to be felt in the wider community. Demetrius, a leader of the guild of silversmiths who made miniature shrines of the temple of Artemis, started a riot against Paul because of the threat his preaching posed to the sale of shrines and to the cult of Artemis (Acts 19:23–41). Paul left Ephesus shortly thereafter. Although Acts does not report it, Paul's letters indicate he suffered more persecution in Ephesus and possibly was imprisoned there for a while (1 Cor 15:32; 2 Cor 1:8). It is likely that after his three-year mission between AD 54 and 57, Paul

---

5. Although some twentieth-century scholars questioned the historical reliability of Acts, subsequent study has led to a more positive assessment. Joseph Fitzmyer typifies recent appraisals in accepting Acts' account of the ministry of Paul as reliable unless Paul's own writings or other strong evidence can be shown to contradict it. See Joseph Fitzmyer, *The Acts of the Apostles*, Anchor Bible (New York: Doubleday, 1998), 124–27; Joseph A. Fitzmyer, "Paul," in *New Jerome Biblical Commentary*, ed. Raymond Brown et al. (Englewood Cliffs, NJ: Prentice Hall, 1990), 1330–32.

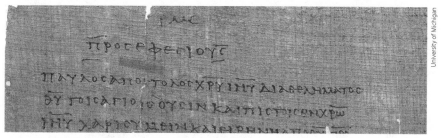

Fig. 1. Superscript (heading) and first verse from first page of the Letter to the Ephesians in Papyrus 46, the oldest manuscript collection of Paul's letters, dated about 200 AD.

left behind a number of house churches consisting of some Jews and many Gentiles, both in Ephesus and in the surrounding region.

Original Readers

The most likely hypothesis is that the Letter to the Ephesians was intended to circulate both among the house churches of Ephesus and among the other nascent churches of Asia. Some of the earliest manuscripts of Ephesians omit the words "in Ephesus" in 1:1.[6] In 1:15, Paul mentions "hearing" about the faith and love of his readers and in 3:2 remarks, "if, as I suppose, you have heard of the stewardship of God's grace that was given to me." These statements suggest a lack of personal acquaintance between Paul and some of the recipients of the letter, which is not surprising in a letter written after several years' absence to a large metropolitan community at the center of a region with a growing Christian population.[7] The most ancient manuscript of Ephesians, Papyrus 46 dating from about AD 200 and lacking the words "in Ephesus" in 1:1, includes a header at the top of the page (see fig. 1) that reads, PROS EPHESIOUS, "to the Ephesians," indicating that the historical tradition linking the letter to the church of Ephesus was already well established.

The content of Ephesians sheds some light on how the author perceived his audience. The most obvious fact is that many among them are Gentile Christians, since they are distinguished from Jewish Christians like Paul (1:11–13; 2:1–3). Gentiles are directly addressed in 2:11 and 3:1 and seem to be the main group the author is addressing. If we assume that the letter's prayers and exhortations

6. The NAB puts this phrase in brackets to indicate that it is missing in some ancient manuscripts of Ephesians and was either dropped from or added to the original.

7. The absence of individual greetings of community members by name in Ephesians is not significant. Paul does not mention many individuals by name in 2 Corinthians, even though he lived there for a year and a half, nor does he mention individuals in Galatians or 1–2 Thessalonians, although it is clear that he has a very close relationship with those churches. In fact, Paul greets the largest number of persons by name in letters written to churches he had not yet visited, i.e., Romans and Colossians.

reflect Paul's perception of his readers, and if we add the information we have from Acts and other ancient sources, we can sketch the following profile of the church of Ephesus and the surrounding region. These Christians are relatively new to their faith and need to be strengthened in their Christian identity. Although they have been baptized and catechized (2:5; 4:20–24; 5:8, 26), they need a deeper awareness and appreciation of the benefits that are theirs through their relationship with Christ. Because they live in a society that worships pagan gods and uses magic to manipulate various spiritual powers (Acts 19:19), they need to grasp Christ's absolute supremacy. It is important that they understand the exalted position and spiritual authority that belongs to believers and to the Church as a whole as a consequence of Christ's death, resurrection, and ascension (1:18–23). These Gentile Christians need to know that their access to God and their standing in the Church is fully equal to that of the Jewish believers who began the community of Ephesus years earlier (2:19; Acts 18:24–19:10) and were probably still its main leaders. These recent believers need to understand how Christ builds up the Church both through specially gifted ministers and through the gifts given to each member of the community (4:7–16) and to understand the basis of the Church's unity, despite a diversity of charisms and of religious and ethnic origins. They need to understand the holiness they share through baptism and its practical implications. While their new identity in Christ does not eliminate the differences in social standing in their culture, it does radically alter the dynamics of relationships among them (5:21–6:9).

Literary Features

Ephesians differs from many of Paul's letters by not focusing on particular problems in a local church. Instead, it presents teaching for Gentile Christians about what God has done for them through Jesus Christ; the implications would have been directly applicable to most local churches in the Roman Empire outside of Palestine during the first century. The generic character of its content supports the hypothesis that Ephesians was intended to serve as a circular letter like some other New Testament writings, including 1 Peter, James, and Revelation.

The eloquent style of Ephesians bears the hallmarks of classical oratory, which would have suited it well to being read aloud during the liturgy as a sermon.[8] The educated members of the house churches in Ephesus might well have noticed and appreciated two types of oratory recognized by Greco-Roman †rhetoric, originally outlined by Aristotle and discussed by other ancient writers.

---

8. In fact, all the New Testament books were read aloud by or to their original recipients.

Demonstrative speech—also called display, laudatory, or epideictic rhetoric—reinforces common values by praising what is to be esteemed or by denigrating what is not. It seeks to move the emotions of its audience and is suitable for speeches at public celebrations or for education. Ephesians employs demonstrative rhetoric in chapters 1 to 3 in its effusive praise, prayer, and narrative about what God has done for us in Christ. *Deliberative* speech aims to persuade for or against a particular course of action, whether as personal advice or in a matter of public policy. Ephesians 4–6 employs deliberative rhetoric to persuade Christians to adopt a mode of conduct suited to their new identity (4:1) and to attaining the glorious future that awaits them (1:18; 2:7).[9]

This division in rhetorical style corresponds to a division in content. Through thanksgiving, prayers, and teaching, chapters 1–3 communicate what to believe, that is, the content of faith. These chapters are written mainly with verbs in the †indicative that depict what God has done, the truth about the present situation, and what God will do. Chapters 4–6 contain advice and exhortation about how to conduct oneself (sometimes called "paranesis"). In these chapters, Paul uses thirty-six verbs in the †imperative as he aims to guide readers' attitudes and behavior. This two-part structure characterizes some of Paul's other letters (for example, Galatians and Romans) and shows the logic of his moral teaching. Because of what God has done for us in Christ, we can and should †live in a way that corresponds to our new identity. Paul is saying, "Become in practice what in reality you already are."

Ephesians employs a variety of literary forms. After the address and initial greeting, it begins with an adaptation of a Jewish prayer form called a *berakah*, a praise of God that begins, "Blessed be God" (1:3–14). In addition Paul employs two prayers in the body of his letter (1:15–23; 3:14–21). Ephesians 5:14 cites what many scholars think was an early Christian baptismal hymn. Four times Paul quotes and comments on the Old Testament (1:20–22; 4:8, 26; 6:2–3). In 5:21–6:9 he employs a form of instruction intended to guide relationships within the ancient household commonly called a "household code."

Theological Themes

Although Ephesians touches on many topics (see the Index of Pastoral Topics for a more complete list), five principal themes characterize this letter.

9. A third type of oratory, *forensic* speech, was employed primarily in the courtroom and aimed to persuade the listener about the guilt or innocence of a person. Rather than categorize Ephesians in terms of persuasive oratory, some scholars examine it in light of the conventions of Hellenistic letter-writing. They conclude that the first half compares to a letter of congratulation and the second half to a letter of advice.

1. *Christ*. The word "Christ" appears forty-five times in Ephesians, a title for Jesus that often stands in place of his name. The Greek word *christos*, from which we get "Christ," is the Greek translation of the Hebrew word meaning "†messiah," the anointed king whom many among the Jewish people hoped would save their nation (1:12, see sidebar on p. 29). Ephesians emphasizes what God has already accomplished through Jesus' death, resurrection, and exaltation to the right hand of God but also points to God's ultimate plan to bring everything under Christ's headship "in the fullness of times" (1:10). Through Christ, God has saved believers from spiritual death caused by sin, from the power of Satan, and from the †flesh (2:1–10). Through the cross, Christ broke down the dividing wall of enmity between Jew and Gentile and reconciled them both to God and to one another, bringing peace (2:13–16). He accomplished all this through his death and resurrection, creating "in himself one new person," uniting human beings to the Father through the gift of the Spirit (2:13–18). Christ is "head over all things" (1:22), "head of the church" (5:23; see 4:15), and the Church's bridegroom (5:25–27, 32).

2. *Union of believers with Christ*. In various ways the letter repeatedly indicates that the benefits Christians enjoy are a result of their being united to Christ in the past (baptism), present, and future (2:5–7). One of the most frequent and important expressions in Ephesians is "in Christ"—and equivalent phrases such as "in him" and "in the Lord"—in reference to this solidarity. Christians have been "brought . . . to life with Christ . . . raised . . . up with him, and seated . . . with him in the heavens in Christ Jesus" (2:5–6). At the same time, union with Christ remains the goal of Christian life and believers must choose now to "grow in every way into him" (4:15). "In the ages to come" they can expect to share "the immeasurable riches of his grace . . . in Christ Jesus" (2:7).

3. *Christian identity*. Union with Christ gives human beings a radically new identity. We have put off the old self, the old humanity, and have put on the new (4:20–24). We have become members of Christ's body (3:6; 4:25; 5:30). Jewish Christians who had hoped for the messiah have obtained their †inheritance (1:11–14).[10] Gentile believers, in dramatic contrast to their former status as outsiders, have now been re-created along with Jews as "one new humanity" (2:15 NRSV) and have been fully incorporated into the people of God as coheirs and copartners in the promise God made to Abraham and his descendents (3:6). All Christians are God's "beloved children" (5:1; see 1:5), chosen "before the foundation of the world" (1:4), and members of God's household (2:19) and are being built together into a †holy temple, a community that is a dwelling place for God himself (2:21–22). We

10. This is how the NJB, NRSV, ESV, and I interpret these verses; other translations interpret them differently.

are "children of light" (5:8) rather than "sons of disobedience" (2:2; 5:6 RSV). In Ephesians, Paul's favorite way of referring to Christians (nine times) is as "the holy ones" (NAB), or, in other translations, "the †saints" (RSV, JB, NRSV, NIV).

4. *Holy and righteous conduct.* Believers' close relationship with God calls for and makes possible a new way of life that corresponds to their new identity (4:1). They are to preserve the unity of the Church (4:2–3) and to use the diverse gifts they have received to build up the body of Christ (4:7, 11–12, 16). They are to renounce their former, Gentile, way of life (4:17–31; 5:3–6). Instead, they are to speak the truth and live in love in a way that imitates God and Christ's sacrificial self-gift (4:25–26, 29; 4:32–5:2). Rather than getting drunk, they are to be filled with the Spirit and offer worship and praise to God (5:18–20). They are to be considerate of one another in their family and household relationships (5:21–6:9), adopt Christlike attitudes and behaviors that will help them hold their ground in times of temptation (6:10–17), and pray in the Spirit at every opportunity (6:18).

5. *The Church.* All of the above themes indicate the distinctiveness of the Christian people. Ephesians develops the theology of the universal Church more than any of the other Pauline writings, which mostly focus on local Christian communities. The Church is Christ's body, his "fullness" (1:23); he is its head (4:15; 5:23). The community that composes the Church is a holy temple, built on the foundation of the apostles and †prophets, with Christ Jesus himself as "the capstone" (2:20). This ecclesial body is being built up in love by leaders whom Christ has given to the Church to equip the members for ministry until the Church attains a Christlike maturity (4:13–16). Finally, the union of Christ and his Church is revealed to be that of a bridegroom and his bride (5:25–32).

The Meaning of Ephesians for Today

This rich theology makes Ephesians an important source of Church teaching, particularly regarding the Church's understanding of her own nature and of the sacrament of marriage. The Liturgy of the Hours makes weekly use of two "canticles" from Ephesians (1:3–10; 3:14–21) in evening prayer. Its beauty and wealth of meaning makes Ephesians a favorite among Paul's letters for Bible study, meditation, memorization, and *lectio divina.*

Although it contains a few texts that must be applied differently because of cultural changes, Ephesians remains as relevant today as when it was first written. Like Ephesians' original readers, twenty-first-century Catholics need to grasp the immensity of what God has done for us through Jesus' death and resurrection, to appropriate the blessings in the Holy Spirit that are ours, and to long for our glorious future with a lively hope (1:18). Perhaps even more than in Paul's day, Gentile Christians need to understand that we have been brought in to share in the promises of God to Israel and that the Church will always consist of Jews and Gentiles united in the Messiah (2:11–19; 3:6–9; Rom 11). Christ's tearing down "the dividing wall of enmity" (2:14) that separated Jews and Gentiles enables us to recognize the unity and equality in him of all our sisters and brothers, regardless of race, culture, or socioeconomic status.

Paul's instruction about Christian conduct still holds true. The same attitudes of humility, gentleness, patience, and forbearance are the key to preserving the Spirit's gift of unity in families, parishes, and religious communities. As in the first century, Christ gives specially gifted leaders to the Church as well as gifts to every member "for the work of ministry, for building up the body of Christ" (4:12). Today as in Paul's day, only "with the proper functioning of each part" will the Church mature and attain "the full stature of Christ" (4:13–16). Today also, Christians must choose to put off the lifestyle of the old fallen human nature and to put on the way of life of the new humanity, that is, to live in union with Christ. Christians must be acutely aware of our true identity in Christ and give shining testimony (5:8–14) in a world that sometimes seems to grow darker by the day. We must learn to defer to one another out of reverence for Christ. Our marriages must emulate and point to the relationship of Jesus and his bride (5:21–33). Finally, it is a time for Christians to draw strength from the Lord in the spiritual battle and to be persistent in prayer empowered by the Spirit (6:10–18).

The letter to the Ephesians is a masterpiece of Christian literature and one of the Bible's greatest treasures. As I submit this manuscript, I am overtaken by an awareness of how much Paul's letter surpasses any commentary. My hope and prayer is that this volume may open a path to the Apostle's treasure house for my brothers and sisters in Christ.

I want to thank those who have helped me so much in my work: Bob Ervin, Daniel Harrington, Janet Smith, and Christi Wensley, who reviewed earlier drafts and offered many helpful suggestions; Oswald Sobrino, who proposed Catechism references; Elizabeth Siegel, who provided lectionary references; Michael Gorman, who allowed me to use his photos of Ephesus; the very capable and cooperative team at Baker Academic; Mary Healy and Kevin Perrotta, my friends (Prov 27:17) and fellow editors; and my wife, Marsha Daigle-Williamson, who prayed, encouraged, advised, and copyedited many versions of this work.

"Now to him who is able to accomplish far more than all we ask or imagine, by the power at work within us, to him be glory in the church and in Christ Jesus to all generations, forever and ever. Amen" (3:20–21).

Outline of the Letter to the Ephesians

Part 1: Proclamation of God's Gracious Plan of Salvation in Christ

    A. Opening greeting (1:1–2)

    B. Opening blessing (1:3–14)
- The Father's plan of salvation (1:4–6)
- Fulfillment through Christ (1:7–10)
- Inheritance through the Spirit (1:11–14)

    C. A prayer to know God and to understand his gifts (1:15–23)
- The motive of Paul's prayer (1:15–17)
- Understanding our glorious future (1:18)
- Grasping the greatness of God's power for us (1:19–23)

    D. Salvation by grace through faith for good works (2:1–10)
- The problem: the human condition apart from Christ (2:1–3)
- God's solution, God's motives (2:4–7)
- Grace, faith, and works (2:8–10)

    E. Reconciliation of Gentiles and Jews in the Messiah (2:11–22)
- The Gentiles' previous status as outsiders (2:11–12)
- Reconciliation for all through Jesus' death on the cross (2:13–16)
- Peace and access to God in the Spirit through Jesus' resurrection (2:17–18)
- Fellow citizens, members of God's household, a holy temple (2:19–22)

    F. Paul's commission to preach God's secret plan (3:1–13)
- Paul and his ministry (3:1–3)
- The mystery of Christ (3:4–6)
- Paul's role (3:7–10)
- God's eternal purpose (3:11–13)

    G. A prayer for divinization (3:14–21)
- Introduction (3:14–15)
- Five petitions (3:16–19)
- Doxology (3:20–21)

Part 2: Exhortation to Christian Conduct

    A. Building up the Church (4:1–16)
- Unity—attitudes that preserve it, facts that establish it (4:1–6)
- Ministry—building up the body of Christ (4:7–12)
- Maturity—the goal (4:13–16)

B. The new self and a new way of living (4:17–5:2)
- Conduct not like the Gentiles' (4:17–19)
- The key to virtuous living (4:20–24)
- Guidelines for conduct (4:25–29)
- Imitators of God (4:30–5:2)

C. Children of light (5:3–20)
- Avoiding suggestive speech (5:3–4)
- Not deceived about the consequences of immorality (5:5–6)
- Living as children of light (5:7–10)
- Shining light on wrongdoing (5:11–14)
- Living wisely (5:15–17)
- Being filled with the Spirit (5:18–20)

D. Instruction about household relationships (5:21–6:9)
- An exhortation to everyone (5:21)
- Wives and husbands, Christ and the Church (5:22–33)
  - An exhortation to wives (5:22–24)
  - An exhortation to husbands (5:25–30)
  - The oneness of wife and husband, Christ and the Church (5:31–32)
  - Concluding exhortation (5:33)
- Children and parents (6:1–4)
- Slaves and masters (6:5–9)

E. A summons to spiritual battle (6:10–20)

F. Closing greetings (6:21–24)

Part 1

Proclamation of God's Gracious Plan
of Salvation in Christ

Blessing God for Every Spiritual Blessing

Ephesians 1:1–14

Like a majestic overture before a symphony, a hymn of praise at the beginning of Ephesians arouses our anticipation of what is to come by sounding the great themes of salvation and setting the tone for the entire letter. The grandeur of these truths inspires awe at God's amazing plan.

Greeting (1:1–2)

---

[1]Paul, an apostle of Christ Jesus by the will of God, to the holy ones who are [in Ephesus] faithful in Christ Jesus: [2]grace to you and peace from God our Father and the Lord Jesus Christ.

NT: Col 1:1–2
Catechism: members of the Church called "saints," 823

Paul briefly introduces himself and salutes his readers with his customary greeting. The word **apostle** comes from the Greek verb "to send" and means someone who has been "sent" as an official representative. Paul refers to the one who sent him by his title, **Christ Jesus.** Just as Jesus' appointment of the Twelve was in accord with the will of the Father—it followed a night of prayer (Luke 6:12–13)—so Paul's appointment as the †Messiah's authorized delegate (Acts 26:15–18) is **by the will of God.**

The **holy ones** or "†saints" whom Paul addresses are the members of the Church.[1] Christians are †holy in the deepest sense not because of heroic virtue but because

1:1

---

1. Most translations use the word "saints" here, but the NAB translates *hagioi* as "holy ones" in order to avoid confusion with those canonized by the Church.

they have been made holy (sanctified) by a holy God and belong to him. God sanctified them through the death and resurrection of Jesus and has communicated this holiness to them through baptism and the gift of the Spirit.[2]

The NAB places **in Ephesus** in brackets because it is missing in some important manuscripts (see the introduction). It is likely that Ephesians was written as a circular letter (an "encyclical") to a number of churches in the Roman province of Asia (located in modern-day Turkey).

Paul also refers to these "holy ones" as **faithful in Christ Jesus**. The Greek word *pistoi* can be translated "faithful," "reliable," or "believing." This adjective often functions as a shorthand way of referring to Christians—"believers" or "the faithful"—since it is †faith in Jesus that makes us Christians.

1:2   Paul's greeting—**grace to you and peace from God our Father and the Lord Jesus Christ**—can be understood either as a prayer-wish, customary in letters of that period, or as Paul's bestowing a blessing on behalf of those he represents, namely, God the Father and the Lord Jesus.

Among Greek-speaking people in Paul's day, the common greeting at the beginning of letters was *chairein*—"rejoice"—indicating that the sender wished happiness to the recipient. Paul's word "†grace" (*charis*) is similar but refers instead to a divine "gift" or "†favor." The common greeting among Jews was *shalom*, usually translated in English as "peace," although the Hebrew word has a wider range of meaning, signifying complete well-being.

It is worth noting how Paul refers here to the first two persons of the Trinity. He refers to God familiarly as *our* Father—in the words Jesus taught his disciples and with the filial confidence that the Spirit inspires (Rom 8:15; Gal 4:6). Paul refers to Jesus by the solemn titles that reveal his identity. He is Lord and Christ (see Acts 2:36; Phil 2:11; Rev 11:15). "Christ" means Messiah (see sidebar on p. 29). Lord, *kyrios*, means "master" and is the way that the †Septuagint, the Greek translation of the Hebrew Bible, translates the divine name "Yahweh." Jesus' divine status is further indicated by the fact that he is named alongside God as the source of "grace . . . and peace."

Opening Blessing (1:3–14)

Paul begins his letter by fervently praising God for his generosity toward the people who belong to Christ. He adopts a form of prayer found in the Old Testament (Gen 14:20; 1 Kings 8:15; Ps 66:20) called a *berakah*, the Hebrew word

2. See Eph 5:25–27; Rom 15:16; 1 Cor 1:2; 6:11.

What Does "Christ" Mean?

The name "Christ" appears three times in the first two verses and forty-six times in the whole of Ephesians. To most people today "Christ" is simply part of Jesus' name. But to the New Testament authors and the first-century men and women who were evangelized by Jewish believers, "Christ" meant "Messiah."

The word "Christ" comes from the Greek *christos*, the Septuagint translation of the Hebrew word *mashiah* (English "messiah"), meaning "anointed." In the Old Testament, priests, kings, and (occasionally) †prophets were consecrated by being anointed with oil. The books of Samuel and Psalms often refer to the king of Israel as the Lord's "anointed" (1 Sam 16:6; Ps 2:2). God promised through the prophets that he would place a descendant of David on the throne of Israel who would save God's people and establish an everlasting kingdom (2 Sam 7:12–13; Isa 9:1–7; Jer 33:14–22). In the two centuries before the birth of Jesus, Jews increasingly used the term "the messiah" ("the christ") to refer to this promised redeemer-king.

When Jesus began his ministry, many Jews were eagerly awaiting the coming of this royal messiah, and some wondered if Jesus was the one (Matt 26:63; John 1:19–25; 7:31). Jesus was born of the line of David (Luke 2:4) and revealed himself as "anointed" by the Spirit (Luke 4:18). Peter confessed him to be the Christ, the promised Messiah (Mark 8:29),[a] and the resurrection confirmed his identity as God's †eschatological savior. The apostles preached Jesus as the Messiah (Acts 5:42; 9:22). Since the messianic promise was fulfilled in Jesus, the title *christos* became affixed to his name—"Christ Jesus" or "Jesus Christ"—much the way people combine name and title when they say "King David" or "Queen Elizabeth." But the meaning of "Christ" remains: the Messiah, the descendant of David whom God anointed to save and reign forever over his people and the world.

a. The NAB and NRSV usually translate *christos* as "Messiah" in the Gospels, as "Christ" or "Messiah" in Acts, and as "Christ" in the rest of the New Testament. The use of "Messiah" better conveys the meaning to contemporary Christians, while the use of "Christ" has the advantage of familiarity and liturgical usage. I will use the terms interchangeably.

for "blessing"—a prayer form that is still used by Jews today. A *berakah* begins with the words "Blessed be God" and immediately states why God should be praised by naming the benefits received from him. Paul's blessing differs from Jewish blessings by identifying God as the Father of Jesus and by making repeated references to Christ.

The Greek text of Eph 1:3–14 forms one complex sentence—the longest in the New Testament. Most English translations wisely break down the blessing into many sentences in two or three paragraphs. Even so, it takes considerable effort to understand the rich cluster of ideas and images contained in it.

Paul begins by blessing (that is, praising) God for having bestowed on Christians every possible divine blessing (that is, every divine gift and favor; 1:3). The rest of the prayer explains what those blessings are (1:4–10) and how they have come both to Jews and †Gentiles who have believed in Jesus (1:11–14). It is possible to count four, six, seven, eight, or more blessings, depending on how finely a reader wishes to distinguish them from one another. Rather than list these blessings in a neat, orderly way, Paul brims over with praises that explain or add to blessings already mentioned.

Although these verses appear as a distinct prayer of praise, they are linked to the rest of Ephesians, introducing themes that occur throughout the letter. This prayer fulfills one of the main purposes of the letter, namely, to help Christians appreciate the extraordinary gifts we have received through Christ.

Scholars hold a variety of opinions about the structure of this blessing. I will follow the division indicated by the paragraph headings in the NAB, which highlights the Trinitarian structure of the prayer, but I will treat the first verse as a separate unit:

Overview of the Blessing (1:3)

The Father's Plan of Salvation (1:4–6)

Fulfillment of the Plan through Christ (1:7–10)

Inheritance through the Spirit (1:11–14)

This three-part structure also highlights three phases of God's plan of salvation: creation, redemption, and †inheritance. To get the full impact of this wonderful prayer of praise, I suggest reading all of 1:3–14 aloud once or twice before continuing with the commentary below.

Summary of the Blessing (1:3)

---

³**Blessed be the God and Father of our Lord Jesus Christ, who has blessed us in Christ with every spiritual blessing in the heavens,**

NT: 2 Cor 1:3; 1 Pet 1:3

Catechism: meaning of "blessing," 1078–79; God revealed as Father of the Son, 240

Lectionary: 1:3–6, 11–12: Immaculate Conception, Commons of the Blessed Virgin Mary; 1:3–10, 13–14: Christian Initiation Apart from the Easter Vigil; 1:3–14: Consecration of Virgins and Religious Profession

This opening makes an extraordinary declaration. It praises (blesses) **God** the 1:3
Father for having already bestowed on us Christians every blessing of †heaven!
Every word of this statement bears further examination.

Rather than referring to God as "King of the Universe" or "the God of Israel,"
as Jewish blessings typically do, this blessing identifies God as the "Father" **of
our Lord Jesus Christ** (as in 2 Cor 1:3 and 1 Pet 1:3). Ever since Jesus' death
and resurrection, Christians cannot think about God apart from Jesus or about
Jesus except as God's Son. Jesus is himself described in a particular way as "our
Lord." The possessive pronoun "our" conveys a warmth of mutual belonging
and the words "†Lord" and "Christ" express a sense of our accountability to
him. Paul likes to speak of "our Lord"; he uses this expression twelve times in
Romans, ten times in 1 Corinthians, and five times in Ephesians (1:17; 3:11;
5:20; 6:24). Paul usually completes the phrase "our Lord" with his name and
title, "Jesus Christ." Jesus is the one whom Christians acknowledge and obey
as our Lord and †Messiah. Pronouncing his name arouses devotion among
those who know him.

Paul now states his reason for praising God: because God **has blessed us**.
There is intentional wordplay on the different meanings of "bless." The verb "to
bless" (*eulogeō*) and the noun "blessing" (*eulogia*) are both related to the first
word of the sentence, "Blessed (*eulogētos*) be God." When people bless God,
they praise him. When God blesses, he confers a benefit.

The text tells us that God has blessed us **in Christ**. The expression "in Christ"
(*en Christō*) occurs very often in Ephesians; if we include equivalent phrases, such
as "in him," it occurs eleven times in this opening blessing alone. In Greek this
phrase is found in the position of emphasis at the end of the clause, stressing that
all of this blessing has come to us through our relationship with the Messiah.

Paul says that God has bestowed on us **every spiritual** (*pneumatikē*) **blessing**.
Although these blessings are benefits for the spirit, or inner self—rather than
physical or material blessings—the adjective "spiritual" here refers above all to
the Holy Spirit through whom the blessings have come to us. This is confirmed
by 1:3–14, which climaxes with the affirmation that Christians have received
the Holy Spirit as the †first installment of our future eternal inheritance. The
first verse thus anticipates the Trinitarian structure of the whole blessing.

Paul describes the blessings we have received as **in the heavens**. Here "the
heavens" refers to the divine realm where God dwells, where Jesus has been
enthroned (1:20–21), and where Christians have in some sense already been
enthroned with him (see 2:6). Heaven is beyond the material universe we inhabit,
in a dimension beyond the time and space of our world (see Heb 9:11–12).

"In Christ"

Although there are subtle variations, we can discern two basic meanings of the Greek phrase *en Christō* in Ephesians. First, it can have an *instrumental* meaning: something happens *by means of Christ*, through his action or will, especially through his death and resurrection. Second, this expression can mean *location* in a metaphorical sense: someone or something exists in the sphere of Christ, *in union with him*. Paul teaches that Christians have been united to Jesus through faith and baptism (Rom 6:3–5; 2 Cor 5:17; Gal 2:20). We have died with Jesus and have been raised with him and now live in a real spiritual union with him (1 Cor 6:17). The New Testament describes the Christian's union with Christ as our living in him, as Christ's living in us (Gal 2:20; Col 1:27), and as a mutual indwelling (John 15:1–7). This spiritual union with Christ is so real that all Christians together are understood as being the body of Christ (1 Cor 12:13, 27). The faithful on earth are a visible, tangible manifestation of Christ's presence. Sometimes when the phrase *en Christō* is used, both *instrumentality* and *location* are intended.

The extraordinary affirmation made in 1:3 is that God has blessed Christians in every possible way through what Christ has done, including giving us the Holy Spirit and uniting us to Jesus, who is enthroned in heaven. This benefit has *already* been conferred and has begun to be experienced.

The Father's Plan of Salvation (1:4–6)

[4]as he chose us in him, before the foundation of the world, to be holy and without blemish before him. In love [5]he destined us for adoption to himself through Jesus Christ, in accord with the favor of his will, [6]for the praise of the glory of his grace that he granted us in the beloved.

NT: Rom 8:14–16, 28–30; Gal 4:5–6; Eph 5:27; Col 1:13, 22
Catechism: Church as holy and blameless, 865, 1426; adoption as children in the Son, 2782; God's gracious plan, 257

The remainder of Paul's opening blessing enumerates the principal benefits that God has bestowed on us in Christ in the order of their occurrence. They are benefits Christians have already begun to enjoy, even though we will not experience their fullness until Christ returns. First, Paul looks back before the dawn of time to the Father's original intention.

The first blessing is that God **chose us**. One of the most important doctrines   1:4
of the Old Testament is the doctrine of election—God chose the descendents of
Jacob, also called Israel, to be his people out of all the peoples of the earth, and
so Israel is called God's "chosen" people (Deut 7:6). The New Testament teaches
that Christians are also God's chosen people, his "elect" (Rom 8:33; 2 Tim 2:10;
1 Pet 2:9). However, rather than being chosen on the basis of physical descent
from a particular ancestor, our election results from being **in him**, that is, from
our union with Jesus, God's "chosen one" par excellence:

> Here is my servant whom I uphold,
>> my chosen one with whom I am pleased,
> Upon whom I have put my spirit;
>> he shall bring forth justice to the nations. (Isa 42:1; see also 41:9;
>> 49:7)

These words about the servant of the Lord were fulfilled in the †Messiah, Jesus
(Matt 12:18; Luke 9:35; 23:35). The divine decision to include as "chosen" each
of us who would be united to Christ through faith and baptism occurred **before
the foundation of the world**, that is, before creation.

Finally, a purpose for God's choosing us is announced, namely, that we
should **be holy and without blemish before him**.[3] God willed that we should
be the kind of people fit to be in his presence. The words "holy and without
blemish" originally came from the language of worship and sacrifice rather
than from the vocabulary of moral conduct. Any person or thing that is to be
in God's presence, "before him," must be perfect, "without blemish," "spot-
less" (JB). In Latin the word is *inmaculatus*, from which we derive the English
"immaculate." Thus in the Old Testament both animals used in sacrifices and
the priests who offered them were required to be without any physical defect
(Exod 12:5; Lev 21:17–21). Even today we choose vestments, chalices, and
other sacred objects that are of the highest quality possible for use in the
Church's liturgy.

In the Bible the primary meaning of the word "holy" is not "virtuous" but
"set apart" from what is ordinary or profane for God, who is himself "holy"
and transcendent. The ancient Israelites, and to a lesser extent the pagans, had
a sense of how utterly different God is from us and observed elaborate rituals
in the hope of bridging the impassible gap between what is merely human and
profane and what is divine and holy. Both the Old Testament and the New Testament affirm that human beings need to be cleansed to dwell in the presence

---

3. The RSV and NRSV, less precisely, say "blameless" rather than "without blemish."

of a holy God. Paul will explain how it is that Christians become "holy and without blemish" in 5:25–27.

In most ancient religions, worship—the means by which one obtained and acknowledged the favor of the gods—and ethics were two separate and unrelated spheres. In Judaism and Christianity, however, an important relationship emerges between the two. Beginning in the †Torah, God makes clear that Israel's call to be a "kingdom of priests" (Exod 19:6), a people qualified to stand in his presence, entails ethical conduct that corresponds to God's nature. "Be holy, for I, the †Lord your God, am holy" (Lev 19:2). Holiness is not possible for those engaged in unjust or immoral activity. Instead, justice and sexual purity characterize acceptable worship. Paul will address the topic of conduct later in the letter, but here he simply tells us that God willed from all eternity that we would somehow become "holy and without blemish before him."

1:5   The next sentence reveals God's motive for choosing us—a fatherly love that moved him to adopt us as his children: **In love he destined us for adoption to himself**. In saying that God "destined us for adoption to himself,"[4] the focus is not on the legal procedure of adoption but on the *result* of adoption, that is, that we become members of God's family, *his* sons and daughters.[5] God intended to accomplish this **through Jesus Christ**, the only way humans can truly become God's children. Although Genesis portrays humans as God's offspring because we were created in his image and likeness (Gen 1–2; see Luke 3:38), sin severely damaged this relationship (see 2:3). When the New Testament speaks of becoming children of God it refers to a far deeper filial relationship with God in Christ and through the gift of the Spirit than was previously possible (John 1:12–13; Rom 8:14–17; Gal 3:26).

Sometimes people are a bit put off by the idea that we are *adopted* children since this term could seem to distance us from God. But as parents of adopted children can testify, adopted children are not loved less.[6] In the Greco-Roman world of the first century, adopted children enjoyed all the rights and privileges of those born into the family. Paul reflects at some length in Rom 8:14–39 about the privilege of being God's sons and daughters, and in Matt 5:44–7:11

4. The NIV has "predestined," also an accurate translation. In fact, Catholics and most Christians believe in predestination in the basic sense that God knew, loved, and chose in advance all those who accept the gospel and become part of his people (see Catechism 600).

5. The RSV says "to be his sons," the NJB "to be adopted sons," and the NRSV "for adoption as his children." The Greek word for "adoption" is *huiothesia*, formed from the words "to place or establish" and "son." The term can be understood inclusively, as the NRSV translates it.

6. While Paul describes us as God's adopted children to emphasize God's choice and our change of status, John speaks of Christians as "born from above" (John 3:3) and "begotten by God" (1 John 3:9; 4:7; 5:4, 18) to emphasize the dynamism of divine life present in us.

Jesus indicates what this relationship entails. We have God as our Father and Jesus as our older brother (Rom 8:29). So intimate is this familial relationship that the Holy Spirit, who unites the Father and the Son, dwells also in us. As children we can count on God's protection, provision, and steadfast love (Matt 6:31–34; 10:29–31; Rom 8:39). As children, we are "heirs of God," with a dignity so extraordinary that creation itself will be transformed when our identity as sons and daughters of God is fully revealed (Rom 8:19–21).

The text emphasizes the Father's free initiative in this plan: our adoption was **in accord with the favor of his will**. The NJB and NRSV speak instead of the "good pleasure" of his will. Adopting us as his sons and daughters was what he really wanted.

Paul next indicates the only fitting response we can make to what God has done: this gift calls **for the praise of the glory of his grace**.[7] In this case, "†glory" refers to the immensity, or splendor, of God's †grace, of unmerited favor that has been revealed and that evokes praise. Paul uses a similar phrase, "the praise of his glory," twice more in this prayer—in verse 12 in reference to Jesus and in verse 14 in reference to the Holy Spirit, making this a Trinitarian blessing in which praise is given for the work of each of the divine persons.

1:6

What moves Paul is not God's character in the abstract but the specific act of generosity **that he granted us in the beloved**, that is, in the gifts of election and adoption as God's children available through our relationship with Jesus. Jesus is described as "beloved," the same word spoken by the Father's voice from †heaven at his baptism (Matt 3:17; Mark 1:11; Luke 3:22) and transfiguration (Matt 17:5; Mark 9:7). "Beloved," like the word "chosen,"[8] indicates the unique favor and love that God the Father has toward his Son Jesus. Because God decided to incorporate believers "in the beloved," we share in the extraordinary favor and love that Jesus receives from the Father.

Reflection and Application (1:3–6)

Children of God. I remember when, at age nineteen, I began to understand what it means that we are sons and daughters of God. At the time I experienced the insecurities and self-image problems common to young people. I was keenly aware of my shortcomings, worried what people thought of me, and searching to discover who I really was. I belonged to an ecumenical prayer group, and one

---

7. Other translations say "to the praise of his glorious grace" (RSV, NRSV, NIV), which means about the same thing.
8. See Matt 12:18; Col 3:12; 1 Thess 1:4.

evening our guest speaker was an Episcopalian pastor. Using texts from Paul, he taught that we are sons of God because God has poured the Spirit of his Son into us, enabling us to address God as "Abba, Father!" (Gal 4:6). He preached the words spoken to Jesus at his baptism, "You are my beloved Son; with you I am well pleased" (Luke 3:22). At the beginning and at the end of his message he prayed that the Holy Spirit would communicate this truth to our hearts. Then he taught us a chorus that repeats the words, "I am a son of God, I am a son of God, I am a son of God, his Spirit lives in me." I could not get that song or that truth out of my mind because it had lodged itself deeply in my heart. I realized that I have a relationship with God that no one can take away, that I have an extraordinary destiny when my identity as a son of God will be fully revealed (Rom 8:19; 1 John 3:2). I realized that our heavenly Father loves me; his pleasure rests on me; he is *for* me. Compared to that, what others might think or say about me does not matter. My self-image problems did not all disappear at once, but the discovery that I am a son of God changed me.

Mary as holy and immaculate. The liturgy's use of this text (1:3–6, 11–12) for the Immaculate Conception and other Marian feasts is fitting, since Mary experienced the benefits that belong to believers before the rest of us and in a unique way. Mary was blessed "with every spiritual blessing in the heavens" (1:3). She was chosen in Christ before the foundation of the world to be "holy and without blemish" before God (1:4) for a very special role. She was among those "who first hoped in Christ" (1:12), both by sharing Israel's longing for the †Messiah and by eagerly awaiting the birth of the promised "Son of the Most High" in her womb (Luke 1:32). She lived completely "for the praise of his glory" (Eph 1:12; Luke 1:46).

Mary's Immaculate Conception was a consecration for a special role. It had precedents in the Old Testament. When God revealed his plan to deliver Israel through Samson, a specially consecrated individual (a Nazirite), his mother was instructed to prepare for his birth by abstaining from alcoholic beverages (forbidden to Nazirites) and from everything that was ritually unclean (Judg 13). When the tabernacle, God's dwelling, was constructed, all the materials had to be of the finest quality and were consecrated by special sacrifices (Exod 35–40; Heb 9:19–23). When Isaiah "saw the Lord" and was called to be a †prophet, one of the seraphim touched his mouth with an ember from the altar of God to remove his sin (Isa 6:1–7). Therefore it should not surprise us that God would prepare the mother of the Messiah by a special consecration, preserving her from sin from her conception so that she might be holy and immaculate, cleansed in advance to have the Son of God dwell in her body. In this, Mary anticipates the cleansing from sin that comes to us through faith and baptism, making us also "holy and without blemish" (1:4; 5:26–27). Baptism consecrates our bodies to be temples of the Holy Spirit (1 Cor 6:19) and begins a transformation of our human nature that will be completed at the resurrection. The source of Mary's consecration and of ours is the sacrificial death of her Son.

Fulfillment through Christ (1:7–10)

> [7]In him we have redemption by his blood, the forgiveness of transgressions, in accord with the riches of his grace [8]that he lavished upon us. In all wisdom and insight, [9]he has made known to us the mystery of his will in accord with his favor that he set forth in him [10]as a plan for the fullness of times, to sum up all things in Christ, in heaven and on earth.

NT: Rom 3:24–25; 1 Cor 15:24–28; Eph 3:4–6; Col 1:14; Heb 2:8; 9:22
Catechism: redemption through Christ, 517, 1992; God reveals his plan, 50, 257; the fulfillment of God's plan, 1043

Paul's prayer of blessing now explicitly describes Christ's role. These verses describe blessings Christians already enjoy, but conclude by directing our attention to God's plan for the ultimate future.

Paul now tells what we have received through Jesus, namely **redemption.**   **1:7–8a** "Redemption" means liberation, for instance, of a slave or captive, often by the payment of a ransom. In our case the liberation needed is **forgiveness** or "release" from the guilt of our **transgressions.** "Transgressions" (or "trespasses," RSV, NRSV) refers to sins that involve direct disobedience of God's commandments. In 2:1–3 Paul will describe the condition due to our transgressions that made this liberation necessary, but here he focuses on the means of our redemption, namely, the **blood** of Christ. The New Testament speaks of Christ's blood as a shorthand way of referring to Jesus' sacrificial death on the cross in atonement for sin.[9] The death of God's "beloved" Son (1:6) was a high price to pay for our freedom (see 1 Pet 1:18–19), but it manifested **the riches of his grace that he lavished upon us**, the extraordinary abundance of his favor that he freely bestowed on us.

The next remarkable blessing with which God has blessed us is a revelation   **1:8b–9** of **the mystery of his will.** In the New Testament the †mystery usually refers to

---

9. The same Greek word for "redemption" is used in Rom 3:24–25. See also Heb 9–10; 1 John 2:2; 4:10.

God's plan to redeem the †world through Christ—a plan that was kept secret in the past but has now been revealed. The **wisdom and insight** refers to the understanding of God's plan given to believers through the Spirit. One of Paul's major aims in this letter is that his readers grasp this transforming †knowledge as fully as possible (1:16–19; 3:14–19; see sidebars on p. 49 and p. 100).

This "mystery" **in accord with his favor**[10] is the plan that God **set forth in him**. In other words, God gladly chose to accomplish his will through Jesus. These verses show us a God who is not reactive but proactive, a God who is in control and working out his good purposes.

1:10   The **plan** that God has revealed has to do with not only the present but also our ultimate future, **the fullness of times**.[11] The content of this plan is that God has decided **to sum up all things in Christ**. "All things" means all creation. The Greek expression "to sum up," *anakephalaioō*, is a verb formed by combining the word for "head," *kephalē*, with a preposition meaning "up" or "again"; literally, it means "to head up."[12] Comparing other translations illustrates its range of meaning: "to unite" (RSV), "to gather up" (NRSV), "to bring . . . under one head" (NIV), "to gather everything together under Christ, as head" (JB).[13] The person in whom God will unify all creation is "Christ," the †Messiah. The Greek text emphasizes once more that all this occurs through Jesus by repeating "in him" (omitted in English translations) at the end of the clause. The phrase **in †heaven and on earth** indicates God's purpose to unite the whole cosmos under Christ's headship. In principle, this has already been achieved through Jesus' death and resurrection, as other texts indicate (Matt 28:18; Col 1:19–20). But here Paul probably speaks of the future, when everything will be under Christ's direct control and will achieve the unity and harmony God intends (1 Cor 15:24–28; Heb 2:8).

Reflection and Application (1:3–10)

What is the relevance of the opening blessing of Ephesians for Christian life today? Besides its rich doctrine, the most obvious value of this text is as a prayer of praise to God. The Liturgy of Hours uses Eph 1:3–10 for Evening Prayer every Monday and on all feasts of Mary, apostles, pastors, and virgins. I use it often in my personal prayer.

10. As in 1:5, the NJB and NRSV read "good pleasure"; the RSV says "purpose."

11. This expression differs from the "fullness of time" (singular) in Gal 4:4.

12. The headship of Christ over all of creation (here and 1:22) and of the Church (4:15; 5:23) is an important theme in Ephesians.

13. This word has also been translated "to recapitulate" or "to restore." This verse was the basis of Pope Pius X's motto, "To restore all things in Christ."

What Is This Summing Up?

LIVING TRADITION

Saint John Chrysostom offers two explanations:

> To "recapitulate" (*anakephalaioō*) is to join together.... In our customary usage a *recapitulation* is a brief summary of what has been said at great length. It is a concise expression of everything that has been detailed. That is what it is here as well. The providential ordering that has occurred over a long time, the Son has once for all *recapitulated*. Everything is summed up in him.... There is also another meaning: In Christ's incarnation God has given a single head to all creation, both angels and humans." (*Homilies on Ephesians* 1.1.10)[a]

a. Mark J. Edwards, ed., *Galatians, Ephesians, Philippians*, ACCS (Downers Grove, IL: InterVarsity, 1999), 116.

Christian worship, whether in the liturgy or personal prayer, entails a continuous reciprocal dynamic: In response to the blessings God has bestowed on us through creation and redemption, we offer praise to our Father through his Son and in the Holy Spirit and ask his continued blessing. He in turn blesses us by pouring out through Christ the grace of his Spirit on our offering, on the Church, and on the whole world, with the result that his divine blessings evoke more "praise of his glorious grace."[14]

Inheritance through the Spirit (1:11–14)

[11]In him we were also chosen, destined in accord with the purpose of the One who accomplishes all things according to the intention of his will, [12]so that we might exist for the praise of his glory, we who first hoped in Christ.

[13]In him you also, who have heard the word of truth, the gospel of your salvation, and have believed in him, were sealed with the promised holy Spirit, [14]which is the first installment of our inheritance toward redemption as God's possession, to the praise of his glory.

NT: Acts 10:34–35, 44–48; 2 Cor 1:22; 5:5; Gal 3:14

Catechism: baptismal anointing with the Spirit, 1241; baptism as seal, 1272–74; the Spirit as seal, 1295–96; confirmation's effects, 1302–5; the Spirit as anticipation of fullness, 1107; prayer of praise, 2639; God's glory, 293–94

14. See Catechism 2627, 1077–79, 1083.

This text has two parts, as laid out above. Paul continues in an exultant tone. Having extolled God's gracious plan from before the foundation of the world to Christ's future headship over everything, Paul now declares how this blessing reaches both Jewish Christians like himself—who had long †hoped for the coming of the Messiah—and †Gentiles, like most of his readers, who had only recently come to hope in Christ. Both groups have received the gift of the Spirit as a foretaste of the good things to come.

1:11–12   According to the NAB translation (the RSV and NIV are similar), Paul celebrates the fact that **we**, meaning Jewish Christians, are God's people **chosen** (*klēroō*) in Christ, having been **destined** according to God's **purpose** to live for God's praise.

However, the NRSV and NJB interpret *klēroō* differently: in Christ we have "obtained an inheritance" (NRSV).[15] According to this interpretation, Paul celebrates that Jewish believers in Christ have finally entered into their long-awaited †inheritance.

Under either interpretation, the God who "destined" the Jewish people for this blessing long ago **accomplishes all things according to the intention of his will**. God is in control of history and works everything according to his plan and for the good of his people (Rom 8:28). Paul says that God's "purpose" and "intention" for Jewish people like himself—**we who first hoped in Christ**—was **that we might exist for the praise of his glory**. God's †glory is the manifestation of his greatness and goodness now revealed in an unprecedented way. Praising God's glory fulfills Israel's reason for existence, namely, to be a priestly people, a nation devoted to proclaiming the praises of God (Exod 19:6; Isa 43:21; 1 Pet 2:9).

1:13–14a   Paul hastens to make clear that his readers, most of whom are Gentiles, have not been left out. Gentile readers, **you also, who have heard . . . the gospel . . . and have believed in him**, have received the gift of the Holy Spirit. †Faith in the †gospel, the good news about Jesus, has been their means of obtaining the same blessings. This message is **the word of truth**—a reliable message that corresponds to reality—and it brings **salvation**, a topic that will be explained in 2:1–10.

Then Paul states three facts about the Spirit.

First, you **were sealed with the . . . holy Spirit**.[16] In the ancient world, when a letter or legal document was marked in wax with the seal (*sphragis*) of its au-

---

15. Translations vary because of different interpretations of the passive form of the verb *klēroō* in this context. Some, like the NAB, take it to mean "to be allotted or destined" to something. I, however, agree with the NRSV, which takes it to mean "to obtain an inheritance" in light of the related word "inheritance," *kleronomia*, in v. 14 and the context in Ephesians of Jews and Gentiles sharing the same benefits in Christ (2:11–3:13).

16. The NAB does not capitalize "holy" probably to reflect that when the New Testament was written, "holy" was not yet part of the Spirit's name, as it would become after the doctrine of the Trinity was defined, but rather a way of indicating that the Spirit is God's own Spirit.

thor, the seal gave evidence of its authenticity. A seal was also used to indicate ownership: sheep and cattle were branded with their owner's seal. When soldiers enlisted in the Roman army, they were often sealed by tattooing the name of their commanding general on their hand or forearm.

Fig. 2. Papyrus document from Egypt, folded, bound and sealed. On the outside the Aramaic word *sefer*, "book."

Several places in Scripture speak of God placing seals on people to indicate that they belong to him (Exod 39:30) and are under his protection (Ezek 9:4–6; Rev 7:2–4). The gift of the Spirit that Christians have received functions as a seal. It marks us as belonging to God and under his protection; it is the proof of our adoption as sons and daughters (Gal 4:6).

Second, the Holy Spirit is described as **promised** because the prophets of the Old Testament promised that one day God would pour out his Spirit on Israel (Isa 44:3; Ezek 36:27) and on the whole human race (Joel 3:1–2). Jesus refers to the Spirit as the "promise of my Father" (Luke 24:49; compare Acts 1:4–5), and he himself promises the Spirit to his disciples (John 14–16). On Pentecost, Peter, referring to Joel's prophecy, describes the Spirit as "the promise" (Acts 2:33, 38–39), indicating that "the last days" of which Joel spoke (Acts 2:17)—the final phase of God's plan for the human race—have begun.

Third, the Spirit is **the first installment of our inheritance.** The expression "first installment," *arrabōn*, also translated "guarantee" or "pledge," is a business term that means "down payment."[17] If someone sells a house and the buyer makes a down payment of 20 percent, that first installment is the *arrabōn*. The initial payment guarantees that the promised remainder will be paid. Notice that it is not merely a promise that something will be transferred in the future; it is actually the beginning of the transfer of goods. Here Paul shifts from addressing Gentile readers ("you also") to speak of *our* inheritance, since both Jewish and Gentile believers have received the same "first installment" on their inheritance. The Holy Spirit is a foretaste and pledge of our inheritance, eternal life in God's presence.

Christians have received the "down payment" of the Spirit **toward redemption as God's possession.**[18] Paul concludes his prayer focusing not on our acquiring our inheritance but rather on God's acquiring *his.* From the beginning God wanted a people for himself as his own treasured possession (Exod 19:5);

1:14b

17. Paul uses this same term for the Spirit in 2 Cor 1:22; 5:5.

18. Most interpreters read the text this way. An alternative possibility is found in the RSV: "until we acquire possession of it."

The "Seal" according to the Fathers of the Church

LIVING TRADITION

While Paul regards the Holy Spirit as the seal (2 Cor 1:22), Church Fathers as early as the second century regarded baptism, the sacrament that conveys the Spirit, as sealing Christians. Just as circumcision was the seal of the Old Covenant (Rom 4:11), baptism is the seal of the New Covenant. It is an indelible seal—like a brand, a tattoo, or circumcision—and therefore not to be repeated. It signifies belonging fully to Christ and enlistment in his army. Other Church Fathers understood tracing the sign of the cross on the foreheads of catechumens as sealing them, that is, marking them as Christ's and protecting them from the devil. Still other Church Fathers regarded the anointing with oil that followed baptism as the seal that conveyed the Spirit.[a]

a. For a more complete account of how the Church Fathers interpreted the seal, see Jean Daniélou, *The Bible and the Liturgy* (Ann Arbor, MI: Servant, 1979), 54–69.

Scripture describes Israel as the Lord's "inheritance" (Deut 32:9 NJB and NIV).[19] Sin intervened and deferred the fulfillment of God's desire for a while. Now, however, through what Christ has done, God can be united to the people he loves by the *arrabōn*, the gift of his Spirit. This, however, is only a step toward his taking full possession of his people in the kingdom of God (Mal 3:17; 1 Pet 2:9). In modern Greek the word *arrabōn* refers to an engagement ring or to the engagement itself. An engagement ring is of great value by itself and even more so as the sign and promise of a future union, the consummation of a relationship already begun. The gift of the Spirit is a first installment of this kind. It both promises and anticipates a wonderful future to a pair of lovers, a mutual possessing.

The words **to the praise of his glory** confirm that the Gentile members of God's people, like the Jewish Christians (v. 12), exist to praise God for his greatness and goodness now revealed. This is the third time a similar phrase is used (vv. 6, 12, 14), this time in regard to the Spirit, completing the Trinitarian hymn of praise. The location of this phrase at the end of this extended prayer (vv. 3–14) gives it special emphasis. Recalling God's blessings leads Paul to worship. His words express an overflow of joy at the generosity of God the Father through Christ and the gift of the Spirit to his adopted children, both Jews and Gentiles who have believed in Jesus.

19. Translations vary: "hereditary share" (NAB), "share" (NRSV), "heritage" (RSV).

What Is "Our Inheritance"?

In ordinary usage the word "inheritance" refers to property that is transferred to someone upon the death of a relative. In the Bible, however, the emphasis falls more on the ownership of some good rather than on the way the ownership is transferred.

God promised the land of Canaan to Abraham and his descendants as their permanent possession (Gen 15:7, 18; Exod 32:13). Before and after Israel took possession of the Promised Land, Scripture describes the land as Israel's inheritance (Deut 1:38; 4:21; Josh 11:23; 1 Kings 21:3) and each tribe or family's allotted portion as their "inheritance" (NAB: "heritage"). Interestingly, the Old Testament describes the people of Israel as God's "inheritance" or "hereditary share," his special possession among all the peoples of the earth (Deut 32:9; Jer 10:16—translated "his very own" by NAB).

In the New Testament, "inheritance" is understood symbolically to refer to the good things that the promised land meant for Israel—life, peace, security, blessing, the reign of God—but which ethnic Israel failed to fully attain (Heb 3–4; 11:38–39). The promise of "the land" to Abraham and his descendants is extended to encompass not only Canaan but the whole world (Rom 4:13; Matt 5:5). God has fulfilled his promise by bestowing the whole world on Abraham's descendant, the Messiah Jesus, who embodies faithful Israel (Matt 28:18; Gal 3:16). Now Jews and Gentiles who believe in Christ have become coheirs through their union with him through faith and baptism (Gal 3:26–29). They will enjoy the fullness of the inheritance at the resurrection when they fully possess eternal life in the kingdom of God. In the meantime, many of the benefits of the inheritance are available through the gift of the Spirit, "the first installment of our inheritance" (Eph 1:14; see 2 Cor 1:22).

Reflection and Application (1:11–14)

All four Gospels record John the Baptist's testimony that the distinguishing characteristic of the one to come is that "he will baptize you with the holy Spirit" (Mark 1:8). In the Church, Jesus bestows the Spirit on Christians through the sacraments of baptism, confirmation (or chrismation in the Eastern Church),[20] and the Eucharist. In the rite of confirmation, the bishop makes the sign of the cross with the oil of chrism on the forehead of a person as he says, "Be sealed with the gift of the Holy Spirit."

A seal is a *visible* mark of ownership, but the Spirit is invisible (John 3:8). How could the Spirit be recognized by the early Christians as a seal? In the

20. See Catechism 695, 1242, 1289.

early Church the coming of the Holy Spirit was accompanied by experiential and often visible effects. This is apparent in the book of Acts when the Holy Spirit came on Jesus' disciples at Pentecost (2:2–4), on the Samaritans (8:17–18), on the first Gentile converts at the home of Cornelius (10:44–46), and on the disciples of John the Baptist (19:6) with gifts of speaking in tongues and other manifestations of spiritual power. Paul presupposes that his readers have a vivid awareness of the past and present activity of the Spirit in their lives (see also Gal 3:2–5).

Today, experience of the Spirit among Catholics varies greatly, especially since most receive baptism as infants and confirmation when they are still quite young. The impact of these sacraments depends on the degree to which people *appropriate* by conversion, prayer (Luke 11:9–13), and [†]faith in Christ's promise (Gal 3:5, 14) the [†]grace the sacraments impart. Catholics today should aspire to experience as fully as they can the seal of the Spirit in a way that is visible to all by manifesting the charisms (1 Cor 12) and the fruit of the Spirit (Gal 5:22–23).[21]

The praise expressed in Eph 1:3–14 is rich with truth about God and our relationship with him that can be summarized by seven blessings this prayer celebrates.

1. Before creation, God the Father chose us to be [†]holy and without blemish, to live in his presence forever.
2. He destined us in love to become his sons and daughters through a relationship with his Son, Jesus Christ.
3. Through the Messiah's sacrificial death on the cross, we have received forgiveness for all our sins.
4. God has revealed to us his previously hidden eternal plan to unite the whole of creation under Christ's headship.
5. Through Jesus, Paul and other Jewish believers who were waiting for the Messiah have entered into their inheritance.
6. In Jesus, Gentiles who have heard the gospel and believed in it were sealed as God's own by the gift of the promised Holy Spirit.
7. The Spirit is the first installment of *our* eternal inheritance, which anticipates the day when God takes possession of *his* inheritance, us, his people.

---

21. For more on appropriating the grace of the Spirit, see reflections on 5:18–20; for more on charisms, see comments on 4:8–16.

A Prayer to Know God
and to Understand His Gifts

Ephesians 1:15–23

It is said that the children of Nicholas II, the last czar of Russia, used to entertain themselves by playing in the royal treasury. They loved the beautiful things they held in their hands—crowns, orbs, scepters, necklaces, and rings—but did not have the slightest inkling of their extraordinary value.

Saint Paul regards his readers as a bit like those royal children; they possess enormous wealth but do not grasp the value of what belongs to them. After praising God and enumerating some of the blessings, Paul prays that his readers will come to understand fully what these blessings mean for their lives. As a good teacher, Paul describes in evocative language the "jewels" that he prays God will help them to appreciate.

In the †Hellenistic culture of the first century it was common to begin letters with a thanksgiving to the gods for the recipient or a commendation of that person to the gods. Paul adapts this familiar practice in a way that reflects Jewish liturgical patterns. Jewish prayers typically begin by blessing God (Hebrew *berakah*, as in 1:3) or by thanking him (as in 1:16 below) and continue with prayers of petition. This pattern, found in most of Paul's letters, became a model for Christian worship and is reflected in the Eucharistic Prayer.

Paul's prayer in verses 15–23 has three sections, although in Greek it is written as a single sentence:

1. The motive of Paul's prayer, 1:15–17
2. A petition to understand the glorious future to which God has called us, 1:18
3. A petition to understand the greatness of God's power on our behalf, 1:19–23

45

The Motive of Paul's Prayer (1:15–17)

---

[15]Therefore, I, too, hearing of your faith in the Lord Jesus and of your love for all the holy ones, [16]do not cease giving thanks for you, remembering you in my prayers, [17]that the God of our Lord Jesus Christ, the Father of glory, may give you a spirit of wisdom and revelation resulting in knowledge of him.

NT: 1 Cor 2:10–16; Phil 1:3–4; Col 1:3–4, 9; 1 Thess 1:2–3
Catechism: intercession, 2632; thanksgiving, 2638; Spirit gives understanding of faith, 94; faith seeks understanding, 158; gift of wisdom, 1831

1:15–16   Paul links his prayer to the preceding blessing (1:3–14): **Therefore.** Recalling the many blessings God has bestowed, Paul is moved to unite his prayer to God's gracious will as it unfolds among his readers. As a prisoner, Paul depends on the reports of others to learn of his churches' progress (see the sections on "Paul in Ephesus" and "Original Readers" in the introduction for discussion of the historical background). He says **hearing of your faith,** as in all likelihood five years have elapsed since he visited Ephesus.

He has heard of their faith **in the Lord Jesus** and their **love for all the holy ones**—two of the qualities that Paul prizes most in the lives of Christians (he will mention their †hope later in the prayer). The Greek word for faith, *pistis*, can mean either "belief" or "faithfulness"; it is likely that Paul refers both to his readers' confidence in Jesus and to their faithfulness to him. While Paul uses "faith" vertically to describe people's relationship with God, he usually uses "love" horizontally to refer to relationships among people. Here Paul commends the Ephesians' love not merely for one another but for "all the †holy ones." That suggests that his readers' love extended to believers in other places, perhaps by sending alms to the poor in the Jerusalem community (as Paul's churches had done a few years earlier) or by ministry to Christians in their region. Genuine believers express a special care for their brothers and sisters in Christ wherever they may be (Gal 6:10). According to St. Augustine, "To the degree that someone loves Christ's Church, to that degree he has the Holy Spirit."[1]

Paul never stops praying: **I . . . do not cease giving thanks for you, remembering you in my prayers.** This characteristic of Paul is revealed in many of his letters (see Phil 1:3–4; 1 Thess 1:2–3). In Phil 4:6 he recommends that believers accompany their petitions with thanksgiving, which is precisely what he does here. Constantly remembering people, thanking God for them, and

---

1. Augustine, *Treatise on the Gospel of John* 33.8.

commending them to God in prayer is another way that Christians demonstrate love (Eph 6:18; Col 4:2).

Paul begins by naming the one to whom he is praying—**the God of our Lord Jesus Christ**. The following phrase, **the Father of glory**, is a †Semitic way of saying, "the glorious Father." We understand that God is a glorious Father because of the revelation of his Son, our Lord (see 1:3). What may disconcert Christians today is referring to the Father as Jesus' God (see also John 20:17)—is not Jesus Christ equally God? He is, as Paul's use of the title "Lord" in other contexts clearly indicates.[2] There is, however, a difference in relation and role between the Father and the Son that this wording reflects. As a man, Jesus was obedient to the Father; he even offered his life as a sacrifice, a gift, to God (5:2; Phil 2:5–11). In response, the Father exalted Jesus to divine authority, as vv. 19–23 indicate.

The essence of Paul's prayer here is for God to pour out his Holy Spirit on them so that they would come to know God more deeply and understand what he has given them through Jesus Christ. Although some scholars interpret the **spirit of wisdom and revelation** as qualities of the readers' human spirit, the fact that the Old Testament refers to the Spirit of God as "a spirit of wisdom" (Isa 11:2; see Exod 31:3; 35:31) and that the other two persons of the Trinity are mentioned here suggests that Paul is referring to the Holy Spirit. Furthermore, in Eph 3:4–5 Paul identifies the Spirit as the means by which God revealed the "†mystery of Christ" to the apostles and †prophets. In this context, Paul prays that the Holy Spirit will likewise impart an understanding of God and his plan to the members of the church. The primary goal of this gift of the Spirit is **knowledge of him**, that is, that Paul's readers know God better. In 1 Cor 2:9–12, Paul teaches that it is the Spirit of God who enables us to know God. This request could seem strange, since the Ephesians already have the Spirit and already know God. But there is always more of the Spirit to receive and more †knowledge of God to acquire. Eternal life involves drinking ever more deeply of the divine Spirit (Rev 22:1, 17) and knowing God as fully as we are known (Isa 11:9; 1 Cor 13:12).

Reflection and Application (1:15–17)

If we love people, we will pray for them. Paul's example of constant prayer for those he pastored as well as other Christians he simply heard about (Rom 1:8–10; Col 1:3–4, 9; 2:1–2) helps us to see how much our love needs to grow. When my father passed away I found a list of prayer requests that he kept in

---

2. For example, Phil 2:10–11 in reference to Isa 45:23; 1 Cor 8:6 in reference to Deut 6:4.

a small notebook and updated regularly. Besides our family members, there were dozens of people for whom he prayed daily, as well as situations and even nations that he prayed for weekly. As prayers were answered, he would move the items to a different page that listed blessings for which he gave thanks.

It is interesting that Paul prays that God will send the Holy Spirit, "a spirit of wisdom and revelation," on his readers. How many of us would think to pray for that? Although we have already received the Holy Spirit through baptism and confirmation, it is always appropriate to ask for more of the Spirit.

Understanding Our Glorious Future (1:18)

---

[18]May the eyes of [your] hearts be enlightened, that you may know what is the hope that belongs to his call, what are the riches of glory in his inheritance among the holy ones,

---

NT: Eph 1:8–10; 3:18–19; Col 1:5, 9, 12; Titus 3:7
Catechism: hope, 1817–21; faith seeks understanding, 158
Lectionary: 1:3–6, 15–18: second Sunday after Christmas

1:18   Besides imparting a personal [†]knowledge of God, the Spirit helps Christians to grasp the value of what God has given us in Christ. In this regard, Paul prays that his readers may understand something about their future.

The phrase **the eyes of [your] hearts** undoubtedly refers to interior understanding (see sidebar on p. 49). In the Bible, the heart is the seat not only of feelings but also of the intellect and will; the heart is our inmost self.[3]

Paul first prays that his readers **may know what is the hope that belongs to his call**. [†]Hope always refers to the future, either as an attitude we have about the future or, as here, the actual content of that future. Paul is praying that his readers will understand the future that was promised in God's "call," the invitation to enter into a relationship with him through the [†]gospel. The basis of this call has already been explained: God knew us, loved us, and chose us before the foundation of the world (1:4–5). The hope contained in this invitation is eternal life with God and one another. Paul wants his readers to grasp that reality more deeply, because clarity about our ultimate future changes our

---

3. Translations differ as to when "the eyes of [your] hearts" are enlightened. Some, like the NAB, interpret it as future, as part of what Paul is praying for. Others, like the NRSV, understand Paul to be saying that the Ephesians have already been enlightened, through initial conversion, and now Paul is asking that they receive more insight. The NAB places "your" in brackets to indicate that not all manuscripts include this word.

Knowledge That Transforms

BIBLICAL
BACKGROUND

Paul often uses words related to knowledge: "wisdom," "insight," "revelation," and "enlighten." In the Bible, knowledge usually means more than mere information or cognitive understanding; rather, it is relational and experiential. A literal translation of Gen 4:1 reads, "The man knew Eve, his wife, and she conceived and bore Cain." Obviously, that knowledge was more than cognitive. To know God is to be in relationship with him. To know the truth about God and his plan—in the way that Paul means—is not to know it in a merely theoretical way but to have an inner understanding and appreciation of it.

Paul commends and prays for three kinds of knowledge for his readers: spiritual understanding of God's plan of salvation (theological knowledge, 1:8–10, 16–23; 3:18); insight about how to live in a way that pleases God (moral wisdom, 4:17–24; Col 1:9–10), and personal knowledge of the love of God and of Christ (Eph 3:14–19, see sidebar on p. 100).

True knowledge of the things of God comes only through the Holy Spirit: "Among human beings, who knows what pertains to a person except the spirit of the person that is within? Similarly, no one knows what pertains to God except the Spirit of God. We have not received the spirit of the world but the Spirit that is from God, so that we may understand the things freely given us by God" (1 Cor 2:11–12; see context vv. 6–16).

Paul regards spiritual understanding as pastorally important because it changes people. In Rom 12:2 he writes, "Do not conform yourself to this age but be transformed by the renewal of your mind." In Ephesians he exhorts his readers, "Be renewed in the spirit of your minds, and put on the new self" (4:23–24).

---

outlook on everything, even our view of crushing hardships and sufferings that can defeat merely human optimism.

If a man were obliged to undertake a miserable job for a year knowing that at the end of his service he would receive fifteen thousand dollars, he would probably remain an unhappy worker. But if he knew that at the end of the year he would receive fifteen million dollars, he might well whistle while he worked.[4] The hope to which we have been invited—eternal life in God's presence—infinitely surpasses any imaginable material compensation and provides a basis for extraordinary courage and joy.

Elaborating on this future, Paul prays that his readers may know **what are the riches of glory in his inheritance**. Again, he is praying for his readers to

---

4. From a sermon given at Redeemer Presbyterian Church in New York by Timothy Keller on Easter 2004, titled "The Hope of Glory."

acquire a deeper appreciation of what they have already begun to experience (the first installment of 1:13) and of what awaits them. He prays that they may grasp the immense value, "the riches of †glory," of what is theirs. By "his inheritance" Paul means the †inheritance that God provides his people (see sidebar on p. 43), described elsewhere as "an inheritance that is imperishable, undefiled, and unfading, kept in heaven for you" (1 Pet 1:4). This present and future blessing is enjoyed **among the holy ones**, not just individually but in communion with the whole people of God.

Reflection and Application (1:18)

Since the kind of knowledge that changes us comes from the Holy Spirit, we must pray for revelation and insight just as Paul does. One of the most effective means of growing in knowledge of God is through prayerful daily reading of the Bible called *lectio divina*. Sometimes it is described as having four aspects: *lectio*, reading; *meditatio*, meditation, that is, thinking about what one has read; *oratio*, prayer; and *contemplatio*, contemplation, or a wordless response of the heart to the Lord that the Holy Spirit sometimes grants.

These valid distinctions can make something very simple sound complicated. To read Scripture daily, find a few minutes when you are not likely to be interrupted. Begin by asking the Lord to speak to you or teach you through his word. Read through a few paragraphs or a chapter of the Bible—more if time allows—once or twice. In the long run, it is most fruitful to work one's way through whole books of the Bible, rather than just selections. When something catches your attention, stop and try to understand it, perhaps pausing to pray. Try to be sensitive to any insight or inspiration that the Spirit may be giving you. Conclude with a prayer thanking the Lord and asking for his grace to understand, believe, and put into practice what you have read. During the day, try to recall what you read. This practice will nourish your prayer and increase your knowledge of God and his ways. I have found it to be the most effective and enjoyable way to become familiar with the Bible. Reading Scripture has become a quiet high point of every day.

Grasping the Greatness of God's Power For Us (1:19–23)

[19]**and what is the surpassing greatness of his power for us who be-lieve, in accord with the exercise of his great might, [20]which he worked in Christ, raising him from the dead and seating him at his right hand in the heavens, [21]far above every principality, authority, power, and dominion,**

and every name that is named not only in this age but also in the one to come. ²²And he put all things beneath his feet and gave him as head over all things to the church, ²³which is his body, the fullness of the one who fills all things in every way.

OT: Ps 8:6; 110:1
NT: Matt 28:18; Mark 16:19; 1 Cor 12:12–13; Phil 2:9–11; Col 1:15–20
Catechism: Christ at the right hand of the Father, 663–64; as Lord of history and the cosmos, 668; as head of the Church, 669; the Church as the body of Christ, 790, 795
Lectionary: 1:17–23: Ascension of the Lord (Year A)

In contrast to the previous petition, which is presented in a couple of phrases, Paul develops this petition to understand God's power to the point that it becomes a proclamation of praise.

The second request that Paul makes for his readers is that they grasp **the**   **1:19**
surpassing greatness of God's **power** exercised on behalf of Christians, **for us who believe**.[5] The vocabulary of power that Paul uses is striking: **in accord with the exercise of his great might**. Translated literally the phrase reads, "in accord with the operative power (*energeia*) of the strength of his might." Why does Paul consider it so important that his readers know about this power? The Christians of Ephesus and the surrounding cities of Asia live in a world in which wealth, political power, and custom are completely enmeshed in the worship of pagan gods. Greco-Roman society understood when Jews did not participate in the pagan religious ceremonies that shaped its civic life, because Jews worshiped the God of Israel, whose temple was in Jerusalem. Gentile Christians, however, had to abandon important parts of their culture and did not enjoy the same understanding. Historian Eckhard Schnabel describes their plight:

> When polytheists in Ephesus were converted . . . they no longer visited the temple of Artemis Ephesia, no longer participated in the sacrificial rites of her cult, no longer marched in processions held in her honor. . . . When they walked across the State Agora, they no longer worshiped [Caesar] Augustus in the Basilike Stoa as they used to do. . . . They no longer dined in the temple, no longer observed the traditional rituals on the doorstep[s] of [their] house[s], [they] removed the statues of deities that stood in the cult niche in their living rooms.[6]

5. The NRSV, NJB, and NIV translate this phrase similarly. The RSV alone says "in us who believe," a less accurate translation although theologically sound. Literal translations propose "toward us who believe."

6. *Paul the Missionary* (Downers Grove, IL: InterVarsity, 2008), 359.

The Apostle is aware that his readers are in a situation in which they could easily feel powerless. They live in a society with radically different values that mocks and sometimes persecutes Christians, whose conduct sometimes appears antisocial. Christians refuse to worship the publicly recognized gods, they reject society's sexual mores, and they confess Jesus rather than Caesar as †Lord. But the divine Caesar and the pagan gods are at the center of Greco-Roman culture and commerce. Paul acknowledges the existence of opposing spiritual powers (6:12) but reassures his readers of the same truth that 1 John 4:4 announces: "the one who is in you is greater than the one who is in the world." Christians must be fully assured of the power of Christ if they are to preach the gospel, find strength to resist temptation, and live faithfully in a powerful culture whose beliefs and values are so mistaken.

1:20–21   Paul often makes his most important theological points by referring to the paschal †mystery. To demonstrate the power that is available for Christians to be victorious in the face of the †world's opposition, Paul recalls the most decisive act of power in history: the power that resurrected the human body of Jesus that lay lifeless in the tomb and that re-created his body for eternal life. This same power raised someone with the same human nature as our own to a position of authority **far above** every human and angelic power in the universe. This is what God did for Jesus.[7] Paul

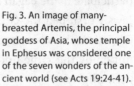

Fig. 3. An image of many-breasted Artemis, the principal goddess of Asia, whose temple in Ephesus was considered one of the seven wonders of the ancient world (see Acts 19:24-41).

Michael J. Gorman

thus includes the ascension of Christ in this more extensive explanation of the resurrection: Jesus was not only raised from death to life, he was also raised to the heights of †heaven. The phrase **seating him at his right hand in the heavens** is a metaphorical way of saying that Jesus received sovereign power from God. Here Paul alludes to Ps 110, a messianic psalm often quoted in the New Testament: "The †Lᴏʀᴅ says to my lord: 'Sit at my right hand, / till I make your enemies your footstool'" (Ps 110:1 RSV). Since the ascension, someone

---

7. This account and most New Testament accounts emphasize the Father's role in raising Jesus from the dead. Some texts, however, speak of the activity of Jesus himself (John 10:17–18) and of the Spirit (Rom 8:11) in the resurrection. The Catechism teaches that in Jesus' resurrection "the three divine persons act together as one" (648).

with our human nature, Jesus of Nazareth, sits on the throne of God wielding divine authority (see Catechism 648, 659, 668).

Paul emphasizes the extent of Christ's power by identifying everything that has been subjected to him: **every principality, authority, power, and dominion**. Although these terms can refer to human political authorities, here, as elsewhere in Ephesians (3:10; 6:12; also Col 1:16; 2:15), Paul uses these words to refer to heavenly, spiritual powers, either good or evil, that direct or influence human affairs. To make clear that there is no exception to the beings that are subject to Christ, he adds, **and every name that is named**. The Ephesians would have known of many "names" of pagan gods, goddesses, and demons invoked in both religious and magic rituals of their day. Paul wants to make it clear that Jesus' supreme authority holds good for both the present and the ultimate future, so he adds **not only in this age but also in the one to come**.[8]

To complete this description of Christ's total sovereignty, Paul quotes Ps 8:7—**he put all things beneath his feet**. The original meaning of Ps 8 was that God has set the human race in authority over creation (Gen 1:26–28):

1:22–23

> What is man that you are mindful of him,
> and the son of man [Hebrew *adam*] that you care for him?
> Yet you have made him little less than the angels,
> and you have crowned him with glory and honor.
> You have given him dominion over the works of your hands;
> you have put all things under his feet. (Ps 8:4–6 RSV Second Catholic Edition; in NAB, vv. 5–7)

But the early Christians understood this text to have a deeper meaning (Heb 2:6–9): Jesus is the "son of man," the new Adam par excellence, who now exercises authority over the entire cosmos in a far greater way than the first Adam.

Paul concludes his account of the greatness of Christ's power by asserting again, in different words, that the risen Jesus is over the entire cosmos and, at the same time, is united to his readers in a marvelous way: God **gave him as head over all things to the church**.[9] Unlike the statements later in Ephesians (4:15–16; 5:23; also Col 1:18) that Christ is the head of the Church,[10] here the point is that God has made the †Messiah the "head," the one in the highest

---

8. Judaism of the first century and early Christianity divided time into two periods, the present age and the †eschatological future, described as the age that is to come.

9. The JB and NJB interpret this as Christ's appointment as head of the Church, but this goes beyond what the text states.

10. The CCSS uses uppercase when referring to the universal Church and lowercase when referring to a local community or when using "church" as an adjective.

53

Resurrection, Ascension, and Universal Mission · LIVING TRADITION

John Paul II describes the implications of the resurrection:

> By raising Jesus from the dead, God has conquered death, and in Jesus he has definitely inaugurated his kingdom. During his earthly life, Jesus was the Prophet of the kingdom; after his passion, resurrection and ascension into heaven he shares in God's power and in his dominion over the world (cf. Matt 28:18; Acts 2:36; Eph 1:18–21). The resurrection gives a universal scope to Christ's message, his actions and whole mission. . . .
>
> Indeed, after the resurrection, the disciples preach the kingdom by proclaiming Jesus crucified and risen from the dead. . . . The first Christians also proclaim "the kingdom of Christ and of God" (Eph 5:5; cf. Rev 11:15; 12:10), or "the kingdom of our Lord and Savior Jesus Christ" (2 Pet 1:11). (*Redemptoris Missio* [*Mission of the Redeemer*] 16)

position (see sidebar on p. 160) over "all things," over the entire universe, animate and inanimate, for the benefit of the Church.[11]

The New Testament attests to both an "already" and a "not yet" dimension to Christ's headship over the universe. On the one hand, after his resurrection Jesus has been exalted as Lord (Phil 2:9–11) and has been given "all power in heaven and on earth" (Matt 28:18). On the other hand, "at present we do not see 'all things subject to him'" (Heb 2:8). In the present phase of salvation history Christ exercises his authority over the cosmos for the unfolding of God's plan, especially for the proclamation of the gospel and the building up of the Church. A day is coming when he will completely destroy evil, "put all his enemies under his feet," including death (1 Cor 15:25–28), and unite the entire creation under his gracious governance (Eph 1:10).

According to Paul, the relationship of the Church to the risen Jesus is quite extraordinary: the Church **is his body.** By †faith and baptism, Christians have become members of the body of Christ (1 Cor 12:12–13) and are henceforth an incarnate expression, a physical extension of Christ in this world. This is more than an analogy—the Church is not merely *like* a body, having various organs and members; it *is* Christ's body. Paul discovered the real union of the Messiah with his Church when the risen Jesus confronted him on the road to Damascus with the question, "Saul, Saul, why are you persecuting *me*?" (Acts 9:4, italics added). Paul understood that to persecute Christians is to persecute

11. The RSV, NRSV, and NIV translations highlight this fact by using a different preposition: God made Christ the head of all things "for the church."

Jesus himself. According to Origen, a third-century theologian, "The whole Church of Christ is Christ's body in that he ensouls it with his Godhead and fills it with his Spirit."[12] In saying that the Church is his **fullness,** *plērōma*, Paul means that the Church is completely filled with the presence of the risen Lord. Saint Augustine speaks of Christ and the Church as *totus Christus*, the whole Christ.[13] However, Paul is not saying that Christ and the Church are identical or co-extensive. Christ is greater still since he **fills all things in every way.** Jesus' power and presence permeates the entire universe because his rule is divine (4:10; see Jer 23:24).

Reflection and Application (1:19–23)

When the powers of the world, the magnitude of our troubles (see Catechism 272), or the obstacles to our ministry or the Church's mission seem overwhelming, we need not succumb to fear or dismay. God has established Christ as head of the universe for the sake of his people, the Church—for our sake! We know whose power is greater because it was demonstrated in Jesus' resurrection; death itself has been defeated. We know that no earthly or spiritual being will ultimately prevail against us, because Jesus—to whose body we have been united—has been raised "far above" every other power to the throne of God. We know that eternal life awaits us because we have tasted the life of the Spirit, the down payment on our inheritance (1:13–14). We know the end of the story, and so we are full of †hope.

---

12. Origen, *Epistle to the Ephesians*, in Mark J. Edwards, ed., *Galatians, Ephesians, Philippians*, ACCS (Downers Grove, IL: InterVarsity, 1999), 126.

13. Augustine, *On the Epistle of John* 1.2.

Saved by Grace through Faith for Good Works

Ephesians 2:1–10

Having declared the greatness of God's power manifested in Jesus' resurrection, ascension, and enthronement (1:20–23), Paul now explains how that power has affected "us who believe" (1:19) to save us from the human predicament. He begins with a brief, stark sketch of the condition of Gentiles and Jews apart from Jesus (2:1–3). Then he announces what God did about it and why (2:4–7). Paul concludes by explaining the roles of grace, faith, and good works in salvation (2:8–10).

The Problem: The Human Condition Apart from Christ (2:1–3)

---

¹You were dead in your transgressions and sins ²in which you once lived following the age of this world, following the ruler of the power of the air, the spirit that is now at work in the disobedient. ³All of us once lived among them in the desires of our flesh, following the wishes of the flesh and the impulses, and we were by nature children of wrath, like the rest.

OT: Gen 2:16–17
NT: Acts 26:18; Rom 3:23; 5:12–19; Col 1:13; 2:13; Titus 3:3
Catechism: sin and death, 400–403; the world and the devil, 407–9, 2852; the flesh, 1852, 2515

2:1–2　　Turning his attention to his †Gentile readers, Paul makes a surprising assertion: **You were dead.**[1] Describing them as "dead" indicates how radically

---

1. The RSV inserts "you he made alive" in this verse, anticipating 2:5.

deficient their former life was. These Gentile Christians were once "dead" to God, incapable of a right relationship with him. The reason for this incapacity was that they †**lived**—literally "walked" (*peripateō*), a word the Bible uses to refer to a person's way of life—in **transgressions and sins**. These two words refer to the totality of ways humans fail to do God's will: by disobeying explicit commandments (1:7) or by falling short in other ways. Paul discusses the link between sin and death in Rom 5:12–19, where he refers to the consequences of the Fall (Gen 2:17). The death that immediately followed our first parents' disobedience was spiritual: they and their descendants, who followed them in sin (Rom 5:12), were no longer capable of free communion with God and of living justly. Alienation from other humans and from nature followed (Gen 3:16–4:8), as did physical death.

Paul explains furthermore that before their conversion to Christ his Gentile readers were subject to two evil powers. The first of these evil influences was social: they "walked" **following the age of this world**.[2] Although Scripture often uses these terms neutrally, in this context "the age" (*aiōn*) and "this †world" (*kosmos*) refer to human society and culture insofar as they oppose God in the present period before his kingdom comes in its fullness.[3]

The second evil power influencing the Gentile readers was demonic: they "walked" **following the ruler of the power of the air, the spirit that is now at work in the disobedient**. This refers to the devil, whom Paul understands to exercise a power in the "air," that is, above the sphere of human activity but below God's supreme power in †heaven. Perhaps it also connotes the idea of an evil social "atmosphere." Paul is expressing the common New Testament understanding[4] that until the coming of Christ Satan exercised broad powers in the world and still continues to exercise power over "the disobedient" (literally, "sons of disobedience"),[5] those who do not keep God's law.

Until now Paul has been addressing Gentile converts who had been especially subject to Satan's power, living in a society that worshiped idols rather than the true God. But in what follows he includes himself and his fellow Jews alongside his Gentile readers. **All of us once lived among them in the desires of our flesh, following the wishes of the flesh and the impulses.** Here Paul refers to

2:3

---

2. The NAB gives the most literal rendering. The RSV and NRSV say "following the course of this world." The NJB paraphrases, "you were living by the principles of this world."

3. See John 8:23; 12:31; 14:17; 1 Cor 2:8; Gal 1:4; James 4:4; 1 John 2:15–16.

4. Matt 4:8–9; John 12:31; 1 John 5:19; Rev 12:9, 17.

5. The RSV translates this literally, "sons of disobedience," a †Semitic way of referring to people who are characterized by disobedience.

fallen human nature in its condition of disordered desires and thoughts.[6] Some people think that "the flesh" refers exclusively to bodily urges—above all, sexual desire—but that is not Scripture's view. The †flesh includes our *minds*, which are also subject to disordered "impulses" such as pride, envy, or greed (see Paul's list of the "works of the flesh" in Gal 5:19–21).

This predicament is shared by Jews and Gentiles alike: **we were by nature children of wrath, like the rest** of the human race. The fact that both Jews and Gentiles are sinners is something Paul treats in greater depth in Rom 1–3. The phrase "children of wrath" is a †Semitic idiom (like "sons of disobedience" in the previous verse) that means "those who are headed for divine judgment." The word "†wrath" occurs fairly frequently in the Bible. Sometimes it refers to human anger, but more often it refers to God's condemnation and punishment of wrongdoing. It is a mistake to think of God's wrath too anthropomorphically, as though God was having an outburst of temper. In Scripture, God's wrath is a manifestation of his holiness and is always just. This fact can actually make the wrath of God a comforting doctrine because it is a way to describe God's unalterable opposition to evil.[7]

How is it that we were "by nature" deserving of God's punishment? It cannot refer to our humanity in its essence, since humans were created good, in the image of God (Gen 1:26–27). Paul uses the same expression, "by nature," in Gal 2:15 ("we who are Jews by nature") to refer to a condition that results from birth. Most interpreters take "by nature" in 2:3 to be a reference to the sinful condition inherited from our first parents, which Paul describes in Rom 5:12–21, and which came to be called "original sin."

To sum up, Paul is saying that before they entered into relationship with Christ, his Gentile readers were spiritually dead because of their sinful actions and were caught in a web of behaviors and relationships influenced by the devil. Jews and Gentiles alike share a sinful human nature and are destined for judgment.

Reflection and Application (2:1–3)

Although most Christians are aware of sin in their lives, the degree to which readers identify with this description of the human predicament will vary. Those who are adult converts to Christianity will identify most easily, since

---

6. The word translated "impulses" by the NAB is more accurately translated "thoughts" (NIV). The JB paraphrases: "living sensual lives, ruled entirely by our own physical desires and our own ideas."

7. John R. W. Stott, *The Message of Ephesians: God's New Society*, The Bible Speaks Today (Downers Grove, IL: InterVarsity, 1986), 76.

their situation resembles that of Paul's readers. It is not uncommon to hear people who lived sinful lives describe suddenly waking up to an awareness of how "dead" they were. Also, many Catholics who came to faith and conversion after baptism can identify with Paul's description. Some Catholics, however, have lived their faith from childhood without being dominated by the world, the flesh, and the devil. Does this text apply to them? Saint Thérèse of Lisieux, who belongs in this category, explains: "I recognize that without Him, I would have fallen as low as Mary Magdalene did, . . . but I also know that Jesus has *forgiven me more* than He did for *Mary Magdalene*, since He forgave me *in advance*, keeping me from falling."[8] In a word, Christians like St. Thérèse were rescued from the same thing—the spiritual death of sin and its consequences—but at a much earlier stage, before its effects became manifest.

Some readers will wonder whether Paul's outlook is too grim. These verses, however, are not intended to provide a complete description of the human condition but rather a thumbnail sketch of the evils from which Christ saves us. A complete biblical theology would affirm that the image of God in which humans have been created has not been obliterated by sin, only disfigured. It would affirm that God reveals himself in the beauty of creation (Rom 1:19–20) and reveals his will for human conduct in conscience (Rom 2:14–15), and thus non-Christian cultures may perceive aspects of truth (Acts 17:22–28). It would acknowledge that there have been men and women, among both Jews and Gentiles, whom Scripture depicts as righteous, people like Enoch and Noah (Gen 5:24; 6:9), Ruth and Job, Zechariah and Elizabeth (Luke 1:6). Nevertheless, even these righteous figures have sinned and depend on Christ for salvation (Rom 3:9–24).

Although the Catholic Church teaches that non-Christians who sincerely seek God and try to do his will can be saved through Christ, it also teaches that "very often, deceived by the Evil One," people choose the way of falsehood and idolatry or reject God altogether and "are exposed to ultimate despair" (*Lumen Gentium* 16; see also Catechism 839–48). While it is charitable to hope and pray for those who have died without an explicit relationship with Christ, it would be extremely uncharitable to presume on the salvation of non-Christians and, for that reason, to fail to proclaim to them the good news of salvation in Jesus.

Paul's depiction in 2:1–3 of human life apart from Christ helps to explain the very great evils we sometimes see in the world. It shows humanity's need for God and our powerlessness to save ourselves from evils that surpass our natural abilities—sin, the world, our disordered nature, and the devil. These

---

8. St. Thérèse of Lisieux, *The Story of a Soul*, trans. Robert J. Edmonson (Brewster, MA: Paraclete, 2006), 86.

verses indicate why Jesus' death on the cross was necessary and why every other religious or secular solution is inadequate. Scripture's diagnosis of the maladies that afflict our race provide a compelling reason for evangelization, for sharing the medicine of the †gospel with every man, woman, and child.

God's Solution, God's Motives (2:4–7)

---

[4]But God, who is rich in mercy, because of the great love he had for us, [5]even when we were dead in our transgressions, brought us to life with Christ (by grace you have been saved), [6]raised us up with him, and seated us with him in the heavens in Christ Jesus, [7]that in the ages to come he might show the immeasurable riches of his grace in his kindness to us in Christ Jesus.

OT: Exod 34:6–7; Ps 103
NT: John 3:16; Rom 5:5–10; Col 2:12–13; 3:1–4
Catechism: God takes the initiative to love us, 604–5; divinization, 1988, 1996; graces and charisms, 2003; seated with Christ in the heavens, 2796
Lectionary: 2:4–10: Fourth Sunday of Lent (Year B)

2:4–6   After succinctly describing humanity's desperate predicament, Paul bursts out with a declaration of the good news, beginning with the hopeful words, **But God**. God has not left us in our misery. God saw the situation of the human race, much as Exod 2:23–25 tells us he saw the plight of his people Israel enslaved in Egypt and acted to save them. Paul describes what kind of God this is: he is **rich in mercy**. Mercy, *eleos*, refers to the good will and kindness that seeks to help someone who is in trouble or need.

God's motive for acting was his desire for our welfare: he acted **because of the great love he had for us**. The Greek is more forceful, using the word for "love" both in its noun and verb forms: "because of his great love with which he loved us." Love (*agapē*) refers to cherishing and caring in a self-giving, disinterested way. To make plain that we did not deserve this love, Paul indicates that God loved us **even when we were dead in our transgressions**. This line recalls Rom 5:8, where Paul says that "God proves his love for us in that while we were still sinners Christ died for us."

Paul interrupts the sentence to reaffirm parenthetically that this initiative on God's part was totally gratuitous, undeserved: **by grace you have been saved**. To save (*sōzō*) means to rescue from any kind of trouble, danger, or affliction and refers to the problems of humanity described in 2:1–3. This salvation is depicted as something that has already taken place. In the Greek, the word "saved" is in the †perfect tense, which describes a past event whose effects continue in the present.

To explain how God saved us, Paul uses three verbs to which he adds the prefix *syn-*, which means "with." The repetition of this prefix links us inextricably to Christ in the action that unfolds. God **brought us to life with Christ . . . , raised us up with him, and seated us with him in the heavens**. When God the Father brought Jesus to life, raised him to †heaven, and enthroned him at his right hand (1:20–21), in a mysterious way he did this for all Christians too. We used to be spiritually dead; now we are spiritually alive. Although he does not say it here, Paul is speaking about our union with Jesus' dying and rising through †faith and baptism. Other Pauline texts explicitly state that faith and baptism unite Christians to Jesus' death and resurrection (Rom 6:3–4; Col 2:11–13).[9] Paul presupposes that his readers already understand this, probably from their pre- or postbaptismal catechesis.

The phrase "seated us with him in the heavens" **in Christ Jesus** goes beyond other texts that speak of the believer's solidarity with Jesus' dying and rising. Paul's words raise obvious questions. To all appearances we are still very much living on the earth, so what does he mean? We could say that Paul uses a spatial metaphor to describe liberation in Christ from the evils that dominated us (2:1–3). God has rescued us by raising us in some sense *above* the spiritual death that was the consequence of our sinful way of life (Rom 5:17–18; 6:2–4), "the age of this world" (see Rom 12:2; Gal 6:14), the power of the devil (Col 1:13), and "the desires of our flesh" (Rom 8:1–10; Gal 5:13–25).

However, there is more to our being seated with Christ in the heavens. If we are "in Christ Jesus," members of his body, and Christ our "head" is in heaven, we also are in heaven in some way. Life in the Spirit is life in God, whose presence defines the boundaries of heaven. Colossians says, "For you have died, and your life is hidden with Christ in God. When Christ your life appears, then you too will appear with him in glory" (Col 3:3–4). Catherine of Siena expresses a similar idea: "All the way to heaven is heaven, because our Lord said, 'I am the way.'" The liturgy and prayer "in the Spirit"[10] are the most obvious ways Christians express participation in the life of heaven (Heb 12:22–24).

---

9. Col 2:12 refers to both baptism and faith, while Rom 6:3–4 mentions only baptism, but in the context of Paul's discussion of faith, beginning in chapter 3. Paul does not conceive of baptism apart from faith in Christ, nor faith in Christ apart from baptism. When one is mentioned, the other is presupposed.

10. Eph 6:18 (see comment on that verse); see also Rom 8:26; Jude 20.

Colossians 3:1–4:6 describes how being exalted with Christ should affect our goals and our conduct.

2:7   Nevertheless, it is obvious that being seated with Christ in the heavens does not mean that Christians now fully experience reigning with Christ, even though we have begun to experience the benefits of salvation. God's purpose for saving us is so **that in the ages to come he might show the immeasurable riches of his grace in his kindness to us.** A glorious future awaits us.[11] As was mentioned earlier (1:21), the fundamental division of time in Scripture is the division between the present age and the age to come. When Paul speaks of "the ages to come," he refers to our eternal future.[12] God plans to "show"—the word could be translated to "demonstrate," "display," or "prove"—how much he loves us. Lovers long to express the immensity of their love. God's purpose in saving us was not merely to rescue us but also to put us in a position that would enable him to express in a tangible way "the immeasurable riches of his grace in his kindness to us."

In the meantime, much of what God has done for us remains hidden. Romans 8:19 says, "For creation awaits with eager expectation the *revelation* of the children of God" (emphasis added). Our true identity as God's children is presently concealed from the world (1 John 3:1–2), but in the age to come, God intends to fully demonstrate his infinite love for us by manifesting it for all to see.

Reflection and Application (2:4–7)

Like the opening blessing of 1:3–14, these verses arouse amazement and gratitude for what God has done for us. They provide a basis for tremendous confidence in God's love, despite our sins, which he knew all about before he acted to save us. These verses explain how God's powerful action in raising Jesus from the dead was really "for us who believe" (1:19). They also shed light on our †hope for the future, something Paul prayed his readers would come to know (1:18).

God raised and enthroned Jesus of Nazareth after his crucifixion, around AD 30. However, none of us and not all of Paul's original readers were born at the

11. The JB and NJB interpret that as a past event with continuing consequences, rather than as a future benefit: "this was to show for all ages to come."

12. Both in the preaching of Jesus and in the life of the Church the new era has already begun but awaits its completion. In 1 Cor 10:11 Paul describes Christians as those "upon whom the end of the ages has come." In Eph 2 this "already" and "not yet" dimension of the kingdom is indicated by the fact that we have already been raised and seated with Christ in the heavens (v. 6) but await the full revelation of God's grace toward us in the future (v. 7).

time of these events. How can he say that we were "brought to life . . . raised up . . . and seated with Christ"? The answer is that these things occurred to Paul's readers and to us at baptism. Though a person may receive baptism centuries after the death and resurrection of Christ, at the moment of baptism, that person is united across time with Jesus in his death and resurrection. All the sacraments enable us to transcend time and place because they unite us to Jesus, the eternal son of God, whose paschal †mystery transcends time and space.

The Roles of Grace, Faith, and Works (2:8–10)

> **8For by grace you have been saved through faith, and this is not from you; it is the gift of God; 9it is not from works, so no one may boast. 10For we are his handiwork, created in Christ Jesus for the good works that God has prepared in advance, that we should live in them.**

NT: Acts 15:11; 2 Cor 5:17; Titus 3:4–8
Catechism: all our merit from Christ, 2006–11; necessity of works, 1815

These verses repeat and then comment on the parenthetical statement in 2:5, "by grace you have been saved." Paul begins with the conjunction **For** to indicate that an explanation is coming, in this case an explanation of a word he used twice in the preceding verses, **grace**. †Grace (*charis*) refers to what is given freely, an unearned, unmerited gift. Paul wants to emphasize that the salvation we have received is entirely God's initiative.   **2:8–9**

The structure of verses 8–9 leaves no opportunity for misunderstanding. Paul begins with the assertion that **by grace you have been saved**. Then he denies we had anything to do with it: **and this is not from you**. Then he repeats the point—our salvation **is the gift of God**—and again he denies that it proceeds from human effort—**it is not from works**. Finally, he states a reason for this fact: **so no one may boast**. It is a consistent biblical and Pauline teaching that God wants his people to realize that he is the source of their salvation and that all the credit belongs to him and not to any human being.[13] In the Christian religion there is no room for pride or self-sufficiency. Our basis for boasting is what God has done (1 Cor 1:29–31).

Paul indicates that this grace of salvation has come **through faith**. In Paul, †faith does not indicate mere belief or mental assent to a truth but rather a personal commitment that includes belief, trust, and obedience. Even the necessary

13. See, for instance, Deut 8:11–18; Judg 7:2; Jer 9:22–23; Rom 3:27; 4:2.

Justification and Salvation

When Paul speaks of grace and faith in Rom 3:21–26 and Gal 2:15–21 he is discussing justification, but here he speaks of salvation. What is the difference? In Paul's usage, justification is generally a narrower concept, referring to the action of God by which Jews and †Gentiles obtain a right relationship with God and become full members of the redeemed community. Paul's concern about justification arose in response to the Judaizers, who said that it was necessary for Gentile Christians to be circumcised and to observe the Jewish law in order to be justified. Paul insisted, however, that because of the universality of sin no one can be justified by works and that all need the grace of God, which is received through faith in the Messiah on the basis of his atoning death on the cross.[a]

In Ephesians Paul does not address the claims of the Judaizers or the issue of justification. Instead, he addresses Gentile Christians and says something analogous: salvation from sin, Satan, the †world, and the †flesh has come to us through the grace of God through Christ's resurrection.[b]

a. In the Christian theological tradition and in the Reformation controversies, justification acquired a wider meaning; in fact, some of the controversy resulted from using the term in different senses. For a description of the Catholic theology of justification, see Catechism 1987–2029. For the ecumenical progress that has occurred in understanding this concept, see the "Joint Declaration on the Doctrine of Justification" signed by the Catholic Church and the Lutheran World Federation in 1997 (available on the internet).

b. In Rom 4:25 Paul links justification with Christ's resurrection.

response of faith in the †Messiah is God's gift (Catechism 153–55), although Paul does not say this explicitly.[14]

2:10   Verse 10 also begins with the conjunction **For** to signal that more explanation is coming. Not only are we not saved because of *our* works, **we are his handiwork**—he made us, and he made us well. The word "handiwork," *poiēma*, from which we get the English word "poem," can bear an aesthetic sense. As the NJB puts it, "we are his work of art." Furthermore, it is not simply that we have been rescued from the evils that oppressed us—we have been made completely new, **created in Christ Jesus**. Since the context speaks of how we have been saved, we know that Paul is not speaking of our original creation but of a re-creation, something he mentions twice more in this letter (2:15; 4:24).

14. Some ancient and medieval interpreters (e.g., Jerome, Chrysostom, Aquinas) understand the phrase, "and *this* is not your own doing" (2:8b NRSV) to refer to the "faith" (2:8a) by which we are saved. While it is true that faith is itself God's gift, most modern interpreters hold that "this" refers to the preceding clause as a whole ("by grace you have been saved through faith"), rather than to "faith."

Making us a "new creation" (2 Cor 5:17; Gal 6:15) is an important aspect of Paul's description of what God has done for believers. "Created" emphasizes the radical newness of life in Christ. Jesus' resurrection began the new creation, and our re-creation was accomplished when we were joined to our risen Lord through faith and baptism.

Both in Paul's day and in our own, some people have drawn the erroneous conclusion that because "works" are not the basis of our justification and salvation, only faith matters. Does being saved by grace through faith mean that works are unimportant? Not at all. Paul explains that we have been created in Christ Jesus **for the good works**. The *purpose* of our salvation and re-creation is to live a different kind of life than we used to when we "walked" in "transgressions and sins" (2:1). Many texts in Paul's letters and the rest of the New Testament insist that proper conduct and good works accompany faith.[15] In fact, after the doctrinal section in Paul's letters to churches, he always devotes substantial space to describing the conduct that corresponds to Christian faith.

Good works are important as a goal and outcome of our faith, and Paul wants us to know that God is also at work in the good works that **God has prepared in advance**. The Catechism follows Paul by teaching, "The merit of good works is to be attributed in the first place to the grace of God. . . . Man's merit . . . itself is due to God, for his good actions proceed in Christ, from the predispositions and assistance given by the Holy Spirit" (2008). Paul says our good works have been "prepared in advance" by God. Saint Thomas sees this as a kind of predestination: "For predestination is nothing else than the pre-arrangement of God's blessings, among which blessings our good works themselves are numbered."[16] Predestination, however, does not eliminate free will. On the contrary, Paul indicates the importance of our willing cooperation in these good works by adding the otherwise unnecessary phrase, **that we should live in them**. Paul uses this word "live"—literally, "walk"—five more times in this letter (4:1, 17; 5:2, 8, 15), each time advising his readers how they should or should not conduct themselves. God's preparation and our free choices cooperate to enable us to fulfill God's will that good works characterize our lives (Catechism 1993).

There are two possible interpretations of what Paul means by saying that our good works have been prepared in advance by God. He could be referring

15. See Eph 5:5–6; Rom 6:12–13; 1 Cor 6:9–10; 15:58; 2 Cor 5:10; Gal 5:13–26; Titus 2:14; 3:8, 14; Heb 10:24–27. Sometimes James 2:14–26 is portrayed as contradicting Paul in our present text. James may well be correcting a misinterpretation of Paul's teaching, but James is not denying the priority of faith. He simply insists that true faith must express itself in works, a fact that Paul's teaching also recognizes.

16. Thomas Aquinas, *Commentary on Saint Paul's Epistle to the Ephesians* 2.3, trans. Matthew L. Lamb (Albany, NY: Magi, 1966), 97.

Two Fathers of the Church on Salvation by Grace through Faith

LIVING TRADITION

Saint Ambrose confirms the teaching of St. Paul and indicates that celebration is the proper response to this blessing:

> Do not rely on your own efforts but on the grace of Christ. "You are," says the apostle, "saved by grace." Therefore it is not a matter of arrogance here but faith when we celebrate: We are accepted! This is not pride but devotion. (*On the Sacraments* 5.4.19)[a]

Saint John Chrysostom also emphasizes that it is all grace from start to finish:

> So that you may not be elated by the magnitude of these benefits, see how Paul puts you in your place. For *by grace you are saved,* he says, *through faith.* Then, so as to do no injury to free will, he allots a role to us, then takes it away again, saying *and this is not of yourselves.* . . . Even faith, he says, is not from us. For if the Lord had not come, if he had not called us, how should we have been able to believe? . . . [Rom 10:14]. So even the act of faith is not self-initiated. It is, he says, *the gift of God.* (*Homilies on Ephesians* 2.8)[b]

a. Mark J. Edwards, ed., *Galatians, Ephesians, Philippians,* ACCS (Downers Grove, IL: InterVarsity, 1999), 133.

b. Ibid., 134. See the footnote on "through faith" regarding 2:8 (page 64 note 14).

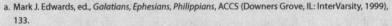

generally to a lifestyle of good works prepared for Jesus' disciples. Or he could be saying here what we also know to be true, that God has a *unique* plan and vocation for each of his sons and daughters.

Reflection and Application (2:8–10)

The necessity of grace. Paul's forceful teaching that salvation is God's gift and not the result of what we do provides an important corrective to the idea that we can and must save ourselves. This is a common assumption of those who strive to solve humanity's deepest problems by means of education, the social sciences, technology, politics, or economics without addressing their spiritual aspects. While all these means can benefit others, they will continue to come up short until people avail themselves of God's grace to address humanity's root problems named in 2:1–3.

Even religious people sometimes believe or act as though their religious and moral exertion is the fundamental way they can win God's favor, but that error leads to various problems. Some who think that correct conduct is the basis of salvation despair of being saved, since they know their sinfulness. Others who share that assumption pride themselves on their religious or moral achievement and feel superior to those whose lack of self-control is more obvious. Still others adopt a legalistic approach to life, weighing their good deeds against their sins, hoping to keep the balance tipped in their favor.

A positive result of the Protestant Reformation was the rediscovery and emphasis on Scripture's teaching about the primacy of grace. Although this was always the genuine Catholic doctrine, faulty teaching and some popular religious practices had obscured this truth. Over the years many Catholics have heard these truths for the first time from Protestants. Protestant teaching, however, often fails to give adequate place to the role of good works. The Council of Trent in the sixteenth century and the Second Vatican Council in the twentieth century reaffirmed the centrality of God's grace while affirming the necessity of human cooperation with that grace.[17]

"Are you saved?" Catholics often do not know how to respond when evangelical or fundamentalist Christians pose this question, since Catholics are not accustomed to using the word "saved" to describe their present condition. Despite the unfamiliar language, there is no need for hesitation, since Paul declares forthrightly, "by grace you have been saved." Catholics can confidently say, "Yes, I am saved, thanks be to God!" But there is more to the story. Paul and other New Testament authors use the word "save" (*sōzō*) to refer to events in the past, the present, and the future. As in Rom 8:24, Paul here speaks of the salvation we have already experienced. Elsewhere Paul says that we are *in the process* of being saved (1 Cor 1:18; Phil 2:12). Finally, many New Testament texts refer to salvation at the last judgment as a *future* good we await (Luke 13:23–24; John 10:9; Rom 5:10). It is one thing for a person to be saved from being lost and set on the right road; it is another to arrive at one's destination. Believers are summoned to continue on the road to salvation, living a life of divinely enabled charity and good works, to reach the destination of eternal life with God.

Some who ask "Are you saved?" hold to a doctrine of "eternal security," sometimes summarized as "once saved, always saved." According to this view, once people believe in Christ, their salvation is absolutely secure and there is nothing they can do to lose it. But the New Testament is quite consistent in

17. For the Church's teaching about grace and the necessary human response, see Council of Trent Sixth Session (1547, "Decree on Justification," esp. chaps. 1–11, 16 [DS 1525–38, 1545–49]); Vatican II, *Lumen Gentium (Dogmatic Constitution on the Church)* 39–42; Catechism 1987–2029.

warning Christians to be vigilant against temptation and not to presume on the status we have already attained (1 Cor 10:1–12; Phil 3:12–14).[18] On this biblical basis the Catholic Church teaches that no one can know "with absolute certitude" that he or she will persevere in following Christ and so be saved at the last day.[19] Our daily choices to follow Christ, especially the decision to repent whenever we fall, are the best indicators of our final destiny. Vigilance does not mean being anxious or fearful about God's attitude toward us at the final judgment. The New Testament provides many strong assurances of God's steadfast love for us and solid reasons for Christians to †hope confidently in their future salvation (John 10:27–29; Rom 5:1–11; 8:28–29). As Paul proclaims in Rom 5:8–10 (RSV):

> God shows his love for us in that while we were yet sinners Christ died for us. Since, therefore, we are now justified by his blood, much more shall we be saved by him from the wrath of God. For if while we were enemies we were reconciled to God by the death of his Son, much more, now that we are reconciled, shall we be saved by his life.

---

18. Other examples include Gal 5:4; 2 Thess 2:3; 1 Tim 1:19; Heb 3:7–19; 6:4–8; 10:26–31; 1 John 2:19. See Catechism 837.

19. Council of Trent, "Decree on Justification," 13 (DS 1541).

Gentiles and Jews Reconciled to God and United in the Messiah

Ephesians 2:11–22

Most of us have had the experience at one time or another of being left out. Perhaps we were not chosen for a sports team or were not accepted by a group we wanted to join. Some of us have experienced the pain of exclusion because of race, religion, nationality, socio-economic status, or gender. Some of us may have had the good fortune of being accepted and included where we previously were not. That can be a rather heady experience, particularly if the group that now welcomes us is a genuinely worthy group. It is this kind of remarkable reversal that Paul now recounts.

Paul reminds Gentile believers that at one time they were the consummate outsiders, separated from God and from his chosen people Israel (2:11–12). He explains that the Messiah's sacrificial death on the cross has brought them in, reconciling Jews and Gentiles to one another and to God in a re-created human race (2:13–18). The upshot is that Gentile believers now enjoy an astonishingly close relationship with God as members of his household and as part of his temple on earth (2:19–22).

The Gentiles' Previous Status as Outsiders (2:11–12)

¹¹Therefore, remember that at one time you, Gentiles in the flesh, called the uncircumcision by those called the circumcision, which is done in the flesh by human hands, ¹²were at that time without Christ, alienated from

the community of Israel and strangers to the covenants of promise, without hope and without God in the world.

NT: Rom 9:4; 1 Thess 4:13
Catechism: role of the Jewish People, 62–64, 839; covenants, 72, 2077

2:11   Paul contrasts the past and present of his readers as he did in 2:1–10, bidding them to **remember** their previous condition. He addresses himself to **you, Gentiles in the flesh**, suggesting that most of his readers are not Jews. He points out that Jews, **the circumcision**, sometimes refer to †Gentiles derogatorily as **the uncircumcision**. In the Old Testament (e.g., Exod 12:48; Ezek 44:7, 9) and in the Judaism of Paul's day, this term referred to those who were considered unclean, or lacking the covenant relationship with God that Israel enjoyed, signified by circumcision. But Paul hints that this difference between Jews and Gentiles is of limited value, for he describes circumcision as **done in the flesh by human hands** and thus *not* a divine action that affects a human being at the deepest level.

2:12   Paul now lists five privileges of Israel from which his Gentile readers were previously excluded, indicating his high view of the blessings that belong to Israel (see also Rom 9:4–5). First, and above all, Gentiles were **without Christ**, that is, they lacked the relationship with Israel's †Messiah that they now enjoy. Second, they were **alienated from the community of Israel**, completely outside God's chosen people. Third, they had no participation in **the covenants of promise**, the solemn agreements that God made with Abraham, Isaac, and Jacob in which he promised to bless them and their descendants and to be their God.[1] The fourth and fifth privileges that the Gentiles lacked follow from the first three. They were **without hope**, in other words, without †hope of experiencing the future blessing promised to Abraham's descendants, and in particular, without hope of resurrection, which was shared by many first-century Jews. Finally, they were **without God in the world** because they lacked a relationship with the true God.

Reconciliation for All through Jesus' Death on the Cross (2:13–16)

---

[13]**But now in Christ Jesus you who once were far off have become near by the blood of Christ.**

---

1. Probably by describing them as "covenants of promise" Paul intends to indicate the covenants with the patriarchs (Gen 15:7–21; 17:1–21; 26:2–5; 28:13–15) rather than the Sinai covenant (see Gal 3:16–19).

¹⁴**For he is our peace, he who made both one and broke down the dividing wall of enmity, through his flesh,** ¹⁵**abolishing the law with its commandments and legal claims, that he might create in himself one new person in place of the two, thus establishing peace,** ¹⁶**and might reconcile both with God, in one body, through the cross, putting that enmity to death by it.**

OT: Isa 9:5; 57:19; 65:17–18

NT: 1 Cor 12:13; 2 Cor 5:18–21; Col 1:21–22; 2:14

Catechism: the Church as the sacrament of unity, 775; the Church as the one People of God, 781; the New Law of freedom, 1972

Lectionary: 2:13–18: Mystery of the Holy Cross

Now Paul explains how Christ's death eliminated the causes of division between Jew and Gentile and united both groups to God.

The first words of verse 13 emphasize the contrast between the †Gentiles' previous and present conditions. **But now in Christ Jesus,** that is, through their union with the †Messiah Jesus, the Gentiles who used to be **far off**—distant from God and his people—**have become near**. Some of the Dead Sea Scrolls and later rabbis employ this metaphor of distance drawn from Old Testament texts (e.g., 1 Kings 8:41; Ps 148:14) to describe the differing status of Gentiles and Jews in relationship to God. They refer to a convert to Judaism, a proselyte, as one who has come or has been brought near. Paul uses the metaphor to describe the change in the Gentiles' status, which has occurred not by conversion to Judaism but by a more radical remedy, namely, **the blood of Christ**, Jesus' sacrificial death on the cross.

2:13

The long and complicated sentence of the next three verses explains how the Messiah's death eliminated the distance that separated Gentiles from God and his people. **For he is our peace.** When Jews like Paul use the Greek word for peace, *eirēnē*, in a religious context, it bears the richer connotations of the Hebrew word *shalom*: wholeness, well-being, fullness of blessing. If Christ is our *shalom*, what did he do?

2:14

First, he **made both one,** that is, he eliminated the essential difference between Jew and Gentile by bringing both into one community united to himself. In Gal 3:27–28 Paul links this unity with baptism: "For all of you who were baptized into Christ have clothed yourselves with Christ. There is neither Jew nor Greek, there is neither slave nor free person, there is not male and female; for you are all one in Christ Jesus." In order to achieve this, Jesus **broke down the dividing wall of enmity** that separated Jew and Gentile. Most scholars believe this "dividing wall" refers to one or the other of the two most important identity markers of first-century Judaism: the temple in Jerusalem and the law of Moses.

Fig. 4. This Greek inscription on a stone plaque warns Gentiles not to enter the sacred precincts of the Jerusalem temple on pain of death.

Only Jews could enter the inner courts of the temple, the place where the God of Israel made himself available in a unique way. Gentiles who worshiped Israel's God, called "God-fearers," could get only as close as an outer court. Beyond that a barrier with warning signs kept them out. Archaeologists have recovered one of these signs bearing the following: "No man of another race is to enter within the fence and enclosure around the Temple. Whoever is caught will have only himself to thank for the death which follows."[2] If this is the division Paul had in mind, the Gentiles' participation in a spiritual temple (2:21–22) indicates an immense change of status.

The other "dividing wall" in Judaism that excluded Gentiles was the law of Moses as it was traditionally interpreted. This constituted a sociological barrier, forbidding Jews to intermarry or even to eat with Gentiles. Some Jewish writers described the Mosaic law, or the †Torah, as a "fence" protecting Jews from Gentile moral and ritual defilement. But human sinfulness transformed a divinely intended distinction between Jew and Gentile into a source of enmity. The legally enshrined practice of separation "often led Jews to have a contempt for Gentiles which could regard Gentiles as less than human. In response, Gentiles would often regard Jews with great suspicion, considering them inhospitable and hateful to non-Jews, and indulge in anti-Jewish prejudice."[3]

2. Quoted in Andrew T. Lincoln, *Ephesians*, Word Biblical Commentary (Waco: Word, 1990), 141.

3. Ibid., 142.

How did Jesus tear down either of these walls? Paul says he "broke down the dividing wall of enmity" **through his flesh**, which here, like "the blood of Christ" in 2:13, alludes to the Messiah's death.

To Paul's original readers there is more than a hint of sacrifice in the mention of Jesus' "blood" and "flesh." In temple worship, sacrifices entailed the separation of the †flesh and the blood of the sacrificial animal. The blood was poured out on the altar and the flesh was divided, some being burnt as a gift to God and some being eaten by the worshipers. To a Christian community that regularly celebrated the Lord's Supper (at which this letter was probably read aloud), mention of Christ's blood and flesh would have called to mind the rite they were about to celebrate. Elsewhere Paul teaches that sharing in Christ's sacrifice by partaking of his body and blood is the basis of the Church's unity (1 Cor 10:16–17).

Jesus' sacrificial death removed the division that led to hostility between Jew **2:15** and Gentile by **abolishing the law with its commandments and legal claims.**[4] "Abolishing" (*katargeō*) might be better translated "vacating" or "nullifying." Paul is saying that by means of Christ's death, a covenant relationship with God no longer depends on observance of the law of Moses. Israel had indeed been graced with a special relationship with God through the covenant God made with Israel at Sinai—a relationship not available to Gentiles unless they became Jews by accepting circumcision and the law. Now the relationship of both Jews and Gentiles to God is founded on "the new covenant in my blood" (1 Cor 11:25), that is, on Messiah Jesus' death on the cross, rather than on the law of Moses that divided them.

Whether or not the law constituted the "dividing wall of enmity," there is no doubt Paul is saying that Jesus' death radically changed the status of the law of Moses.[5] We need to proceed carefully here, since Paul clearly does not think that the law has ceased to be important (see 6:2–3 and sidebar on p. 181). Elsewhere he recommends love of neighbor as a *means* of keeping the commandments (Rom 13:8–10; Gal 5:14) and even says that Christ's death took place "so that the righteous decree of the law might be fulfilled in us" (Rom 8:4). Later theological

---

4. The NJB offers a possible alternative translation: "destroying . . . the hostility, that is, the Law of commandments with its decrees."

5. Paul explains in Gal 2:15–16 that Jewish believers like himself have come to rely on faith in Jesus and his death on the cross in order to be in a right relationship with God ("justified"). He suggests that through solidarity with Jesus' death in baptism (Rom 6:3–4; Gal 2:19–20; Col 2:12), Jewish believers have "died to the law" (Gal 2:19–20; see Rom 7:1–4) in order to belong to Jesus Christ along with Gentiles who have been justified the same way. Paul does not explain here God's relationship with the Jewish people who have not believed in Christ (see Rom 11:25–29) or why Jewish Christians like himself continued in some degree to observe the law (Acts 16:1–3; 21:23–26).

reflection distinguishes between the law's moral requirements that continue to reveal God's will and its ritual requirements that are no longer binding since they have been fulfilled in Christ's sacrifice.

The next phrase, **that he might**, indicates Jesus' purpose for what he did. His goal was nothing less than to **create in himself one new person in place of the two, thus establishing peace**. The Greek word translated as "person" is *anthrōpos*, which can be translated "human being" or "man" (understood inclusively, RSV, ESV, NIV, NJB). The NRSV renders it as "humanity" to indicate that Paul is speaking of humans in a collective sense. Jews regarded humanity as divided in two parts: the people of Israel and the Gentiles (every other nationality). Jesus' purpose was to remove that division once and for all and create one new human race in himself. It is highly significant that Paul repeats the word "create" (used in 2:10) to describe what God has accomplished. Through Jesus' death and resurrection, God has initiated the "new creation" (2 Cor 5:17; Gal 6:15) promised in Isa 65:17–18. He has created a new humanity without divisions in Jesus, who is a second Adam (see Rom 5:12–19; 1 Cor 15:45–49). God has opened a new possibility for the "dead" (2:1) and divided descendants of the first Adam: to be united in the Messiah, to share in peace (2:14) and wholeness.

2:16   Paul attributes a second purpose to Jesus' sacrifice that is even more important: that he **might reconcile both with God**. Prior to this point Paul has focused exclusively on what the Gentiles lacked, but now he reminds us that Israel was also estranged from God. Despite being the chosen people and receiving the "covenants of promise" (2:12), Israel had broken the covenant God made with them at Sinai and needed forgiveness (Jer 31:32–34). In Eph 2:3 (as in Rom 1–3) Paul indicates that sin and its consequences are universal: "All of us once lived among them in the desires of our flesh, . . . and we were by nature children of wrath, like the rest."

Jews and Gentiles are reconciled to God **in one body**. Surely this refers to the body of Jesus, but in what sense? By including the word "one," Paul indicates that he is referring to the ecclesial body of Christ, the Church, which unites Jews and Gentiles who are themselves united to Jesus through baptism and the Holy Spirit: "For in one Spirit we were all baptized into one body, whether Jews or Greeks, . . . and we were all given to drink of one Spirit" (1 Cor 12:13). The church of Antioch (from which Paul was originally sent on mission) and the churches Paul founded included both Jewish and Gentile believers in the same community (Acts 11:19–26; 13:43–48; 18:1–8). The Church thus provided visible proof of the reconciliation in Christ of divided humanity.

Keeping Enmity Dead

Saint John Chrysostom exhorts us to take full advantage of Jesus' victory over enmity in relationships:

> No expression could be more authoritative or emphatic [than 2:16]. His death, [Paul] says, killed the enmity, wounded and destroyed it. He did not give the task to another. And he not only did the work but suffered for it. He did not say that he dissolved it; he did not say that he put an end to it, but he used the much more forceful expression: He killed! This shows that it need not ever rise again. . . . So long as we remain in the body of Christ, so long as we are one with him it does not rise again but lies dead. (*Homily on Ephesians* 5.2.16)[a]

a. Mark J. Edwards, ed., *Galatians, Ephesians, Philippians*, ACCS (Downers Grove, IL: InterVarsity, 1999), 141.

The next phrase underscores how we have been reconciled, namely, **through the cross**. This is the third time (vv. 13, 14, 16) Paul points to Jesus' death on the cross as the means by which reconciliation with God and one another has been achieved (see 2 Cor 5:19, 21).

Paul completes this account of our reconciliation with an exclamation. What happened to the enmity that existed between Jew and Gentile? Jesus put **that enmity to death by it**, that is, by the cross.[6] A literal translation of the Greek is even more forceful: by the cross "he killed the enmity"!

Reflection and Application (2:13–16)

Developing Paul's affirmation that God has created a new humanity in Christ, the *Epistle to Diognetus*, an anonymous second-century writing, describes Christians as a "new" or "third" race.[7] This assumes a difference between Jews and Gentiles and underscores an even greater difference between those who have been created as a new humanity in Christ and those who have not.

It also raises a legitimate question: rather than bringing unity, has not the coming of Christ had the effect of adding yet one more division to the human race? In one of his earliest theological writings, Joseph Ratzinger (later Pope Benedict XVI) wrestled with the paradox of brotherhood that we know from

---

6. The pronoun translated "it" could refer either to the cross or to Christ. The NJB renders this phrase, "in his own person he killed the hostility"; the JB is similar.

7. *Epistle to Diognetus* 1.

our experience, namely, whenever any group of people becomes closely united, a separation occurs from those who are not part of that union.[8] This problem arises both when God calls Israel into a special relationship with himself in the Old Testament and when Jesus establishes a special relationship among his disciples in the New.

According to Ratzinger, Paul's teaching that Christ is the Second Adam helps resolve this tension since "though men are not yet brothers in Christ they can and must become so. The *philadelphia* [brotherly love] owed to one's fellow Christian does not exclude, but rather implies, the appropriateness of the *agapē* [self-giving love] offered to every man."[9] Brotherly love begins with a removal of all barriers within the Christian community, including those of nationality and social class, and requires that roles of leadership in the Church be exercised in a spirit of humble service. Finally, the separation of Christians into one body needs to be understood not as an end in itself but as a means of serving and reaching out in the hope of saving all. This responsibility of those who are already part of the new humanity toward the rest of the human race is to be exercised by proclaiming the †gospel, by works of charity, and by suffering that is united to Jesus' paschal mystery. In this way the "third race" exists for the benefit of the other two.

Peace and Access to God in the Spirit through Jesus' Resurrection (2:17–18)

---

[17]He came and preached peace to you who were far off and peace to those who were near, [18]for through him we both have access in one Spirit to the Father.

OT: Isa 52:7; 57:19
NT: John 20:19, 21, 26
Catechism: Christ the source of peace, 2305; Trinitarian communion and the Church, 738, 747

Just as Jesus' death on the cross eliminated the estrangement between Jews and †Gentiles and between God and the human race, his resurrection brought both Jews and Gentiles into an intimate relationship with the Father through the Holy Spirit.

---

8. Joseph Cardinal Ratzinger, *The Meaning of Christian Brotherhood* (San Francisco: Ignatius, 1993 [German original, 1960]).

9. Aidan Nichols, summarizing Ratzinger, in *The Thought of Pope Benedict XVI: An Introduction to the Theology of Joseph Ratzinger* (New York: Burns and Oates, 2007), 48.

The Greek for **preached** is *euangelizō*, to proclaim good news, the origin of   2:17
our word "evangelize." Paul uses the phrase "preached peace" (literally, "proclaimed good news of peace") because key Old Testament prophecies promise
that God will send someone to proclaim the good news of salvation, of **peace**
(Isa 52:7; Nah 2:1; Zech 9:10). Paul is saying that the risen Jesus has announced
the eschatological messianic peace, the peace that belongs to the end of history
and that entails the fullness of salvation.[10]

Paul says that Jesus came and preached peace **to you who were far off and
peace to those who were near**. He alludes here to Isa 57:19, a text that speaks
of †YHWH announcing peace and bringing healing: "Peace, peace to the far
and the near, / says the †LORD; and I will heal them." Paul thus interprets the
incorporation of Gentiles into the people of God as fulfilling God's ancient
promise. When did Jesus preach to the "far off" Gentiles of Ephesus and Asia
Minor? Paul probably refers to the time when he and other evangelists preached
the †gospel there. Whenever the good news is preached it is Jesus himself who
speaks through the members of his body.[11]

The proof that the Gentiles are co-recipients with the Jews of the messianic   2:18
peace is that **through him we both have access in one Spirit to the Father**.
Through a relationship with Jesus, both Jews and Gentiles can experience God
as Father (Gal 4:6), and the same Spirit of God is the medium of access for
both. Paul's concise phrase sums up the Trinitarian dynamic of liturgical prayer
addressed to the Father, through the Son, and in the Holy Spirit.

What is so special about "access"? Some years ago a political brouhaha
erupted in the United States when it was discovered that large contributors to
the president's political campaign were routinely rewarded for their generosity
by invitations to stay as guests at the White House. The scandal was that their
money gained them unfair access. People understand that having the ear of the
person in authority gives one a better chance of their request being granted.

Every Gentile and Jewish believer now has "access" in prayer to the king of
the universe. In the Bible, the word "access" also denotes the special privilege
of priests to come into the presence of God (Zech 3:7). All baptized believers have access to God for priestly worship and intercession (1 Pet 2:5, 9).
The Gentiles, previously unable to enter the inner courts of the temple, now

10. Although the entire ministry of Jesus can be described as "preaching good news of peace" (see
Acts 10:36), Paul's statement here follows an account of the cross, suggesting that he has in mind Jesus'
proclamation of peace after the resurrection. When Jesus appears to the disciples in Luke 24:36 and
John 20:19, 21, 26 he says, "Peace be with you."

11. Paul's words in Acts 26:23 seem to identify Christ's proclamation to Jews and Gentiles with the
Church's evangelization.

Access in One Spirit

LIVING TRADITION

Marius Victorinus, a fourth-century scholar who converted to Christianity, relates Paul's teaching to Christian experience: "Both Jews and Gentiles *have access to the Father* through Christ himself. But how? *In one Spirit.* For the Spirit, who is one with Christ, enters into us when we believe in Christ. We then feel God's presence, know God and worship God. Thus we come to the Father in that same Spirit through Christ" (*Epistle to the Ephesians* 1.2.18).[a]

a. Mark J. Edwards, ed., *Galatians, Ephesians, Philippians*, ACCS (Downers Grove, IL: InterVarsity, 1999), 142.

have direct, personal access to God himself through Jesus in the Holy Spirit. Hebrews 10:19–22 expresses the same idea by summoning Christians to enter confidently through Christ's sacrifice into the †holy sanctuary that previously only the Jewish high priest could enter.

Reflection and Application (2:17–18)

Peace be with you. The crucified and risen Jesus signaled the beginning of the messianic age when he proclaimed peace to his disciples. We acknowledge this peace at every liturgy when the priest proclaims the Lord's peace on behalf of Christ to those present. The exchange of peace that follows signifies our acceptance of Jesus' gift of peace and indicates reconciliation with one another before approaching the altar (in accord with Matt 5:23–24). In the second half of the letter, Paul discusses maintaining peace in the Christian community (4:1–6; 4:25–5:2).

The peace that the †Messiah announces is not a peace that depends on external circumstances and certainly does not mean that Christians will be spared conflict and troubles, as Jesus makes clear in John 16:33. Rather, the peace that Jesus gives is an interior peace, founded on his resurrection victory over sin, Satan, and death, communicated by the Spirit, and received by faith. It is a peace that enables Christians to resist fear (John 14:27) and to find courage in the midst of any trial. It is renewed and deepened by prayer (Phil 4:4–7).

Every human being is now invited to share in the fullness of peace with God through Christ in the fellowship of the Holy Spirit and in the fellowship of the Church. This motivates Christians to be peacemakers by sharing the good news with others to bring them to the fullness of peace and by working to overcome all enmity in human relationships.

Christ has died, Christ is risen. Paul realizes that the paschal †mystery contains the most important truths a person needs to know, so he recalls it constantly. Ephesians 2:13–18 is Paul's fourth reference to Jesus' death and resurrection (1:7, 19–23; 2:5–6), and he will return to it again (4:8–10; 5:2, 25). Is the death and resurrection of Jesus at the center of our own thinking, speaking, and acting?

Fellow Citizens, Members of God's Household, a Holy Temple (2:19–22)

> [19]So then you are no longer strangers and sojourners, but you are fellow citizens with the holy ones and members of the household of God, [20]built upon the foundation of the apostles and prophets, with Christ Jesus himself as the capstone. [21]Through him the whole structure is held together and grows into a temple sacred in the Lord; [22]in him you also are being built together into a dwelling place of God in the Spirit.

OT: Ps 118:22
NT: Matt 16:18; 1 Cor 3:9–16; Phil 3:20; 1 Pet 2:4–10; Rev 21:14
Catechism: the Church as apostolic, 857; the Church as Temple of the Spirit, 797, 809; the Church as God's building and household, 756
Lectionary: 2:19–22: Feasts of Sts. Simon and Jude and St. Thomas; Anniversary of the Dedication of a Church; Mass for the Holy Church; Mass for the Unity of Christians

Paul now describes the present situation of †Gentile Christians, in contrast to their previous status described in 2:12.

So then—as a result of what Christ has done—**you are no longer strangers and sojourners, but you are fellow citizens with the holy ones**. Previously foreigners or resident aliens (Deut 14:21) among God's people, Gentiles now enjoy full citizenship in the kingdom of God along with "the †holy ones," all God's faithful people of the Old and New Covenant. This explanation, combined with 2:12, makes clear that what God has done through the Messiah Jesus brings Gentiles into relationship with Israel. That God has inaugurated a new creation that includes believing Jews and Gentiles in the body of the crucified and risen Messiah does not make the covenant people of the Old Testament irrelevant; they remain the root and trunk of the olive tree into which Gentile believers have now been grafted (Rom 11:17). Although a new people of God, the Church consisting of baptized Jews and Gentiles is a continuation of the family of Abraham, Isaac, and Jacob.

Paul adds, **you are . . . members of the household of God**. The Greek word used here for household members refers to family and other close relations (it

2:19

also appears in Gal 6:10; 1 Tim 5:8). Gentile Christians are not only citizens, they are also members of God's family. They are in close relationship with him and can be confident of his loyalty toward them.

2:20–21   Rather than elaborate on household relationships, Paul shifts metaphors to speak of the house itself. He describes the universal Church as a structure **built upon the foundation of the apostles and prophets.** Since the foundation stones are humans, it is quite likely Paul is implying that his readers are also stones placed on this foundation (see 1 Pet 2:5). The

Fig. 5. A Roman arch supported by a capstone in Avdat (southern Israel).

apostles are those whom Christ himself appointed to proclaim the †gospel and to exercise leadership in his Church. This number is not limited to the Twelve—Paul, an apostle, was not one of the Twelve—but includes a broader group whom Christ had authorized (see 1 Cor 15:5, 7–9; see sidebar on p. 116). The prophets are most likely New Testament prophets, judging by other references to them in this letter (3:5; 4:11; see sidebar on p. 88). Although in 1 Cor 3:11 Paul speaks about Jesus Christ as the only foundation that can be laid for the Church, here he chooses a different metaphor and speaks of the apostles and prophets as the foundation stones with Christ as the **capstone.**[12]

There is a disagreement among translations regarding whether the Greek word should be interpreted as "capstone" or "cornerstone" in this context. According to ancient building practice, the *cornerstone* was laid first and then the other foundation stones were lined up to it; the *capstone* was the trapezoidal-shaped stone placed at the top of an arch, typically at the entrance to a building,

12. See other references to apostles as foundations in Matt 16:18 and Rev 21:14.

that held all the other stones in place. Since in this text Paul identifies the apostles and prophets as foundation stones, it is quite possible that he distinguishes Jesus' role by referring to him as the capstone, which occupies the highest place. This fits well with the next phrase: **Through him the whole structure is held together**.[13] Christ's role in his Church remains crucial for uniting all its parts and keeping them together. Paul shifts the metaphor once again and says this structure **grows into a temple sacred in the Lord**. The temple grows because it is a living organism. The Church is simultaneously a temple and the body of Christ.

Paul now applies this final image to his readers by saying **in him you also are being built together into a dwelling place of God in the Spirit**. All three of the verbs in verses 21–22 are †present tense: the Church *is held* together, *grows*, and *is being built* together. Although the Church is already the temple of God and the body of Christ, it is a work in progress—God has not finished building us yet! The phrase "a dwelling place of God" is used to describe God's temple on earth as well as his heavenly dwelling. We Christians, the Church, are being made into a community in which God himself resides.

2:22

The Gentiles have come a long way. From standing far off, having no relationship with Christ or with the people of God and no covenant with God, they have now been united with Jewish believers in the body of Christ, have gained access to God through Christ in the Spirit, have obtained full citizenship and membership in God's family, and have themselves become a flesh-and-blood house where God lives. That, to say the least, is extraordinary.

Reflection and Application (2:19–22)

The Church as the temple of God. It is harder for Christians today than for those in the first century to grasp the significance of the Church being the temple or dwelling of God on earth. Because God is present everywhere, we sometimes fail to appreciate that he chooses to make himself present in a special way in particular places and in particular people. In ancient times, Jews and pagans shared an awareness that places could be sacred because they were inhabited in a special way by a god. Catholics have an inkling of this because we reverence the presence of Christ in the Eucharist reserved in the tabernacles in our churches. The New Testament, however, teaches that God is really present and can be accessed in every gathering of Jesus'

---

13. The JB and NJB present another possible translation: "every structure" instead of "the whole structure."

God's "Dwelling," or "Temple," in the Old Testament

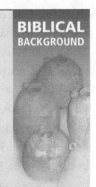

The theme of God living or "dwelling" among his people appears again and again from Genesis to Revelation. The Garden of Eden was a place where God walked among the human beings he had created and conversed with them (see Gen 3:8); Jewish interpreters understood God's work of creation as his building a temple in which to dwell. The patriarch Jacob named a shrine "Bethel" (Hebrew "house of God") because he dreamed of a stairway connecting that spot to God's dwelling in †heaven (Gen 28:11–19). On Mount Sinai, God gave Moses instructions about building the "dwelling" (other translations use "tabernacle") in whose inner sanctuary, called the holy of holies, the ark of the covenant was kept and God lived among his people (Exod 25:8–9).

When Israel arrived in the promised land, God "dwelt" among his people in various shrines, wherever the ark of the covenant was located. Eventually King David moved the ark to Jerusalem and his son Solomon built the temple there as a dwelling place for God, although he acknowledged that no building can contain God (1 Kings 8:27). God's †glory filled the temple, and Solomon's prayer of dedication (1 Kings 8:10–13, 22–61) expressed what this meant to Israel: a close relationship with God and a place to worship him, to obtain forgiveness, and to seek his help on every occasion of communal or personal need. When the Babylonians destroyed the temple in 586 BC, the prophets led Israel to understand that †YHWH had withdrawn his presence from the temple because of their sin (Ezek 10) and led them to hope for a new, more-glorious temple where God would live with his people (Ezek 40–48). After their return from exile the Jews built a second temple in Jerusalem, which they completed in 515 BC and which most of the Jewish people—including Jesus and the early Christians (Mark 11:17; Acts 5:12)—regarded as God's holy dwelling.

disciples in his name (Matt 18:19–20). Reverence and †faith are the appropriate responses to God's holy presence in the universal Church, in our dioceses and parishes, in our small communities, and even in our own bodies. We do not adore him in one another and in the Church as we adore the Host, because there still exists in us a mixture of what is divine and what is sinful; the temple of the Church is still under construction (2:21–22). Nevertheless, God is truly present in Christ's body, the Church, and we must treat our brothers and sisters and the life of the Church with an awareness that God lives within and among us.

God's "Dwelling," or "Temple," in the New Testament

BIBLICAL BACKGROUND

In the Gospel of Luke, Gabriel tells Mary that the Holy Spirit will "overshadow" her (Luke 1:35), using the same Greek word that described the descent of God's presence on the tabernacle in the wilderness (Exod 40:35 LXX). For nine months the womb of the Virgin was God's dwelling, his tabernacle on the earth. The prologue of the Gospel of John informs us that "the Word became flesh / and made his dwelling among us" (John 1:14). Other texts in the Gospel of John indicate that the human body of the incarnate Word was the true temple, the "place" on earth where God was present and available to his people (John 2:19–21; 10:38; 14:7–11). When that "temple" was destroyed by crucifixion, Jesus "rebuilt" it by rising from the dead. When he poured out his Spirit on his disciples, the Church became his body, the temple of God, the new location of God's dwelling on earth. The New Testament uses the metaphor of a temple for the universal Church (Eph 2:21–22; 1 Pet 2:5), for the local church (1 Cor 3:16–17), and for the human body of every Christian (1 Cor 6:19) because of the indwelling presence of the Holy Spirit.

The last chapters of Revelation reveal that the final stage of God's dwelling among his people will occur when the New Jerusalem, God's heavenly dwelling, descends to earth. Then God's people will dwell with him forever, worshiping God and the Lamb and seeing his face (Rev 21:2–3; 22:3–4). Revelation depicts the New Jerusalem symbolically as a perfect cube, like the holy of holies (1 Kings 6:20; Rev 21:16), and explains that "its temple is the Lord God almighty and the Lamb" (Rev 21:22). No other temple will be needed, since the access of God's people to God will be complete, unrestricted, and unmediated.

Grace again. In Eph 2:1–10 we saw that we have been saved not because of our good works but by the action of God's †grace. In 2:11–22 we see that his choice of us was not because of our nationality or race. We Christians who are Gentiles were not born into the chosen people but were like a "wild olive shoot" that has been grafted on to the cultivated tree (see Rom 11:17–24). Our membership in God's family is sheer grace (1 Pet 2:10).

Unity of Jew and Gentile. For 1,900 years the vast majority of Christians have been Gentiles. Ephesians 2:12–22 might seem to address a unique circumstance at the beginning of the Church's history without much meaning for us today. However, in these verses Paul is indicating that the unity of Jew and Gentile in the Messiah Jesus is a permanent and essential characteristic of the Church. God made an eternal covenant with Abraham, and the Jewish people continue to have a unique role in God's plan of salvation.[14] According to Rom 11:15, 23–31, someday "all Israel" will acknowledge Jesus and so be saved (see Catechism 674). Throughout history there have been many Jews, such as Edith Stein (St. Teresa Benedicta of the Cross), who have confessed Jesus as Israel's Messiah without renouncing their Jewish identity. It is likely that more Jews have professed faith in Jesus during the past hundred years than in any period since the first century.[15] The Church of Jesus Christ is therefore a communion of Jews and Gentiles at the beginning, at the end, and in between. The Church has a special relationship with the Jewish people: we welcome among us those like Paul and Peter and the first generation of Jewish believers who recognize Jesus as Israel's Messiah. We reach out with esteem, hope, and love to those who do not yet realize that the one they are waiting for has already come. We pray for the day when the veil will be removed (2 Cor 3:15–18) from the hearts of the people who were chosen first.

Unity of all races and nationalities. The breaking down of the barrier between Jew and Gentile in Christ gives us hope that in Jesus all walls and all hostility between peoples can be overcome. This fact summons Christians now to root out racism or ethnic prejudice and all hatred or disrespect toward people who are different from us. If they are Christians, they are our brothers and sisters in the Lord; if they are not, they still are created in the image of God and are potentially members of our spiritual family. God fervently desires that every person come to know him and be joined to his people. This should be our fervent desire and prayer as well (1 Tim 2:1–4).

---

14. Rom 9–11 describes two categories of Jews in relationship to God's plan: those who have accepted the Messiah and are part of his New Covenant people (Rom 11:1–5) and those who have not accepted him yet (Rom 11:25–31).

15. For a history of this movement, see Dan Cohn-Sherbok, *Messianic Judaism* (New York: Continuum, 2000).

Commissioned to Proclaim God's Secret Plan

Ephesians 3:1–13

Have you ever started to say something and then realized that you needed to back up to provide background information that the listener might not already know? The next section of Ephesians provides information about the plan of God and Paul's apostleship that he may not originally have intended to write. Writing from Rome in the early 60s,[1] Paul may have realized that the churches of Ephesus and the surrounding region now included many new believers since his previous visit and that he needed to address the questions that likely lay in the minds of new †Gentile converts. Why is Paul in prison and what exactly is his role in this new inclusive form of Judaism (which is how they would have understood Christianity)? Why were the pagan poets and teachers of the past ignorant of this teaching?

In this digression (3:1–13), Paul explains (1) that his imprisonment is actually for the benefit of his Gentile readers; (2) that his message has to do with a secret divine plan that God has now revealed and entrusted to Paul and others to announce to the world; (3) that the other spiritual beings learned of this plan only through the Church; and (4) that this chain of events is the outworking of God's eternal purpose.

Introducing Paul and His Ministry (3:1–3)

> [1]Because of this, I, Paul, a prisoner of Christ [Jesus] for you Gentiles—
> [2]if, as I suppose, you have heard of the stewardship of God's grace that was

1. For this commentary's approach to historical background and authorship of Ephesians, see the introduction.

given to me for your benefit, [3][namely, that] the mystery was made known to me by revelation, as I have written briefly earlier.

NT: Phil 1:12–14; Col 4:18
Catechism: the Father reveals the mystery by sending Christ, 50

3:1   Paul begins, **Because of this**, referring to what he has just written in 2:11–22 about the wonderful things God has done for the [†]Gentiles, and continues, **I, Paul, a prisoner of Christ [Jesus] for you Gentiles**. Suddenly he realizes that his readers may not understand why *his* imprisonment is on *their* behalf, so he interrupts his thought to explain.

When he calls himself "a prisoner of Christ [Jesus],"[2] Paul's wording is intended to make us think. The obvious meaning, of course, is that Paul is a prisoner *for* Christ, because he has been preaching the [†]gospel about Christ. But another meaning is implicit in this phrasing: he *belongs* to the [†]Messiah Jesus. Elsewhere Paul refers to himself as a slave of Christ (Rom 1:1; Gal 1:10) and speaks warmly of having been captured by him (Phil 3:12; 2 Cor 2:14).

Paul describes himself as a prisoner "for you Gentiles." This confirms that most of Paul's readers must be Gentiles, but it raises the question of how Paul can be a prisoner on their behalf, especially since this letter will be heard by many people who do not know him personally.

3:2   He supposes that they **have heard of** his ministry, which he describes as a **stewardship**, *oikonomia*, which means management or administration. "Stewardship" is an apt translation here, since Paul refers to something that is not his but has been entrusted to him, namely, **God's grace**. Paul goes on to say that this was **given** to him for **your benefit**.

3:3   What is this [†]grace that Paul has received not for himself but for Gentile Christians? It is, Paul says, a **mystery . . . made known** to him **by revelation**. "[†]Mystery" (*mystērion*) refers to something that is secret, especially a religious secret. When Paul uses the term "mystery" (twenty-one times throughout his letters, six times in Ephesians alone), he is referring to God's previously hidden plan of salvation that has now been revealed through the coming of Christ and the gospel (1:9; 1 Cor 2:1; Col 1:26–27). Paul says that he has **written briefly earlier** on this subject. It seems that Paul is referring to what we have just read in chapters 1 and 2 of Ephesians, where he does indeed speak about God's plan, which has now been revealed.[3]

2. Brackets in the NAB indicate that a word is absent from some Greek manuscripts.
3. The Greek text says only, "I have written briefly"; the NAB and some other translations interpret this by adding "earlier." Other translations interpret it as I do: "as I wrote above in a few words" (NRSV).

The Mystery of Christ Now Revealed (3:4–6)

[4]**When you read this you can understand my insight into the mystery of Christ,** [5]**which was not made known to human beings in other generations as it has now been revealed to his holy apostles and prophets by the Spirit,** [6]**that the Gentiles are coheirs, members of the same body, and copartners in the promise in Christ Jesus through the gospel.**

NT: Rom 16:25; Gal 3:27–29; Col 1:25–27
Catechism: the Apostolic Tradition, 75–76; a new People of God not based on physical descent, 781–82
Lectionary: 3:2–3a, 5–6: Epiphany of the Lord

Paul expresses confidence that what he has written in the first two chapters   **3:4–5** of Ephesians will have impressed his readers with his **insight into** the plan of God. He now refers to that plan as **the mystery of Christ**, indicating the content of the secret: it is about the †Messiah. He goes on to say that this secret was kept from previous **generations** of the human race. To the ancient world with its esteem for the past, one of the strongest arguments against Christianity was that it was a *new* religion. Paul's †Gentile readers would have wondered why the great Greek and Roman philosophers and poets, and the oracles of the gods (like the oracle of Apollo at Delphi), did not know about Christ.[4]

Paul explains that this secret has only **now been revealed** by God **to his holy apostles and prophets.** Paul is including himself in this group, since he has already described himself as an apostle (1:1). To modern readers, Paul might seem proud or presumptuous, referring to himself as †holy, as though he were speaking of his moral excellence; but Paul considers all the members of the Church to be holy, since "holy" means to be in a close relationship with God, to belong to him. This is true of the whole Christian people (1:1, 15; 2:19), and it is especially true of God's servants, the apostles and †prophets. Here the reference is not to the Old Testament prophets, since the †mystery was not fully revealed in the past, but to prophets in the Church. The mystery has now been revealed **by the Spirit,** who imparts understanding of the things of God (John 16:13; 1 Cor 2:9–16). The Spirit has entrusted to the apostles and prophets an understanding of Jesus' death and resurrection and its meaning, which is foundational (2:20) and authoritative for the Church.[5]

4. Later Christian reflection did find anticipations of the gospel and "seeds of the Word" (*semina Verbi*) in the writings of ancient poets and philosophers and in the oracles of Delphi.
5. While Paul usually emphasizes apostolic authority, both here and in 2:20 he includes prophets with apostles as the authorized bearers of divine revelation. The two New Testament ministries are also mentioned together in 4:11; 1 Cor 12:28–29; Rev 18:20.

New Testament Prophets

BIBLICAL
BACKGROUND

In his Pentecost sermon, the apostle Peter explained what was happening to the disciples in the upper room by quoting the prophet Joel:

> In the last days it will be, God declares,
>   that I will pour out my Spirit upon all flesh,
>   and your sons and your daughters shall prophesy,
>   and your young men shall see visions,
>   and your old men shall dream dreams. (Acts 2:17, quoting Joel 2:28 NRSV)

The spontaneous praise of God in various languages at Pentecost was divinely inspired speech, a form of prophecy, and a sign that the messianic age had begun and the end of history was drawing near. Paul distinguishes tongues from prophecy in 1 Cor 12–14; many other biblical texts and early Christian writings attest to the wide dissemination of the gift of prophecy in the early Church.

New Testament prophecy was not focused on foretelling the future or critiquing social injustices. Paul explains its function in 1 Cor 14:3–4: "Those who prophesy speak to other people for their upbuilding and encouragement and consolation. . . . [They] build up the church" (NRSV). They understand mysteries, receive revelations, disclose the secrets of hearts, and strengthen the community through inspired exhortation and praise (Luke 1:67–79; Acts 15:32; 1 Cor 13:2; 14:12–32).

Among the many who prophesied (Rom 12:6; 1 Cor 14:5, 24, 31), some came to be called "prophets" and to fulfill a recognized ministry in the Church. Acts mentions several prophets (13:1; 15:32) and recounts two incidents in the prophetic activity of the prophet Agabus (11:27–29; 21:10–14). Revelation, the only book of prophecy in the New Testament (22:18–19), makes numerous references to Christian prophets besides the author (10:7; 16:6; 18:20). Christian prophets held a position of honor and authority in the early Church second only to that of apostles (1 Cor 12:28). The New Testament warns against false prophets (Matt 24:11, 24; 1 John 4:1; Rev 2:20) and teaches that prophecies should be discerned (1 Cor 14:29; 1 Thess 5:19–22) and prophets evaluated by their fruit (Matt 7:15–23). See the reflection on 4:11–12 regarding prophets in the Church today.

3:6   Now Paul tells us the content of this secret: the Gentiles have been brought into all God's promises to Israel. To emphasize that the Gentiles have been included on an equal basis, Paul says it in three different ways. In the Greek the emphasis is even more striking, because these three words (translated here as

coheirs, **members**, and **copartners**) all begin with a form of the same prefix, *syn-*, which means "with" or "co-." Gentile Christians are now "coheirs" with the descendants of Abraham of the †inheritance God had promised Israel (see 1:13–14). More than that, they have become members **of the same body**, the body of Christ. More than that, they are copartners **in the promise**. This refers to the promises made by God to Abraham in Genesis 12. There are two ways in which the Gentiles become partners in this blessing: **in Christ Jesus** and **through the gospel**. They share in the blessing through union with the Messiah Jesus as members of his body. The way they were joined to Christ was by believing the gospel message (1:13). The words "promise" and "promises" are used throughout the New Testament to refer to all the gifts that God has said he would give to the descendents of Abraham—"the inheritance"—now understood at a higher level to refer to the Holy Spirit and eternal life (see sidebar on p. 43, and comments on 1:14, 18).

Reflection and Application (3:4–6)

Gentiles welcome. To Christians of the twenty-first century, most of whom are Gentiles, it is hard to grasp the significance of this "mystery." It seems old news that Gentiles can belong to the people of God. But for the nineteen centuries between the time of Abraham and the time of Christ, only the Jewish people had been the heirs of God's promises, and these promises distinguished them from all the other peoples of the earth (Deut 7:6–7). It might be possible to think that this is simply Jewish chauvinism on Paul's part, but that would be mistaken. Jesus himself, when the Canaanite woman sought deliverance for her daughter from a demon, confirms that the Gentiles did not have an equal claim to God's provision that had been promised to the children of Israel (Matt 15:22–28).

Beginning with the death and resurrection of Jesus and the gift of the Spirit, however, a new age has dawned in which all the peoples of the earth are invited to share in the blessings previously promised to one particular nation. This is the "mystery," the secret plan of God, that has now been revealed. God always loved and took concern for all peoples of the world (Jon 4:10–11; Acts 14:16–17) and intended from the beginning to bless all †nations through Abraham and his descendents (Gen 12:3; 18:18; Gal 3:8–9). Although the prophets spoke on many occasions of God's future blessings for the nations (e.g., Isa 49:6; 66:18–20), Israel never imagined this would involve making the Gentiles "coheirs," and "copartners in the promise," joining

An Epiphany for the Nations

This text from Ephesians (3:2–3, 5–6) appears as the second reading every year for the Feast of Epiphany, which celebrates the manifestation of Christ to the †Gentiles, that is, to the nations. (The same Greek word, *ethnē*, can be translated as either "Gentiles" or "nations.") It follows the reading of a prophecy from Isa 60:1–6 in which God says to Jerusalem, "Nations shall walk by your light"— referring to the light of God's †glory that will shine forth from Israel to the nations. This was fulfilled in the coming of Christ, in whom God's glory is fully revealed (John 1:14; 2 Cor 3:18; 4:6). The Gospel reading for Epiphany is the story of the Magi (Matt 2:1–12), the first Gentiles who came to worship Christ, fulfilling the prophecy of Isa 60:5–6 and prefiguring all the Gentiles who will later be joined to God and his people.

them "in the same body." Israel was chosen, as we Christians have now been chosen, to bring God's blessing to others. Christians do this by proclaiming the gospel.

The basis of church teaching. Catholic doctrine rests on the apostles' testimony to what Christ did and taught and what the Holy Spirit revealed to them after Jesus' death and resurrection, including an understanding of the Old Testament in light of Christ (*Dei Verbum* 8–9). The apostles' teaching has been handed on to us in Scripture and Tradition that together "form one sacred deposit of the word of God, entrusted to the Church" (*Dei Verbum* 10), authoritatively interpreted by the apostles' successors, the pope and bishops.

Paul's Role (3:7–10)

[7]Of this I became a minister by the gift of God's grace that was granted me in accord with the exercise of his power. [8]To me, the very least of all the holy ones, this grace was given, to preach to the Gentiles the inscrutable riches of Christ, [9]and to bring to light [for all] what is the plan of the mystery hidden from ages past in God who created all things, [10]so that the manifold wisdom of God might now be made known through the church to the principalities and authorities in the heavens.

NT: Acts 9:15; Rom 16:25; 1 Cor 2:6–8; 15:9; Gal 1:11–16; 2:7–9
Lectionary: 3:2–12: Mass for the Evangelization of Peoples; 3:8–12: Common of Doctors of the Church

Paul's role in relationship to this †mystery is that of **minister,** *diakonos.* This   3:7
word means "servant" and in the New Testament can refer to one who fulfills
the office of deacon or other roles of service in the Church. Paul indicates that
his ministry is a **gift of God's grace** and an **exercise of his power**. Genuine
ministry in the Church is never an activity accomplished simply by human
intelligence and effort; it requires God's action if it is to do any lasting good:
"What is born of the flesh is flesh, and what is born of the Spirit is spirit" (John
3:6 NRSV).

In obvious humility and awe, Paul expresses his amazement that he has been   3:8
chosen for such a †grace, such a ministry. He calls himself **the very least of all
the holy ones**. Elsewhere Paul describes himself as the "foremost" of sinners
(1 Tim 1:13–15) and the "least of the apostles" because he formerly persecuted
the Church (1 Cor 15:9). Then he explains his specific role in relationship to
the †Gentiles, **to preach to the Gentiles the inscrutable riches of Christ**. The
NAB's "inscrutable" becomes clearer when supplemented by other translations of the same Greek word: "unsearchable" (RSV), "boundless" (NRSV),
"unfathomable" (NJB). Paul is saying that in Christ there is found a treasure
without limits and that it is his special privilege to share that treasure with the
Gentiles. According to Gal 2:8–9, Peter was the apostle to the Jews and Paul to
the Gentiles (Acts 9:15; Rom 11:13; 1 Tim 2:7).

Paul repeats what he already said in another way: **to bring to light [for all]**   3:9
what is the plan of the mystery.[6] Isaiah had prophesied that the Servant of the
Lord would bring a light of revelation to the Gentiles (Isa 42:6; 49:6), and the
early Church understood this to be fulfilled directly by Christ (Luke 2:32; Acts
13:47) through the preaching of the apostles (Acts 26:23). Now Paul tells us
that the secret was **hidden from ages past in God who created all things**. In
other words, it was concealed in an inaccessible place, namely, with the God of
Israel, who is described as the creator of the universe to emphasize his greatness
in contrast to the "gods" of the Gentiles.

The grace that Paul received to preach Christ to the Gentiles has a conse-   3:10
quence that may surprise us: **so that the manifold wisdom of God might now
be made known through the church to the principalities and authorities**.
Paul is saying that the purpose, or at least the result, of his preaching the †gos-
pel is that the spiritual powers that exercise authority **in the heavens** and who
thus influence earthly events from above should learn "the manifold wisdom

---

6. Other translations capture a nuance of the Greek by rendering the last phrase as "the administration" (NIV) or "the inner workings" (NJB) of the mystery, or in a paraphrase, "explaining how the
mystery is to be dispensed" (JB).

Fig. 6. This fourth-century apse mosaic in the Church of Saint Pudentiana in Rome depicts Christ enthroned among his apostles beneath a jeweled cross, the symbols of the four evangelists, and the heavenly Jerusalem. The two women standing behind the apostles symbolize the Church of Jewish believers and the Church of Gentile believers. On Christ's left, the Church of the Jews crowns Peter; on his right, the Church of the Gentiles crowns Paul (see Gal 2:7–9).

of God," that is, God's multifaceted plan, by observing what is happening in the Church.

Who are these †principalities and authorities, and what is the significance of their learning God's secret plan? Paul has already introduced these beings in 1:21 and will return to consider them in 6:12 (see the comments there). These terms can refer to either good or evil ranks of angelic beings. If the principalities and authorities referred to here are good, readers are invited to consider how amazing the mystery is that even the angels did not know it until they saw it unfold. A similar idea is expressed in 1 Pet 1:12, where the content of the gospel is described as "things into which angels longed to look."

But it seems likely that Paul is including, if not focusing on, the hostile spiritual powers (as in 6:12), and that opens a fascinating cosmic perspective on God's plan. In chapter 1 Paul explained that Christ has been exalted "far above every principality, authority, power, and dominion" (1:21). Now it has become evident that God is freeing the Gentiles from the control of the evil principalities and authorities and is uniting them to his people (2:2; Col 1:13). This recalls Jesus' saying in the Gospels that only when the strong man has been bound

The Principalities and Authorities

BIBLICAL BACKGROUND

Sprinkled through Romans, 1 Corinthians, Ephesians, and Colossians are a number of terms that refer to spiritual beings that exercise power in the world: principalities, rulers, authorities, powers, dominions, thrones, and world rulers. Although all of these terms can be used to refer to human political authorities, the contexts in which they occur indicate that ranks of spiritual beings are intended. Paul uses these terms somewhat flexibly without explaining the differences among them.

Paul presupposes an understanding held by many Jews for the previous two centuries, as the book of Daniel bears witness (Dan 10:13, 20–21; 12:1). On the basis of Deut 32:8–9 it was understood that God allowed angelic beings to exercise power over territories and nations. Events on earth are influenced by what is happening in the †heavenly realm among these beings. God's people are under the protection of the archangel Michael, while the affairs of other nations are influenced by principalities opposed to God and his people. Jewish understanding linked the pagan gods that the Gentiles worshiped with these spiritual beings (Exod 12:12; Deut 32:17; 1 Cor 10:20).

The Pauline letters uphold this worldview but insist on several points: all heavenly powers were created in, through, and for Christ (Col 1:16); Christ triumphed over them in the cross (Col 2:15) and has been raised to a place "far above" them (Eph 1:21); evil powers and authorities under the control of the devil presently wage warfare against Christians (Eph 6:11–12); Christians can stand against them (Eph 6:10–11); and Christ will destroy them at his second coming (1 Cor 15:24–26). The Johannine literature offers similar perspectives on the devil and other evil spiritual beings.[a] The canonical Scriptures do not explain the relationships among the various heavenly beings or how some of them came to oppose God. (See sidebar on p. 191.)

a. John 12:31; 16:11; 17:15; 1 John 5:18–19; Rev 2:10; 12:9–12; 13:1–15; 20:10.

---

can his possessions be taken from him. Christ has bound the strong man, that is, the devil, and is now taking from him (Luke 11:20–22) the men and women who were his slaves, his property, and is joining them to God's people in the Church. The way the evil principalities and authorities have learned of God's mysterious plan, kept secret until now, is by counting their losses as they watch the Church grow through the preaching of the gospel.[7] In 1 Cor 2:8 Paul tells

7. Some interpreters understand Paul to mean that the principalities and authorities learn God's plan through the apostolic preaching. But that meaning would be more clearly conveyed without the phrase "through the church," which points to the Church's life as somehow revealing the mystery.

us that God's marvelous wisdom manifested in Jesus so surprised the spiritual "rulers of this age" that if they had known it, "they would not have crucified the Lord of glory."

And this is only the beginning—do the principalities and authorities see where this is headed? Paul says in 1:9–10 that God has "a plan for the fullness of times, to sum up all things in Christ, in heaven and on earth." The preaching of the gospel to the Gentiles and their incorporation into the Church is a sign to the evil spiritual powers ruling the †world that the age of their dominion is coming to an end. They are losing control. It should come as no surprise that they attempt to resist what God is doing. Paul probably understands his imprisonment as a reflection of the spiritual conflict (6:10–20) that is taking place.

God's Eternal Purpose (3:11–13)

¹¹This was according to the eternal purpose that he accomplished in Christ Jesus our Lord, ¹²in whom we have boldness of speech and confidence of access through faith in him. ¹³So I ask you not to lose heart over my afflictions for you; this is your glory.

NT: Heb 4:16; 10:19; 2 Cor 4:1, 8–18
Catechism: Christ's whole life as mystery of revelation, redemption, and recapitulation, 514–18; boldness in prayer, 2777–78; cooperating with the divine plan through our sufferings, 307

3:11–13   The declaration that the proclamation of the †gospel is fulfilling **the eternal purpose** of God assures Paul's readers that God is in control of history. Christians have reason for confidence about a positive outcome since God's purpose has been **accomplished**[8] through ("in") **Christ Jesus our Lord**. In the Greek the word "our" is in the position of emphasis to underscore the mutual belonging between ourselves and the †Messiah Jesus. United to him ("in whom"), we have **boldness of speech and confidence of access** to God. This probably refers to boldness in preaching the good news (as in 6:19–20) and to confidence in prayers of praise and petition. The basis of this boldness and confidence is either **faith in him** or "his faithfulness"—the Greek can be translated either way.

Like Jewish believers, Gentile Christians have a place in Christ and in the Church because of God's eternal plan. This fact marks a cosmic change and an overturning of the spiritual powers of darkness—a new day, a new hope. Paul's **afflictions** serve that goal and are no cause for discouragement; rather,

8. The JB and NJB differ from most translations by interpreting this verb to refer to God's *establishing* his plan in the past, rather than accomplishing it.

they are **your glory**—something his readers can be glad about, since Paul's imprisonment reflects the fact that he has fulfilled his mission of proclaiming the riches of the Messiah to the Gentiles. If, as seems likely, Ephesians was written during Paul's imprisonment described in Acts 24–28, his very imprisonment was due to the accusations of Jews from Asia (probably from Ephesus; see Acts 21:27–29). Perhaps there is a hint of celebration (as in Rev 12:10–12, 17) that the †principalities and authorities were not able to prevent their loss and now vainly vent their anger at Paul through Roman prosecution. Paul concludes this portion of his letter in the same way that he began it, reminding his Gentile Christian readers that his condition as a prisoner is for their sake.

Reflection and Application (3:1–13)

In this personal digression we catch a glimpse of Paul the man and find much to admire and to imitate. First there is the attractive combination of Paul's absolute confidence in the truth of the gospel and the importance of his ministry with a deep personal modesty. He never tires of repeating that the truth and ministry he possesses is God's †grace. Postmodern culture regards certainty about truth as arrogant and potentially violent—but Paul the prisoner demonstrates that it can be humble and gentle.

Next there is Paul's intense awe and wonder at what God has done in Christ. Paul does not take his faith for granted even though twenty-five years have elapsed since his conversion. Rather, he has reflected deeply on all the implications of the gospel and seeks to cultivate that same appreciation in others.

Third, Paul exhibits boldness and courage in proclaiming the gospel. He is not afraid of spiritual "principalities and authorities" or of political authorities because he is confident in the ultimate victory of God's plan. Paul also approaches God confidently and does not allow guilt about his past as a persecutor or any other faults to undermine his hope in God's love and forgiveness—he has "confidence of access through faith in him" (3:12; see Rom 8:32–39).

Finally, Paul keeps his own personal sufferings in perspective, seeing them in the larger context of God's plan of salvation. Being a Roman prisoner was nothing anyone would desire. Yet Paul takes it in stride and encourages his readers not to lose heart over his afflictions, but to glory in them!

A Prayer for Divinization

Ephesians 3:14–21

With this section Paul comes to the end of his exposition of the mystery, God's eternal plan that has now been revealed. He realizes that his readers have only begun to understand the magnitude of what has been given them. So, like Jesus after his profound farewell conversation with the disciples in John 14–16, Paul offers a fervent prayer that God will bring his good purposes to completion in the Christians of Ephesus. Paul began the doctrinal portion of Ephesians by praying that God would enlighten the eyes of his readers' hearts (1:18); he concludes by praying again for a deepening of their knowledge, but even more for the goal of this knowledge—union with God.

Paul's Introduction to His Prayer (3:14–15)

---

¹⁴**For this reason I kneel before the Father, ¹⁵from whom every family in heaven and on earth is named,**

NT: Acts 7:60; 21:5
Catechism: divine fatherhood as source of human fatherhood, 2214; Paul as intercessor, 2636

3:14   **For this reason**—in Greek the words are identical to those with which Paul began chapter 3, indicating that he is resuming where he left off before digressing to explain his own role in God's plan. The fact that Paul says **I kneel** indicates a special intensity to his prayer. In Scripture, kneeling can indicate humility before God or it can accompany supplication, expressing the earnestness of the request. Here humble gratitude for the ministry God has given him (3:7–8) and supplication are joined. His prayer is to **the Father**, a familiar way of speaking to God made possible by an intimate relationship with him through his Son and his Spirit (Gal 4:6). Paul is exercising the "boldness of speech and confidence of access" (v. 12) that Jesus has obtained for us.

In adding that God is the Father **from whom every family in heaven and**   **3:15**
on earth is named, Paul draws on a relationship between two Greek words. The word for father is *patēr*; the word for family, *patria*, is derived from it. Paul is saying that every family—including every †Gentile family—owes its origin to God. Paul's mention of "every family in †heaven" probably alludes to the ranks of spiritual beings. Some Jewish writers after Paul used the word "family" for the angels. Angels can be regarded as part of God's family as rational creatures who also owe their existence and identity to God.

Five Petitions (3:16–19)

---

[16]that he may grant you in accord with the riches of his glory to be strengthened with power through his Spirit in the inner self, [17]and that Christ may dwell in your hearts through faith; that you, rooted and grounded in love, [18]may have strength to comprehend with all the holy ones what is the breadth and length and height and depth, [19]and to know the love of Christ that surpasses knowledge, so that you may be filled with all the fullness of God.

NT: John 14:23; Rom 8:10, 35–39; 2 Cor 13:5; Phil 4:13; Col 1:9–11
Catechism: prayer as communion, 2565, 2714; asking for the Spirit, 2671; deification, 460, 398
Lectionary: 3:8–12, 14–19: Solemnity of the Most Sacred Heart (Year B); 3:14–19: Common of Holy Men and Women; feasts of Sts. Bonaventure and Margaret Mary Alacoque

As Paul explains what he is asking for his readers, he furnishes an example of what to desire and ask for ourselves and for one another. I have laid out the text to show the structure of this prayer, numbering the five petitions that Paul presents to God the Father.[1]

That he may grant you in accord with the riches of his glory
    1. to be strengthened with power through his Spirit in the inner self,

1. This layout reflects the grammatical structure of the underlying Greek text. The five petitions are framed in three clauses that begin with *hina*, translated as "that" or "so that," followed by a verb in the subjunctive mood ("that he may grant you," "that you . . . may have strength," and "that you may be filled"). The first two of these clauses are each completed by two infinitive clauses.

2. and that Christ may dwell in your hearts through faith;
that you, rooted and grounded in love, may have strength
3. to comprehend with all the holy ones what is the breadth and length
and height and depth,
4. and to know the love of Christ that surpasses knowledge,
so that
5. you may be filled with all the fullness of God.

3:16   The first thing Paul prays for is that his readers may be **strengthened** by the action of the Holy Spirit **in accord with the riches of his glory**, in other words, as much as God's infinite resources make possible. Paul does not merely say "strengthened," but strengthened **with power**. The Greek word for "power" here is *dynamis*, the root from which we derive the English word "dynamite." The place where this strengthening occurs is **the inner self**, or inner person (*anthrōpos*), precisely where we need God's power the most to make choices to love God and others in the face of pressures from the †world, the devil, and our own fallen nature.

3:17   Paul's second request is similar to the first yet adds a new element. He prays that **Christ**, the risen Jesus, **may dwell in your hearts**. In modern culture the heart usually refers to a person's feelings, the seat of one's emotional life, but in Scripture the heart refers to the core of the whole person, the deepest part of a human being where a person thinks, feels, and chooses.

It is more common for Paul to speak of Christians living "in Christ" than it is for him to speak of Christ living in us. Nevertheless, in some places Paul speaks of Christ dwelling in believers: "It is no longer I who live, but Christ who lives in me" (Gal 2:20 RSV).[2] Jesus teaches his disciples about the mutual indwelling he intends for us in John 14–17, especially in the figure of the vine and the branches (John 15:4–5).

But why is Paul praying that the †Messiah dwell in the hearts of his readers if they are already "in Christ" and therefore already have Christ living in their hearts? The fact is that there are *degrees* of living in Christ and of having Christ live in us. There is plenty of room for growth here, and Paul is praying that his readers may go all the way, allowing Christ to live in them to the fullest and to shape their thinking, feeling, and acting. The means by which Christ comes to dwell more deeply in our hearts is **faith**, the same way that we were initially saved from sin, Satan, and the world. For Paul, faith means more than mere mental assent; the Apostle is praying that his readers

2. See also Rom 8:10; 2 Cor 13:5; Col 1:27.

may believe, trust, obey, and be faithful to Jesus, so that he may live in them more and more.

Before naming his third and fourth requests Paul mentions something about the condition of his readers that makes possible what he is about to ask. He describes his readers as being **rooted and grounded in love**. Paul again employs a mix of botanical and architectural metaphors as he does at the end of Eph 2 (and in 1 Cor 3:6–11) to describe the Church. Here Paul indicates that "love" is the bedrock on which we are built and the soil in which we are planted. But whose love? The text does not say, but in light of Eph 1–2, Paul is probably referring to the "great love" (2:4) with which God "destined us for adoption to himself" (1:4–5) to give us a future filled with "the immeasurable riches of his grace in his kindness to us" (2:7). God's love for us is the basis of our love for him and for others and is the reason Paul can make the requests that follow.

In his third and fourth requests, Paul asks that his readers **may have strength**,   **3:18**
a synonym for the "power" he prayed for in the first petition (3:16). In his third request, Paul prays that his readers may be strengthened **to comprehend** something **with all the holy ones**, referring to all Christians. Paul is praying that the Ephesian Christians may understand something together with the whole people of God, the Church.

What is that something? He says, "to comprehend . . . **what is the breadth and length and height and depth**," but he does not make clear what these dimensions refer to. Many exegetes think Paul is referring to the love of Christ mentioned in the next verse (3:19). But the larger context suggests Paul is referring to the immensity of God's plan explained earlier in this chapter (3:3–10). Or it could refer to the dimensions of God's wisdom, since physical dimensions are used of wisdom elsewhere in the Bible (Job 11:5–9). Some Church Fathers suggest that these four dimensions refer to the four arms of the cross on which Christ was crucified. Although none of Paul's other references to the cross refer to its shape or dimensions, this interpretation has the advantage of being vivid and inspiring. In the end, there is not so great a difference among these interpretations. The †mystery of God's plan reflects his infinite wisdom, which in turn manifests Christ's infinite love revealed above all in the cross.

In his fourth request, Paul prays that his readers may be able **to know the**   **3:19**
love of Christ that surpasses knowledge, a reality that exceeds the capacity of words to explain. Paul prays that his readers may realize—may have personal, experiential †knowledge of—Christ's love for them. The word for "love" is *agapē*, gift-love that withholds nothing and seeks the good of the other. Paul never ceases to wonder at "the Son of God who has loved me

Knowing God

In the Bible, "to know God" means not merely to know about him but to have a relationship with him. To know God is to acknowledge who he is and therefore to obey him (1 Sam 2:12; Jer 24:7). Often in Scripture, to know God implies experiencing or being guided by him, sometimes indicated by the use of verbs of sensation: hearing, seeing, thirsting, or tasting (1 Sam 3:7; Ps 42:2–3; Heb 6:4–5). Through the prophet Jeremiah, God promises that in the days to come all his people will know him, from the least to the greatest (Jer 31:31–34; see also Hosea 2:19–23).

In the New Testament, knowledge of God comes through Jesus Christ (John 1:18; 14:9; 1 Cor 1:21–24) and the gift of the Spirit. Through the †gospel, God "has shone in our hearts to give the light of the knowledge of the glory of God in the face of Jesus Christ" (2 Cor 4:6 NRSV). The Holy Spirit is the one who enables Christians to know God, to understand his gifts, and even to "have the mind of Christ" (1 Cor 2:10–16). Those who truly know God conduct themselves uprightly (Matt 7:21–23; 1 Thess 4:5; Titus 1:16; 1 John 2:3–5). Their lives are characterized by love, as is God himself (1 John 4:7–8).

Many Scripture texts indicate that those who come to know God experience delight in knowing him, as well as intense longing to know him more deeply.[a] Hosea 6:3 invites us to "press on to know the Lord" (RSV). Paul, who certainly knew Christ, still expresses a fervent desire "to know him and the power of his resurrection" (Phil 3:10).

The full knowledge of God is something we await in the life to come when "the earth will be full of the knowledge of the †LORD as the waters cover the sea" (Isa 11:9 NRSV), and Paul says, "I will know fully, even as I have been fully known" (1 Cor 13:12 NRSV). (See sidebar on p. 49.)

a. See Ps 27:8; 34; 42; 63; 73; John 7:37–39; Rev 22:17.

and given himself up for me" (Gal 2:20; see Eph 5:2). The cross stands as irrefutable proof of a love that can never fail and from which we can never be separated (Rom 8:31–39). The love of Christ provides a firm †hope of future salvation (Rom 5:6–10) and the compelling motive for mission and ministry (2 Cor 5:14–15).

The fifth request sums up all the others and expresses the real goal of Paul's prayer—**that you may be filled with all the fullness of God**. There is an implicit metaphor here. Paul's readers are likened to containers, which, Paul prays, will be filled up to the maximal level. But rather than say "filled to the brim," Paul prays that his readers may be filled with God's divine life and love

"Divinization" in the Liturgy and the Catechism

At every Mass, the Church prays for the divinization of her members. During the preparation of the gifts, the priest pours a drop of water into the wine that will be consecrated and prays, "May we come to share in the divinity of Christ, who humbled himself to share in our humanity." The Catechism (460) also teaches this truth:

> The Word became †flesh to make us *"partakers of the divine nature"*:[a] "For this is why the Word became man, and the Son of God became the Son of man: so that man, by entering into communion with the Word and thus receiving divine sonship, might become a son of God."[b] "For the Son of God became man so that we might become God."[c] "The only-begotten Son of God, wanting to make us sharers in his divinity, assumed our nature, so that he, made man, might make men gods."[d]

a. 2 Pet 1:4.
b. St. Irenaeus, *Adversus haereses* 3.19.1.
c. St. Athanasius, *De incarnatione* 54.3.
d. St. Thomas Aquinas, *Opuscula* 57.1–4.

to the measure of God's own fullness,[3] in other words, that they may be infinitely full. As he often does, Paul stretches human language to communicate what transcends it.

Paul prays according to God's will that we Christians be so strengthened by the Spirit, so inhabited by Christ, so personally acquainted with the love, wisdom, and plan of God revealed in Jesus' life, death, and resurrection that we would be transformed, becoming containers as full of God as God's fullness. This prayer points toward our ultimate goal as Christians, what some of the Church Fathers daringly describe as "divinization" or "deification" (*theosis*).[4] First John 3:2 says it this way: "Beloved, we are God's children now; what we shall be has not yet been revealed. We do know that when it is revealed we shall be like him, for we shall see him as he is."

Reflection and Application (3:14–19)

These five marvelous petitions of St. Paul for his readers arouse in me a desire that God would grant me these same gifts. I desperately need to be strengthened

3. Literally, the Greek says "*to* all the fullness of God."
4. See Daniel A. Keating, *Deification and Grace*, Introductions to Catholic Doctrine (Naples, FL: Sapientia, 2007), for an excellent introduction to the theology of deification.

by the mighty power of the Spirit in my inner self so that I can love, so that I can pray, so that I can endure, so that I can say no to all the impulses of my fallen nature. I want Christ to take possession of my heart, his dwelling place, and to drive out all the squatters who take up residence whenever I leave my heart untended.

> Heavenly Father, I know how little I grasp of the greatness of your love and of the immensity of your plan for me and for the whole human race. Give me strength of mind and of heart and of imagination so that with your holy people I can understand your plan of salvation so that we can proclaim it to whole world.
>
> Lord Jesus, I believe. Help my unbelief, and make your home in my heart. As I gaze on your cross and adore you in your sacrament, let me understand, as Paul understood, that you loved me and gave yourself for me.
>
> Heavenly Father, change me into that which I adore. Let me be completely filled with your divine life to the extent of your infinite fullness!

Doxology (3:20–21)

---

²⁰Now to him who is able to accomplish far more than all we ask or imagine, by the power at work within us, ²¹to him be glory in the church and in Christ Jesus to all generations, forever and ever. Amen.

NT: Rom 11:36; 16:25; Phil 4:13; 1 Tim 1:17
Catechism: the Father's generosity, 305, 2830; praise, 2639, 2641

3:20–21   Paul concludes his prayer with a doxology (literally, a "word of glory," from *doxa* and *logos*). Like the prayer that precedes it, this expression of worship is addressed to God the Father.

Paul describes God, the one to whom this praise is expressed, as **able to accomplish far more than all we ask or imagine**. In view of his extraordinary requests, it is striking that Paul declares God able to do even greater things. God can accomplish this **by the power at work within us**.[5] By the power of the Holy Spirit living in us, God can grant all five of the extraordinary requests of 3:14–19 and anything else as well. These words provide a firm basis for praying confidently for whatever we need, especially for whatever is necessary to accomplish God's will.

---

5. English translations conceal a play on words here. The root *dyn-* is found both in the verb translated "is able" (*dynamenō*) and in the word "power" (*dynamis*). Literally, "to him who is powerful [enough] . . . by the power at work within us."

Paul concludes with the doxology proper: **to him be glory in the church.** "†Glory," when it is directed to God, refers to praise and honor given to him. This occurs "in the church" since the Church is the community of those who have received his †grace and who return thanks and praise and honor to God, especially in the liturgy.

But what does it mean to ascribe glory to God **in Christ Jesus**? Jesus brought glory to the Father by doing his will on earth, especially by laying down his life on the cross (John 12:28; 17:1–4). He continues to glorify the Father when he acts in power on behalf of his Church (Eph 1:22) and when he answers prayer offered in his name (John 14:13). The Church likewise gives glory to the Father "in Christ Jesus" when, in union with Christ, she does the Father's will and when in the Eucharist she unites herself to Jesus' own self-offering to the Father. Paul declares that God will receive glory in the Church and in Christ **to all generations, forever and ever**, in other words, through all of human history that remains and to eternity. **Amen.**

Reflection and Application (3:20–21)

One of the most frequent and important themes of the New Testament is the exhortation to bold, confident prayer. Many Christians today, however, ask and expect far less from God than he wants to give us. If St. Paul were addressing contemporary Catholics, I suspect he might repeat what James said to his readers: "You do not possess because you do not ask" (James 4:2).

In the Gospels, Jesus repeatedly exhorts his disciples to ask for what they need: "Ask and it will be given to you; seek and you will find; knock and the door will be opened to you. For everyone who asks, receives; and the one who seeks, finds; and to the one who knocks, the door will be opened" (Matt 7:7–8; see Luke 11:9–13).

Jesus instructs his followers to expect that their prayers will be answered: "All that you ask for in prayer, believe that you will receive it and it shall be yours" (Mark 11:24; see Matt 21:22). In parables, Jesus urges his listeners to pray and never lose heart (Luke 18:1–8; 11:5–8). In the Gospel of John, Jesus tells his disciples five times that if they ask "in my name"—uniting themselves to him and asking in accord with his will—they will receive whatever they request (John 14:13, 14; 15:16; 16:23–24, 26).

We know from his letters that Paul prayed constantly for the needs of the churches and also for himself. When he found himself experiencing "a thorn in the †flesh," probably a physical ailment, he prayed three times that God would remove it, until the Lord finally told him, "My grace is sufficient for you, for power is made perfect in weakness" (2 Cor 12:7–9). In this incident we see Paul's faith, his persistent prayer for his own needs, and his joyful surrender when Christ revealed that his will was different from what Paul thought.

As our †faith grows by hearing the word of Christ (Rom 10:17) and as we conform our lives to the incarnate Word, our prayers will become more and more effective. Let us, like Paul, pray for our needs, the needs of others, the needs of the Church, and the needs of the world (1 Tim 2:1–4). Let us offer our prayers with expectant faith and praise to God, who is "able to accomplish far more than all we ask or imagine."

Exhortation to Christian Conduct

The Letter to the Ephesians divides rather neatly into two parts: chapters 1 to 3 describe what God has done for us in Christ; chapters 4 to 6 describe how we ought to conduct ourselves in light of that. Because the second part of Paul's letter builds on the first, let us briefly review what Paul has just said.

In chapter 1, Paul praises God for blessing Christians with every spiritual blessing in the heavens, enumerates these blessings, and prays that God might grant his readers understanding.

In chapter 2, he explains how God saved us from spiritual death, the world, the flesh, and the devil and raised us up to heaven as an act of pure grace through our union with Christ. Through the death of Jesus on the cross, Gentile and Jewish believers have been united in one body, reconciled with God, and built into a spiritual temple.

In chapter 3, Paul explains how he was given a revelation of God's previously hidden plan of salvation and was entrusted with proclaiming this mystery to the Gentiles. Paul concludes by praying that his readers may grasp the magnitude of what God has done for them, fully know Christ's love, and be filled with divine life.

The doctrinal teaching of chapters 1–3 gives readers a powerful motive to respond generously to God's gracious work of salvation. In chapters 4–6, Paul summons Christians to conduct themselves in a way that corresponds to the profound change that God has made in them and instructs his readers in five essential dimensions of Christian conduct:

1. Building up the Church (4:1–16)
2. Embracing the holy lifestyle that belongs to their new identity and renouncing evil conduct in relationships (4:17–5:2)
3. Living as children of light rather than according to the immoral patterns of the surrounding society (5:3–20)
4. Deferring to one another out of reverence for Christ (5:21–6:9)
5. Persevering in spiritual battle and in prayer (6:10–24)

Building Up the Church

Ephesians 4:1–16

Sometimes our need for growth, as individuals and as communities, is painfully obvious. How often do we hear fellow Catholics, or ourselves, express dissatisfaction with parish life, with our Church's witness in the world, or with some other aspect of the Church's life? And when we turn our gaze on our own discipleship, we notice many shortcomings.

Ephesians 4:1–16 explains how spiritual growth comes to the Church, to our local communities, and to ourselves. Paul teaches us that as each member strives for unity and fulfills his or her role of ministry, the body of Christ advances toward maturity. Paul begins his teaching about Christian conduct by talking about life in the Church rather than individual behavior because he understands that individual Christians are transformed through community life in the body of Christ.

The first part (4:1–6) of this teaching on growth addresses the subject of unity. The second part (4:7–12) discusses ministry in the Church. The third part (4:13–16) describes the outcome of effective ministry, namely, Christian maturity.

Unity—Attitudes That Preserve It, Facts That Establish It (4:1–6)

¹I, then, a prisoner for the Lord, urge you to live in a manner worthy of the call you have received, ²with all humility and gentleness, with patience, bearing with one another through love, ³striving to preserve the

unity of the spirit through the bond of peace: ⁴one body and one Spirit, as you were also called to the one hope of your call; ⁵one Lord, one faith, one baptism; ⁶one God and Father of all, who is over all and through all and in all.

NT: John 17:20–23; 1 Cor 12:4–6, 12–13; Gal 3:27–28; Phil 1:27–2:4; Col 3:12–15

Catechism: one faith, 172–75; the Church is one, 813–22; baptism as foundation of communion among Christians, 1271

Lectionary: 4:1–6: Christian Initiation apart from Easter Vigil, Confirmation, Blessings of Abbots and Abbesses, for the Laity, for the Unity of Christians

4:1   In Greek, the first word of the second half of this letter is *parakaleō*, meaning "I exhort." Although chapters 4–6 contain teaching, their primary character is exhortation, an appeal to the will. Paul begins his summons to Christian conduct by reminding his readers that he is **a prisoner for the Lord** and appeals to them on that basis. The Greek literally says "a prisoner *in* the Lord" (JB, NJB, NRSV), a slightly different wording than 3:1 that emphasizes Paul's union with Jesus in his imprisonment. He exhorts his readers **to live in a manner worthy of the call you have received**. The word translated "to ᵗlive" (*peripateō*) means "to walk." In the Old Testament, the way a person "walks" refers to that person's path in life, whether good or evil. The fact that Paul uses *peripateō* four more times in the next chapter and a half (4:17; 5:2, 8, 15) shows his attention to ethical behavior in this section.

In ordinary Greek the word translated "call"[1] means "invitation." As in the Gospel story of the man who invited his neighbors to a banquet (Luke 14:16–24), so Christians have received an invitation to a celebration of the good things that God has for us. If you were invited to a banquet of the world's most famous and important people, you would think carefully about what to wear and how to comport yourself. Paul is saying that since his readers have been invited into a relationship with God and his ᵗholy people that begins now (2:19–22) and culminates in the age to come (2:7; 3:14–21), they should adopt a pattern of conduct that corresponds to such an exquisite invitation.

4:2   Then, paradoxically, Paul plunges into describing a type of conduct that might appear to have little in common with the exalted state of being filled with "the fullness of God" (3:19): **with all humility**.[2] The Greek word Paul uses for humility, *tapeinophrosyne*, comes from *phroneō* ("to think") and *tapeinos* ("low," "insignificant," or "poor"). The verb form of this word, *tapeinoō* ("to make oneself low") is used by Jesus in his teaching: "Everyone who exalts himself will

---

1. The JB and NJB say "vocation."
2. The JB translates this as "selflessness."

be humbled, but the one who humbles himself will be exalted" (Luke 14:11). Humility was an attitude that the pagan world despised; Christians were the first in the ancient world to regard it as a virtue.[3] In Philippians as well, Paul urges humility for the sake of unity, expressed in his exhortation to "regard others as more important than yourselves" (Phil 2:3). He points to the attitude of Jesus, who was willing to become low through his incarnation and the cross, and whom God exalted "because of this" (Phil 2:9).

Paul next recommends **gentleness**, *prautēs*, sometimes translated "meekness" (RSV), which does not mean being soft or weak. Aristotle described this virtue as the desired middle ground "between being too angry and never being angry at all."[4] It can have the character of kindliness. When ascribed to someone in authority, it means a reasonable lenience. Gentleness is a virtue of peacemakers, namely, the inner strength not to retaliate when provoked. It enables a person to bring correction in a fraternal manner when it is needed (Gal 6:1; 2 Tim 2:25). Paul speaks of the "gentleness" of Christ (2 Cor 10:1) and includes gentleness among the fruit of the Spirit (Gal 5:23).

The word translated **patience** literally means "long-tempered." Many times in the †Septuagint (e.g., Exod 34:6; Ps 103:8 [102:8 LXX]) this word is used to depict God as "slow to anger," that is, someone who has a long fuse. Paul uses this word in describing Christ's attitude toward him: "I received mercy, so that in me, as the foremost [of sinners], Jesus Christ might display the utmost patience" (1 Tim 1:16 NRSV). The book of Proverbs teaches that patience marks a person who is wise (14:29; 16:32; 19:11) and that "those who are slow to anger calm contention" (15:18 NRSV). This peacemaking potential of patience is probably what Paul has in mind, since he links it with **bearing with one another through love**. This means kindly putting up with people's faults and idiosyncrasies rather than reacting the way we instinctively feel like reacting. Paul is well aware that relationships even among Christians can be trying and sometimes require extraordinary charity and self-restraint.

Now Paul explains the reason for prioritizing these virtues: **striving to preserve the unity of the spirit**. It would be more accurate to capitalize "Spirit" as most translations do, since Paul refers to the profound unity that already exists because Christians share the same Holy Spirit: "In one Spirit we were all baptized into one body . . . and we were all given to drink of one Spirit" (1 Cor 12:13). The discussion of unity and the Spirit builds on chapter 2, where

4:3

---

3. Jews also, to some degree. This precise Greek word is not found in the LXX, but the concept is present (2 Sam 22:28; Ps 25:9; Isa 66:2).

4. William Barclay, *Letters to the Galatians and Ephesians*, 3rd ed. (Louisville: Westminster John Knox, 2002), 158.

Fig. 7. Lacking church buildings, the early Christians met in the homes of wealthy members with large rooms, like this one, that could accommodate a small congregation.

Paul speaks of Jews and Gentiles being re-created as "one new person" and sharing "access in one Spirit to the Father" (2:15, 18). This unity is defended **through the bond of peace**, that is, by an active effort to preserve peaceable relationships among the members of the church. We know how easy it is for conflicts to arise and divisions to appear in family and church life. Paul exhorts us to adopt the Christ-like attitudes that protect peace and unity: humility, gentleness, patience, and forbearance in love. Jesus the †Messiah "is our peace," established peace, and "preached peace" (2:14, 15, 17); let us remain at peace with one another.

In the next three verses Paul expands on his affirmation that Christians are already one by naming seven points of unity that we share:

4:4   1. We form **one body**, the body of Christ. The Church is not merely a human association but the continuing visible expression of the Messiah on earth (1:23). Being united to Christ in one body implies a profound mutual belonging and responsibility: "God has so constructed the body . . . that the parts may have the same concern for one another. If [one] part suffers, all the parts suffer with it; if one part is honored, all the parts share its joy" (1 Cor 12:24–26).

2. We share **one Spirit** that is the source of life for every Christian. *Pneuma*, the Greek word for "Spirit," also means "breath," an essential for our biological life. According to Gen 2:7 (NRSV), when God created the first man he "breathed into his nostrils the breath of life." The gift of God's Spirit, breathed into us by Christ (John 20:22), gives us divine life.

3. We have been **called to the one hope of** our **call**. God has invited all Christians (see 4:1) to the same banquet; we are not going to different celebrations. In the New Testament, "†hope" (here as in 1:18; 2:12) often refers not to a feeling or attitude but to the objective future blessing we await—the second coming of Christ and life with God forever.

4. We have **one Lord,** namely, Jesus. In the Septuagint, *kyrios*, "the †Lord," was used in place of God's name, †YHWH, which Jews then and now refrain from pronouncing out of reverence. In secular Greek, the title "lord," *kyrios*, was used for the emperor and by slaves for their masters. In the early Church, the affirmation "Jesus is Lord" was a way of acknowledging Jesus as the supreme ruler and God and of confessing allegiance to him over every other power (Phil 2:11; Rom 10:9; see 1 Cor 12:3). **4:5**

5. We share **one faith**. This refers to the content of faith, the apostolic doctrine that has been handed on and received by the Church. Here Paul speaks of the "one faith" as something already shared; later in the chapter he will indicate that the "unity of faith" is something that still remains to be fully achieved (4:13).

6. We share **one baptism**, that is, we have all been "baptized into Christ" (Rom 6:3–8; Gal 3:27–28; Col 2:12–13). By means of this baptism, we died and rose with Jesus and were joined to his body, the Church. Just as Christians are headed toward the same destination, the same "hope," so we share the same point of origin, baptism.

7. Finally, Paul concludes, Christians share **one God and Father of all, who is over all**. Although some commentators take this "all" to refer to the universe and others to the whole human race—and God is certainly over both—the context emphasizes the unity of Christians. At the climax of his list of seven unities Paul affirms that Jewish and †Gentile believers are under the care and protection of the same Father God. This one God and Father works **through all**—this probably refers to God's presence and activity in the gifts Paul is about to describe (as in 1 Cor 12:11). Finally, the "one God and Father" is **in all**, referring to the fact that we are already a "dwelling place of God" (2:21–22; 3:19). **4:6**

Overcoming Obstacles to Unity

LIVING
TRADITION

Father Raniero Cantalamessa, the preacher to the papal household under John Paul II and Benedict XVI, suggests how we may
overcome obstacles to unity, which he compares to embolisms
in the body of Christ:

> Embolisms pose a mortal danger to the human body. Abnormal
> particles called emboli obstruct veins and arteries and, if not cleared in
> time, hinder the free circulation of blood. This can cause great damage,
> leading to paralysis or even death. The church, which is the body of
> Christ, faces its own kind of embolisms. These obstacles to communion
> include the refusal to forgive, lasting hostility and the bitterness, wrath, anger,
> slander and malice [Eph 4:31]. . . .
>
> If we want to "maintain a unity of the spirit in the bond of peace," it is necessary
> to periodically take an x-ray—that is, a thorough examination of conscience—to
> be sure that there are no blockages for which we are responsible. At the level of
> ecumenism we must work patiently to remove the enormous barriers that have
> been built between the churches. This work has to take place at the capillary level:
> between communities and denominations; within each church—for example,
> between clergy and lay people—and finally between individuals.[a]

a. Raniero Cantalamessa, *Loving the Church* (Cincinnati: St. Anthony Messenger, 2005), 32–33.

As Jesus says in John 14:23, "Whoever loves me will keep my word,
and my Father will love him, and we will come to him and make our
dwelling with him."

Reflection and Application (4:1–6)

As much as any text in the Bible, this text describes what unites Christians.
This unity encompasses believers of different races and different cultures, rich
and poor, educated and uneducated. We have been baptized and worship in
the name of the Father, the Son, and the Holy Spirit. We confess the Apostles'
Creed, a baseline of Christian doctrine, and accept the Bible as the word of
God.[5] We look forward to Christ's coming in glory and his establishment of the
kingdom of God in fullness, a hope all Christians share. As Pope John XXIII
said, "What unites us is much greater than what divides us."[6]

5. Some churches differ from the Catholic Church regarding which books of the Old Testament they
accept as canonical, although virtually all accept the same twenty-seven books of the New Testament.
6. As quoted by John Paul II in *Ut Unum Sint* (*On Commitment to Ecumenism*) 20.

This unity in Christ is deeper than the unity we have with the rest of the human race. It is more important than the unity we share with others who are citizens of our country or who share the same language or culture. I am a middle-class, middle-aged professor teaching Scripture at a Catholic seminary in the United States. Yet spiritually I am more deeply united with an Orthodox believer in a factory in Russia and with a Pentecostal tribesman on an obscure island in the South Pacific than I am with American professors who share my ethnic background and political views but are not Christians.

Nevertheless, the unity that exists among Christians of different churches is incomplete. Although for the most part we agree on the Apostles' Creed, significant doctrinal differences divide us. Although we have all been baptized into the one body of Christ, we are not united in a visible communion as the apostolic Church was[7] due to disagreements regarding doctrine and church authority. Visible unity is something Christ intended, something the Church experienced to a considerable degree before the break between the Catholic Church and the Eastern Church in 1054, and something we pray God will bring to pass again. The Second Vatican Council teaches that "men of both sides were to blame" for the separation of large communities from the Catholic Church.[8] A longing for unity among Christians in response to Christ's prayer (John 17:20–23) is the basis of the ecumenical movement, a movement the Catholic Church supports. "At the Second Vatican Council, the Catholic Church committed herself *irrevocably* to following the path of the ecumenical venture, thus heeding the Spirit of the Lord."[9] Thus Pope John Paul II urged Catholics to seek unity in the truth, to overcome the roots of division in human sinfulness, and to pray and work to make the spiritual communion that exists among Christians effective and visible.

Although we do enjoy visible unity in the Catholic Church, we also realize that this unity is imperfect and requires our constant attention. The task of preserving unity begins at home—in our families, parishes, and places of ministry. It is no easy thing to stay united to the people who are closest to us. It is here that we need to embrace the qualities of humility, patience, gentleness, and forbearance in love.

---

7. Although the Church was spread in local communities around the Mediterranean, these communities recognized one another and the leadership of Christ's apostles, among whom Peter exercised a particular role. Paul worked to strengthen the unity of this visible worldwide communion by collecting alms from the predominantly Gentile churches in Greece and Asia Minor for the Jewish church in Jerusalem (Rom 15:31; 1 Cor 16:1–4; 2 Cor 8–9).

8. Second Vatican Council, *Unitatis Redintegratio* (*Decree on Ecumenism*) 3.

9. *Ut Unum Sint* 3; emphasis original.

Ministry—Building Up the Body of Christ (4:7–12)

> [7]But grace was given to each of us according to the measure of Christ's gift. [8]Therefore, it says:
>
>> "He ascended on high and took prisoners captive;
>> he gave gifts to men."
>
> [9]What does "he ascended" mean except that he also descended into the lower [regions] of the earth? [10]The one who descended is also the one who ascended far above all the heavens, that he might fill all things.
>
> [11]And he gave some as apostles, others as prophets, others as evangelists, others as pastors and teachers, [12]to equip the holy ones for the work of ministry, for building up the body of Christ,

OT: Ps 68

NT: Acts 1:9–11; 2:33; Rom 12:3–9; 1 Cor 12:7–11, 27–31; Heb 4:14

Catechism: charisms, 768, 791, 798–801, 910, 2003; apostles and pastors, 1575; laity share in Christ's prophetic and kingly offices, 904–13

Lectionary: 4:1–13: Ascension (Year B); 4:1–7, 11–13: Feast of St. Matthew; Common of Pastors; Common of Doctors; Mass for Conferral of Holy Orders, for Priests, or for Ministers of the Church

Having just described the Church's unity, Paul now indicates that the Church is characterized by a diversity of gifts. These gifts come from the risen and exalted [†]Messiah, who has given them to build up his body.

4:7–8   Every member of the Church has received a gift of [†]**grace**. The phrase **according to the measure of Christ's gift** means that Jesus is the giver and decides the measure and kind of spiritual gifting each person receives.[10] Verses 11–12 make clear that the gifts are not for the benefit of the individual but for the benefit of the Church. The idea is very similar to what Paul writes in Rom 12:6: "Since we have gifts that differ according to the grace given to us, let us exercise them" (see 1 Cor 12:7).

Stating the Messiah's role in giving these gifts prompts Paul to support this affirmation by interpreting Ps 68, which Paul understands to foreshadow Christ's resurrection, ascension, and bestowal of charisms on the Church.

In its original context, Ps 68 was a hymn for a liturgical celebration (vv. 25–28) of God's victories over Israel's [†]Gentile enemies, his taking captives and receiving tribute from them (vv. 19, 30, 32), and his bestowing blessings on his people (vv. 13b–15, 36). One part of the psalm (vv. 17–19) describes God ascending to

---

10. In 1 Cor 12:11 Paul attributes this role to the Spirit. This is not a problem, however, since the Holy Spirit is Christ's own spirit (Rom 8:9; Gal 4:6) and the risen Christ acts by means of the Spirit.

Jerusalem to establish his dwelling, the "holy place." Summarizing rather than quoting the psalm, Paul applies it to Jesus. Having conquered his enemies through his death and resurrection, Christ has **ascended on high** . . . "far above all the heavens." Ephesians has already referred to the Messiah's ascension and exaltation above everything (1:20–21). Drawing on Ps 68:19, Paul says Christ **took prisoners captive**.[11] Here interpretations vary. Some think this refers to Christ's taking captive the hostile †principalities and powers, an idea suggested by Col 2:15. Others think it refers to Jesus' liberation after his death of those who were captives in Hades (1 Pet 3:18–20). Still others think it refers to the Messiah's taking and liberating those who were prisoners of the principalities and powers (Eph 2:2), especially the Gentiles. This last interpretation seems to fit the context best both in Ephesians and in Ps 68, which concludes by summoning the conquered Gentiles to praise the Lord and confess the power of God (Ps 68:33–35).

Paul edits Ps 68 slightly to make his point. Rather than *receiving* tribute from his enemies,[12] Christ *gives* gifts to human beings, gifts of the Holy Spirit. This parallels what St. Peter says at Pentecost: "Exalted at the right hand of God, he received the promise of the holy Spirit from the Father and poured it forth, as you [both] see and hear" (Acts 2:33). Paul's main point is that the risen Jesus is the source of gifts of ministry in the body of Christ.

The next verse is also difficult: **What does "he ascended" mean except that**   **4:9–10**
he also descended . . . ? What is Paul's logic? Paul is interpreting Ps 68:19, which addresses God, saying, "You went up." He makes the logical inference that to speak of God ascending implies that he had previously descended, since God's dwelling is in †heaven, above everything else. The Old Testament sometimes describes God's intervention in human affairs as his coming down or descending (e.g., Gen 18:21; Exod 3:8).

Paul understands Ps 68 to be speaking of Christ. After all, it begins, "Let God arise, let his enemies be scattered" (RSV). When did God *arise* and scatter his enemies? At the resurrection of the Messiah, of course! And Paul tells us to where the Messiah descended: he went down **into the lower [regions] of the earth**. There are various interpretations of this descent. Most likely it refers either to Christ's incarnation, when he emptied himself of heavenly †glory (Phil 2:7) and came down among us (John 3:13), or to his burial in the earth. Alternatively, as was mentioned above, it could refer to Christ's descent into the realms of the dead upon his death, where he preached "to the spirits in prison" (1 Pet 3:18–22).

11. Most translations say "captives" rather than "prisoners." The NRSV opts for an alternate meaning of the Greek word and translates the phrase "he made captivity itself a captive."
12. Ps 68:18 says that God "receiv[ed] gifts among men" (RSV) rather than *gave* gifts, although other parts of the psalm mention God bestowing blessings on his people (11–15, 36).

Who Were the Apostles?

BIBLICAL
BACKGROUND

The Greek word *apostolos* literally means "one who is sent, a messenger." From the Gospels we know that Jesus appointed twelve. After Judas's death, the remaining apostles chose his replacement from among those disciples who had been witnesses of Jesus' ministry and resurrection (Acts 1:21–26). The Twelve then continued to exercise a special leadership role in the earliest years of the Church (1 Cor 15:5; Acts 6:2; Rev 21:14). But the New Testament also refers to other apostles (Acts 14:14; Rom 16:7; 1 Cor 15:7), and Paul firmly insists that he too was appointed an apostle (1 Cor 9:1–2; Gal 1:1; 2 Tim 1:11). We do not know exactly by what criteria the early Church recognized apostles or how many there were. Besides preaching, teaching, and founding new communities (local churches), apostles appointed presbyters and supervised to some degree the communities that emerged (Acts 14:23; 20:17).

In any case, the **one who descended** is the same person who has now **ascended far above all the heavens**, namely, Christ. As in Phil 2:6–11, Paul marvels that the one who came so far down has now been raised so high up. God had a purpose for this: **that he might fill all things**. Here, as in 1:23, "fill" means to exercise divine authority everywhere (echoing Jer 23:24) so that the Messiah might be Lord over all.

4:11   Now Paul names some of the gifts Jesus bestowed after his ascension and explains their purpose. I say "some" of the gifts, because this list differs in two respects from most other lists of charisms found in the New Testament (Rom 12:4–8; 1 Cor 12:7–11; 1 Pet 4:10–11).[13] First, this verse identifies the gifts of 4:8 as *persons* who fulfill certain roles of ministry rather than as divinely empowered abilities, such as prophecy, tongues, or healing.[14] God gives people to serve the Church, and he equips them with the natural and supernatural abilities necessary to fulfill those roles. Second, in contrast to the wider range of gifts in the other lists, the list given here is narrow in scope: it focuses on those who speak the word of God and those who fulfill major leadership roles.

Paul has already mentioned **apostles** three times in Ephesians (1:1; 2:20; 3:5). He indicated that the household of God is "built upon the foundation of the apostles and prophets" (2:20) and that they are the ones to whom God's

13. The ways God works in the members of the Church to build up the body of Christ are many and various, so there is no exhaustive biblical list of "gifts" and "charisms."

14. The list of charisms in 1 Cor 12:27–31 mixes gifts of persons and special abilities.

†mystery "has now been revealed . . . by the Spirit" (3:5). Here the emphasis is not on the foundational and revelatory role of the apostles but on their role as ministers who build up the Church.

We know only a limited amount about New Testament †**prophets** (see sidebar on p. 88). Besides their role in receiving revelation of God's mystery (3:5), we know they fulfilled a speaking ministry in the early Church (Acts 15:32; 1 Cor 14:3–4), occasionally prophesying future events similar to the Old Testament prophets (Acts 11:27–28; 21:10–11). While some were resident in local communities (Acts 13:1), others had an itinerant ministry.[15] We also know rather little about **evangelists** in the early Church, since that word—related to the Greek words for "evangelize" and "†gospel"—appears only three times in the New Testament. In one of those instances, Acts describes Philip as an evangelist (Acts 21:8). He preached the gospel in Samaria and evangelized the Ethiopian eunuch (Acts 8:5–13, 26–38). Second Timothy 4:2–5 exhorts Timothy to do "the work of an evangelist," constantly proclaiming the word of God. It seems that evangelists, like apostles, announced the good news of salvation in Jesus and summoned their hearers to conversion. The use of the term "evangelist" to refer to authors of the Gospels came later.

The final two gifts Paul mentions, **pastors and teachers**, are more familiar. We know that there were itinerant teachers who, like the apostles and prophets, traveled among the early Christian communities. Apollos was one of them (Acts 18:24–28; 1 Cor 3:4–6). While it is possible this text refers to two distinct ministries, pastors (literally, "shepherds") *and* teachers, the way it is written in Greek[16] suggests that pastor-teachers are intended. These would be the resident church leaders who presided over the community, shepherding the flock (see John 21:15–17; 1 Pet 5:1–4) and teaching. Of the ministries mentioned here, this role is most similar to what our bishops and priests do—they also are "gifts" whom Christ has given to the Church.

Why has the Messiah established these roles of leadership in the Church? The purpose is **to equip the holy ones for the work of ministry**,[17] in other words, to prepare the members of the church, particularly the laity, to accomplish all that ministry entails. Ministry, *diakonia*, in the New Testament covers a broad range of service, from hospitality (Luke 10:40) to providing for the poor (Acts 6:1;

4:12

---

15. For some obscure but tantalizing hints regarding the ministry of itinerant apostles, prophets, and teachers, and their relationship to bishops and deacons, see chapters 11–15 of the *Didache*, an early Christian writing from the late first or early second century (available online).

16. There is a definite article in front of the first three terms that identify ministries but only one article before the words for "pastors and teachers."

17. The JB and NJB interpret the role of these leaders as *uniting* God's people for service.

2 Cor 8:4; 9:1) to preaching and teaching the word (Acts 6:4). According to Paul, the work of ministry is not confined to those with overall leadership gifts—the apostles, prophets, evangelists, and pastor-teachers. Rather, it is carried out by all the "holy ones," the baptized believers, whom the leaders have "equipped."

The ultimate goal of equipping members for ministry is **for building up the body of Christ** (see 1:23 and 4:4 for a discussion of what Paul means by "body of Christ"). As in 2:20–22, Paul uses a mixed metaphor, describing the church in both organic ("body") and architectural terms ("building up"). To "build up," sometimes translated "edify," is a favorite term of Paul's (Rom 15:2; 1 Cor 14:4, 12, 26; 1 Thess 5:11) and refers to strengthening the Church and its members.

Reflection and Application (4:11–12)

Apostles, prophets, evangelists, pastors, and teachers after the apostolic age. Besides bishops, ordained as successors to the apostles, and the priests and deacons who assist them, how have the ministries of apostle, prophet, evangelist, pastor, and teacher continued? Throughout history Christ gives anointed individuals to the Church to fulfill important roles of ministry. Missionaries like St. Francis Xavier, who established the Church in new territories, or founders of religious communities and spiritual movements, like St. Elizabeth Ann Seton and St. Francis of Assisi, might well be seen as exercising apostolic charisms. Others who spoke in God's name, such as St. Catherine of Siena and St. Vincent Ferrer, may well be regarded as prophets. More recently, those preaching to large audiences through the mass media or winning many individuals to conversion one by one have done the work of evangelists. Certainly there have been many anointed teachers in the Church who have expounded the word of God luminously and with great fruitfulness. The Catholic Church recognizes some of the most outstanding of these by naming them doctors (which means "teachers") of the Church. The gifted people whom Jesus gives to the Church are by no means confined to popes, saints, or ordained ministers. Many anointed ministries in our local communities have been given by Jesus as gifts to his bride to build up the body of Christ, whether in teaching, music, youth ministry, works of mercy, or evangelization.

Christians of other churches also exercise spiritual gifts for building up the body of Christ, as Vatican II affirmed:

> Very many of the significant elements and endowments which together go to build up and give life to the Church itself, can exist outside the visible boundaries of the Catholic Church. . . . Catholics must gladly acknowledge and esteem the

truly Christian endowments from our common heritage which are to be found among our separated brethren.[18]

Orthodox Christians are especially known for their theological, liturgical, and artistic contributions. Protestant brothers and sisters are recognized for their contributions in missions, evangelism, music, and biblical studies.

How can leaders equip church members for ministry? Since ministry "in the Spirit" draws on graces received in baptism and confirmation, the first priority is to lead lay Catholics to an active faith and personal acquaintance with Jesus Christ. Ephesians offers an order for this task: proclaiming the central truths of the gospel followed by teaching about the Christian way of life, since "living the truth in love" is the goal of pastoral ministry (see 4:13–15). After that comes teaching about the variety of spiritual gifts given for building up the body of Christ and wisdom about discerning the charisms the Spirit has given to the members of the community.[19] In this regard it is important to teach and model an attitude of servanthood that does not aim at self-promotion (Phil 2:3–8) and that values charity over natural and spiritual gifting (1 Cor 13).

Since some gifted persons are hesitant to come forward, wise leaders do not rely exclusively on volunteers but pray about whom to choose and then personally invite people to serve, as Jesus and Paul did (Luke 6:12–13; Acts 16:3). Those who are new in roles of ministry need formation to acquire skill and confidence. Ministry in the Church entails more than accomplishing tasks; it entails building loving relationships among brothers and sisters (*communio*). Formation occurs best in the context of these relationships. Jesus mentoring his disciples and Paul collaborating with coworkers provide models to imitate.

The Lord himself builds up his body through the action of the Holy Spirit, so it is wise to pay attention to those through whom he is working. Are some music leaders particularly effective in leading the congregation to sing joyfully and prayerfully? Are there youth leaders whose influence results in real conversions? Are there teachers or religious educators whose students particularly seem to manifest faith and fervor? Are there individuals who have a knack for bringing organization to aspects of the community's life and do so in a way that others find gracious and effective? Encouraging such people and providing them with opportunities to serve is a way of cooperating with what Christ is doing to build up his body.

18. *Unitatis Redintegratio* 3.
19. The Catherine of Siena Institute (www.siena.org) and other organizations provide resources to parishes and dioceses to help Catholics discern the charisms they have received.

Maturity—the Goal (4:13–16)

>[13]until we all attain to the unity of faith and knowledge of the Son of God, to mature manhood, to the extent of the full stature of Christ, [14]so that we may no longer be infants, tossed by waves and swept along by every wind of teaching arising from human trickery, from their cunning in the interests of deceitful scheming. [15]Rather, living the truth in love, we should grow in every way into him who is the head, Christ, [16]from whom the whole body, joined and held together by every supporting ligament, with the proper functioning of each part, brings about the body's growth and builds itself up in love.

NT: 1 Cor 14:20; Eph 2:21; Col 1:28; 2:19; Heb 5:12–6:3

Catechism: teaching of bishops, 888; Church as the body of Christ, 792–95; doctrine, catechesis, maturity, 4–7, 25, 426–27, 1248, 1308, 2688

Lectionary: 4:11–16: Mass for the Election of a Pope or a Bishop

The apostle now speaks about the outcome of ministry. The goal of the work of apostles, prophets, evangelists, and all pastoral ministry and teaching is that the Church may reach maturity.

4:13 Paul describes maturity first positively (4:13), then negatively (what it is not, 4:14), then positively again (4:15a). Finally he sums up the dynamic by which maturity is achieved (4:15b–16).

The goal of ministry that builds up the body of Christ is to lead the members of the church **to the unity of faith**. The RSV and NRSV translate this more precisely as "the unity of *the* faith." This expression refers to agreement regarding the *content* of what we believe, that is, Christian doctrine, rather than a vague unity based simply on "having faith" or being "persons of faith." Paul precedes this goal with the words **until we all attain**, which might seem to contradict 4:5, where he spoke of Christians already having "one faith." However, there are degrees of unity in the faith, just as there are degrees of holiness. On the one hand, unity of faith is given by the Spirit, who enlightens through the preaching of the †gospel and interior revelation (1:17–18; 1 John 2:20, 27). On the other hand, humans learn gradually.

Doctrine, the faith in which Christians are to be united, is vitally important. Paul's letters warn against distortions of the gospel (Gal 1:6–9; 2 Tim 4:3–4); he corrects immature understandings (1 Cor 3:1–4; see also Heb 5:12–14) and provides guidelines for handling disagreements about the gospel's application to life (Rom 14:3–6). Preaching and teaching must aim at leading Christians to understand the truth together. To correct opponents effectively requires a teaching gift, kindness, patience, and gentleness (2 Tim 2:24–26) grounded in an uncompromising commitment to the gospel as contained in Scripture, Tradition, and Church teaching.

Paul links the "unity of the faith" with the **knowledge of the Son of God**. We have already explained that "†knowledge" of God and of Christ entails personal familiarity and relationship in addition to conceptual understanding (see sidebars on p. 49 and p. 100). Again, there are degrees of knowing Jesus, just as there are degrees of unity in the faith and holiness. Christian preachers and teachers aim to lead their hearers toward an understanding of the word of God that goes beyond cognitive learning to knowledge of the person of Christ. This can be accomplished only by yielding to the Spirit and allowing Christ the teacher to speak through them.

The final goal of ministry is to lead the body of Christ **to mature manhood, to the extent of the full stature of Christ**. These two phrases are roughly synonymous, the second becoming more specific. By "mature manhood" Paul means adulthood, preparing the contrast with "infants," which he makes in the next verse.[20] It is not just the likeness of any mature person to which the Church must attain, however, but rather "to the measure of the stature of the fulness of Christ" (literal translation, RSV), something that happens as the members of the Church unite themselves to him. The Church is to fully resemble Messiah Jesus, to grow into his likeness, to his full stature.

The focus is on *corporate* maturity. We are accustomed to thinking about Christian maturity in individual terms, but here the emphasis is on the Church. When we consider how to "equip the †holy ones for the work of ministry, for building up the body of Christ" (v. 12), we must think of our local communities. What would a mature *parish* or *diocese* look like? Ephesians 4:1–16 suggests that a mature body of Christians has three characteristics: (1) unity in relationships characterized by humility, gentleness, kindness, and forbearance in love (4:2–3); (2) unity and stability in doctrine and in relationship with Christ (4:13–15); and (3) fruitful ministry according to the diverse gifts of the members under the guidance of their pastors and other leaders (4:8, 11–12, 16).

Now Paul describes the characteristics of Christians who are *not* mature: **4:14** **so that we may no longer be infants, tossed by waves and swept along by every wind of teaching**. New believers, and sometimes older ones who should know better, quickly embrace the latest fashions of thought and action, whether secular or religious, without measuring them against Scripture and the faith of the Church. Stability in the truth is a mark of maturity.

---

20. The Greek adjective translated "mature" (*teleios*) means perfect, complete, or fully developed.

"An Adult Faith"

The following is from a homily by Joseph Cardinal Ratzinger immediately before his election as Pope Benedict XVI.

What does it mean to be an infant in faith? Saint Paul answers: it means "tossed by waves and swept along by every wind of teaching arising from human trickery" (Eph 4:14). This description is very relevant today!

How many winds of doctrine we have known in recent decades, how many ideological currents, how many ways of thinking. The small boat of thought of many Christians has often been tossed about by these waves—thrown from one extreme to the other: from Marxism to liberalism, even to libertinism; from collectivism to radical individualism; from atheism to a vague religious mysticism; from agnosticism to syncretism, and so forth. . . . Having a clear faith, based on the Creed of the Church, is often labeled today as a fundamentalism . . . [while] relativism, which is letting oneself be tossed and "swept along by every wind of teaching," looks like the only attitude acceptable to today's standards. We are moving towards a dictatorship of relativism which does not recognize anything as for certain and which has as its highest goal one's own ego and one's own desires.

However, we have a different goal: the Son of God, true man. Being an "adult" means having a faith which does not follow the waves of today's fashions or the latest novelties. A faith which is deeply rooted in friendship with Christ is adult and mature. It is this friendship which opens us up to all that is good and gives us the knowledge to judge true from false, and deceit from truth. . . . In Christ, truth and love coincide. To the extent that we draw near to Christ, in our own life, truth and love merge. Love without truth would be blind; truth without love would be like "a resounding gong or a clashing cymbal" (1 Cor 13:1).[a]

a. Joseph Cardinal Ratzinger, Homily, Dean of the College of Cardinals at the Mass for the Election of the Roman Pontiff, April 18, 2005.

Paul discerns an evil ingenuity behind such harmful teaching. It arises **from human trickery, from their cunning in the interests of deceitful scheming.** Paul uses three Greek synonyms that mean "craftiness" or "trickery" and a qualifier meaning "error" or "deceit." Other biblical texts identify motives for teaching (or embracing) error: love of money (1 Tim 6:5), desire for human approval (John 5:44; Gal 4:17), lust (Rev 2:14, 20), and the desire to justify one's own immoral conduct (Rom 1:24–32; 2 Thess 2:10–12). False teachers may not consciously know what they are doing; 2 Tim 3:13 refers to such individuals as "deceivers and deceived."

4:15–16   **Rather** than being deceived and unstable, Christians should be **living the truth**. The Greek here uses the participle of a verb derived from "truth"—comparable to "truthing"[21]—that contrasts with the "trickery," "cunning," and "deceitful scheming" that precedes it. Paul calls us not only to be loyal to the truth, but to do so without being arrogant or harsh: he urges us to live in the truth out of a desire for the good of others, acting **in love**. Several translations express this as "speaking the truth in love." Whether speaking or living, our conduct is to be truthful, sincere, and motivated by love.

The second half of v. 15 and v. 16 sum up 4:11–16, which in the Greek forms one long sentence. The result of "living the truth in love" will be that we **grow in every way into him**. Maturity means growing in union with Christ. Christ himself is our goal, but there are degrees of unity and maturity. Christian faith entails an "already" and a "not yet." Although the Church is already "in Christ," there is plenty of room to be more fully united with our †Lord Jesus the Messiah, **who is the head** of "the body, the church" (Col 1:18; see sidebar on p. 160), the source **from whom the whole body**, the Church, derives its unity, growth, and flourishing. The vivid anatomical analogy of head and body in 4:15–16 underscores the organic unity of Christ and the Church.

This body, the Church, is **joined and held together by every supporting ligament**—other translations say "joint." These ligaments provide structural support for the body and probably refer to those with special leadership roles; the Greek word for "supporting" suggests that providing nourishment is part of their role.

Notice the intensely communal vision of the Church's nature: the parts are touching one another, fastened together, in a way that supports and empowers the body's activity. This activity depends, however, on the **proper functioning of each part**. As in 1 Cor 12:15–21, no part is dispensable. The ministers with gifts of teaching and overall leadership do their part in equipping other members of the body to fulfill their respective roles. In this way the whole body, head and members in concert, **brings about the body's growth and builds itself up in love**. The emphasis rests on the final word of the sentence both in Greek and in English. The Church can be strengthened only if her members conduct their relationships and fulfill their ministries "in love."

To summarize, Paul is saying that the goal of the diverse gifts Jesus gives the Church is ministry that leads to Christlike maturity in the body as a whole and in its individual members. This maturity is characterized by a unity in doctrine, relationship with Christ himself, and stable adherence to the truth. It involves sincere conduct and love and requires that each member of the body of Christ fulfill his or her role of service.

---

21. A similar idea—although not the same Greek verb—is found in John 3:21 and 1 John 1:6.

Reflection and Application (4:13–16)

Since the growth and health of the body depends on the "proper functioning of each part," it is vital for the Church that each of us discovers his or her role in the body of Christ. But how? The most important means is prayer. A friend of mine recommends always praying after communion, "Lord, show me what you want me to do, and give me the grace to do it!" A few questions can help show us how we are meant to serve.

First, *where has Divine Providence placed me*? My state in life, vocation, and occupation make a difference in how and where I can serve. Am I already a "joint" or "ligament" that helps hold together or supply God's people? Sometimes people are called to serve in faraway places, but usually our place of ministry is the place where we are already planted. Of course, we need to listen to the Holy Spirit. Some like Abraham are called to leave home in answer to God's call.

Second, *what natural and spiritual gifts has God given me*? How has God worked through me in the past to make a difference for others? How do I experience him working through me now? Every Christian can be certain that God has given him or her gifts for ministry, for St. Paul teaches that "grace was given to each of us according to the measure of Christ's gift" (4:7) and "to each individual the manifestation of the Spirit is given for some benefit" (1 Cor 12:7).

Third, *what needs do I see that I can help meet*? Who are the people around me for whom I could make a difference? What is the greatest unmet need in the parish, prayer group, or community that others would be willing for me to help meet? How can I contribute to the common good in my workplace, profession, civic community, or nation? The unmet need that God is summoning me to address will usually correspond to my natural abilities, education, skills, spiritual gifts, available time, and the money at my disposal. Sometimes God summons people to take on tasks that are much bigger than themselves. God does not always call the equipped, but he always equips those whom he calls, as we see in the lives of Bible heroes and saints.

Finally, *what desires has the Spirit placed within me* for serving God and others? This takes discernment, since selfish desires can also motivate us. But as we present our desires to God in prayer and take counsel with others, we will discover the role Christ is calling us to fulfill in his body at the present time.

The New Self and a New Way of Living

Ephesians 4:17–5:2

After beginning his exhortation to Christian conduct with teaching about unity, ministry, and maturity in the Church (4:1–16), Paul now turns to other aspects of the Christian way of life. First, Paul calls for a complete break from the immoral conduct of the surrounding culture (4:17–19). He reminds his readers that Christian moral life follows from the fundamental change brought about by faith and baptism, the new person we have each become in Christ (4:20–24). Then he zeroes in on specific patterns of appropriate and inappropriate behavior, especially in our relationships with one another (4:24–31). Finally, he summons all to love by recalling the love of God our Father and Christ our Savior and inviting us to imitate them (4:32–5:2).

Conduct Not Like the Gentiles (4:17–19)

[17]So I declare and testify in the Lord that you must no longer live as the Gentiles do, in the futility of their minds; [18]darkened in understanding, alienated from the life of God because of their ignorance, because of their hardness of heart, [19]they have become callous and have handed themselves over to licentiousness for the practice of every kind of impurity to excess.

NT: Rom 1:18–32; Eph 2:1–3, 12; 1 Pet 1:18; 4:3–4
Catechism: proliferation of sin, 1865–69; obstacles to knowing God, 37; culpable ignorance, 1791–92

4:17   Paul starts by warning against the kind of conduct his readers practiced before they were converted to Christ. Beginning solemnly—**So I declare and testify in the Lord**—Paul puts them on notice, invoking the authority of the risen †Lord: **you must no longer live as the Gentiles do**. The use of the word "†Gentiles" here is interesting. This is another indication that Paul no longer really considers his non-Jewish Christian readers to be Gentiles (see 2:11), although he addresses them as "you Gentiles" in 3:1. Now that they have been brought into the people of God and have become coheirs of the †inheritance promised to Israel (1:14; 2:12–19), their conduct needs to change to be consistent with their new identity. The conduct of the Gentiles in pagan society is the result of shallowness in their thinking—**the futility**, or vanity, **of their minds**. The NJB catches the sense nicely: "do not go on living the empty-headed life that the gentiles live." The way of life of the surrounding culture makes sense only if people do not think very deeply about it.

4:18   Paul reinforces his exhortation by an explanation of the conduct of people who do not know Christ, as he did in 2:1–3.[1] People who live this way are not merely empty-headed but **darkened in understanding**. One of the consequences of the Fall is that human reason has become clouded by disordered desires so that even if people do think hard about what is right and wrong they often do not get it right. That is why many secular people today who have high moral aspirations fail to reach the right conclusions about sexual morality, abortion, or end-of-life issues. Moral reasoning without the aid of divine revelation often misses the mark. Yet the spiritual condition of the pagans is even graver than their intellectual condition: they are **alienated from the life of God**. The reason for this estrangement is **because of their ignorance** of God's will. We know from experience that when someone does not understand what another person expects, alienation is often the result. The same is true in people's relationship with God.

But Paul is not finished. It turns out that Gentiles who are estranged from God are culpably ignorant: they are estranged **because of their hardness of heart**. Reason and conscience have made their appeal, but the Gentiles have chosen to do as they pleased. In these verses Paul condenses an explanation of human sinfulness that he expounds at greater length in Rom 1:18–32. There he says that humans refused to acknowledge the testimony to God in creation or to respond to him properly in worship and love. Instead we suppressed the truth

---

1. John Stott explains what could seem an overly negative depiction of non-Christians: Paul "is generalizing of course. Not all pagans were (or are) as dissolute as those he . . . portray[s]. Yet just as there is a typical Christian life, so there is a typical pagan life (John R. W. Stott, *The Message of Ephesians: God's New Society*, The Bible Speaks Today [Downers Grove, IL: InterVarsity, 1986], 174).

about God, which led to moral depravity. The Greek word translated "hardness" is *pōrōsis*, as in the medical term *osteoporosis*—a condition in which a person's bones become brittle and lose their flexibility. But here the hardening is more serious, since it is of the "heart," the center of human choice and personality.

The moral consequence is that **they have become callous**; as the NRSV   **4:19** says, "they have lost all sensitivity." An alternative translation of the Greek for "callous" is "despondent." Whether they lacked moral sensibility or became hopeless, they **have handed themselves over to licentiousness,** delivered themselves like freight to be shipped off to a degrading destination. Perhaps they think of licentiousness as freedom, since it knows no restraint; but in fact it is only a life without self-control. The result of their darkened understanding and hardness of heart is that they **practice . . . every kind of impurity**—that is, sexual immorality—**to excess.**[2] The licentious treat themselves and others as objects rather than as persons.

The Key to Virtuous Living (4:20–24)

---

[20]**That is not how you learned Christ,** [21]**assuming that you have heard of him and were taught in him, as truth is in Jesus,** [22]**that you should put away the old self of your former way of life, corrupted through deceitful desires,** [23]**and be renewed in the spirit of your minds,** [24]**and put on the new self, created in God's way in righteousness and holiness of truth.**

OT: Ps 51:12; Isa 65:17–18; Jer 31:33; Ezek 36:25–37
NT: Rom 6:4–6; 10:14; 12:12; 2 Cor 5:17; Col 3:8–11
Catechism: the new life in Christ, 1691–96; conversion of the baptized, 1427–33; catechesis, 1697–98

Having depicted the degradation of the pagan lifestyle, now Paul reminds his readers of the profound change in their identity brought about through their conversion to Christ. He says, in essence, "That degraded way of life is not what you learned from Jesus!" and explains that the key to †holy living is that they have been created anew in baptism.

Paul's way of speaking is arresting. He says his readers **learned Christ . . .**   **4:20–24** **have heard of him and were taught in him.** He does not speak of assimilating Christian doctrine as if it were a set of facts or ideas one could simply master intellectually. He speaks instead of *learning Christ* through what they "heard of

---

2. Other translations help convey the sense of the final words, *en pleonexia*: "with a continual lust for more" (NIV), or "*greedy* to practice every kind of impurity" (NRSV, italics added).

him," that is, the †gospel preaching. Becoming a Christian means *hearing* Jesus Christ proclaimed (1:13; Rom 10:14; 16:25) and responding to him in faith. Then comes catechesis, being "taught in him."[3] Christ is the content and the medium of what is preached and taught, since **truth is in Jesus**. The plain use of the name "Jesus" without the titles "Lord" or "Christ" focuses on a *person* who embodies truth.[4] This truth contrasts with the **deceitful desires** that shaped their **former way of life**. Although Paul gives specific instructions about right and wrong behavior, he recognizes that right conduct flows from knowing the truth and from a relationship with Jesus.

Paul then reminds his readers of the basic teaching they received: (1) **put away the old self** of "your former way of life," (2) **be renewed in the spirit of your minds**, and (3) **put on the new self**.[5] Although baptism is not explicitly mentioned, there is little doubt that Paul is referring to this event, since his other writings speak about baptism using this vocabulary.[6] When they were baptized, adult converts were called to a change of attitude and behavior that corresponded to the real change from the "old self" to the "new self" that was taking place. The verbs "put away" (or "put off," RSV) and "put on" in 4:24 commonly referred to taking off and putting on clothing. In the ancient world, clothing often symbolized a person's identity and standing (e.g., Luke 15:22; Rev 3:3–4, 18). At least as early as the mid-second century, Christian baptismal practice entailed removing one's clothing, receiving baptism, and then donning a white garment that signified the new life of righteousness in Christ.

Paul's teaching in other writings helps to explain what is said here very concisely. Through baptism a person dies with Christ and rises to a new life, freed from the slavery to sin that is endemic to the human race (Rom 6:3, 6–7). This does not mean that a Christian cannot sin—the evidence is against that!—but that we acquire a new freedom to reject sin that we can choose to exercise (Rom 6:11–19).[7] The baptized person, united to the risen Jesus and filled with the Spirit (Rom 8:1–4; 1 Cor 6:17; Gal 3:27–28), has become a "new self." The Greek word translated "self" in 4:22 and 4:24 is *anthrōpos*, "man"

3. See Catechism 1248.

4. Peter T. O'Brien, *The Letter to the Ephesians*, Pillar New Testament Commentary (Grand Rapids: Eerdmans, 1999), 326. This is the only place in Ephesians where Jesus is named without the title Christ or Lord.

5. The RSV presents these three actions as commands for the present, in the †imperative. The NAB and other translations, however, reflect the Greek more closely, indicating these were past instructions that have implications for the present.

6. Rom 6:3, 6; Gal 3:27–28; Col 2:12; 3:9–11.

7. See Catechism 1990–2002 on grace and justification.

Fig. 8. A cross-shaped baptismal font from a fourth century church in Avdat (southern Israel).

in the sense of "human being."[8] The "old self" we put off is the sinful heritage received from Adam, and the "new self" we put on is the transformed life we receive from Christ.[9] In a real sense it is Jesus himself, the new kind of human, whom we "put on" (unite ourselves to) by faith and baptism (Rom 13:14). Paul indicates that this change is nothing less than the re-creation (Eph 2:10, 15) of a human being in the likeness of God. This new self is **created in God's way** (a parallel verse in Col 3:10 says, "in the image of its creator") **in righteousness and holiness of truth**,[10] a phrase that describes people who live devoutly according to God's will (also found in Luke 1:75). Paul thus reminds his readers of the radical change that has taken place and of their decision to set aside the inclinations of the old self and live by the inclinations of their new self, the true self that is united to Jesus.[11]

8. The word *anthrōpos* in the †Septuagint and the New Testament can refer to an individual or to humanity as a whole. God created *anthrōpos* in Gen 1:26–27 and 2:7. Sin and death entered the world through one *anthrōpos*, Adam (Rom 5:12). †Grace and life have now been restored through the one *anthrōpos* Jesus Christ (Rom 5:15; see also 1 Cor 15:21).

9. In an attempt to convey these ideas, the RSV translates *anthrōpos* in vv. 22 and 24 as "nature," although the Greek word for nature is not present in the text.

10. An alternative translation is "in true righteousness and holiness" (RSV, NRSV).

11. Elsewhere Paul describes the same choice as the decision to live according to the Spirit rather than living according to the †flesh (Gal 5:16; see Rom 8:4–6).

The key to putting on "the new self" in everyday life is to "be renewed in the spirit of your minds," that is, in your innermost thoughts.[12] The †present tense of the Greek verb—"be renewed"—indicates an ongoing activity, while the †passive voice indicates that God himself is at work in this process. To be renewed in one's mind entails a change of basic attitude, repentance as well as ongoing growth in understanding divine revelation. This is the "wisdom" and "†knowledge" of God and his plan that Paul prays for earlier in 1:17–18 and 3:18–19 (see sidebar on p. 49). Prayerful reading of Scripture, participation in the liturgy, and study of revealed truth can contribute to acquiring a renewed mind and a transformed life (Rom 12:2; Col 3:9–12). This spiritual understanding contrasts with the "ignorance," "darkened . . . understanding," and "futility of their minds" (4:17–18) of those who do not have a relationship with Christ.

Reflection and Application (4:20–24)

Paul is reminding his readers about baptism, which the Catechism describes as "the principal place for the first and fundamental conversion" (1427). But since most Catholics were baptized as infants, before they had the ability to make a personal response of faith and repentance, Paul's teaching applies differently today than it did to his original readers. Ideally, Christians baptized as babies receive preaching and teaching about Christ from their earliest days and turn to the Lord as children. Ideally, their families and parishes prepare them well for the sacraments of penance, Eucharist, and confirmation, and they continue on this path into adulthood, growing in their understanding of their faith and progressing in holiness and ongoing conversion (Catechism 1428–29).

But often it does not work this way. Some receive little or no Christian formation as children; others receive it, but cease to practice their faith along the way, succumbing to the influence of the surrounding non-Christian culture. These baptized but unconverted Catholics need to be evangelized in order to experience the grace of the sacraments they have received. They need to be introduced (or reintroduced) to the person of Jesus Christ through a proclamation (*kerygma*) of the good news in the power of the Holy Spirit, accompanied by the testimony of those who already believe. Only when they (re)discover the truth that is in Jesus (4:21), believe, and decide to turn from sin will they be able to benefit fully from catechesis about prayer, doctrine, the sacraments,

12. Most interpreters take "the spirit" here to refer to the inmost center of the mind. Some, however, take it to refer to the activity of the Holy Spirit in the mind of the believer.

and the moral life (the major themes of the Catechism). Only then will the divine life received in baptism be able to flourish and grow through a renewal in the spirit of their minds (4:23).

It is commonplace to attribute every kind of pastoral problem to the lack of adequate catechesis, but that analysis fails to take into account that catechesis builds on evangelization, as the order of the verbs in 4:21 suggests: you have "heard" of him and were "taught" in him. Until people have been brought to conversion by hearing a proclamation of Jesus as Lord, catechesis will have a limited effect. To make catechesis more effective, some parishes and dioceses have incorporated evangelization programs (e.g., Alpha Course, Cursillo, Philip Course, or Life in the Spirit Seminar) at the front-end of their RCIA (Rite of Christian Initiation for Adults) and confirmation preparation. Some seminaries employ these programs both to deepen the conversion of seminarians and to familiarize them with evangelization methods.

Guidelines for Conduct (4:25–29)

[25]Therefore, putting away falsehood, speak the truth, each one to his neighbor, for we are members one of another. [26]Be angry but do not sin; do not let the sun set on your anger, [27]and do not leave room for the devil. [28]The thief must no longer steal, but rather labor, doing honest work with his [own] hands, so that he may have something to share with one in need. [29]No foul language should come out of your mouths, but only such as is good for needed edification, that it may impart grace to those who hear.

OT: Exod 20:15–16; Ps 4:5; Zech 8:16
NT: Acts 20:35; Col 3:8–9; 4:6; Titus 3:14; James 3:1–13
Catechism: the virtue of truthfulness, 2505; offenses against truth, 2475–87; anger, 1866, 2302; passions and moral life, 1762–75; varieties of stealing, 2408–12

Here Paul briefly lists some of the behavior patterns that belong to the "old self" and contrasts them with the behavior patterns that belong to the "new self" united to Christ. All of these instructions concern relationships, especially with fellow Christians. Paul gives particular attention to conduct that can build up or tear apart unity in a community. For that reason he focuses on how people are to handle anger and how they are to speak.

Paul bases his moral guidance on two authorities. First, he draws repeatedly from the Old Testament, which the Church recognizes as divinely inspired and as "a storehouse of sublime teaching on God and of sound wisdom on human life" (Catechism 122, quoting *Dei Verbum* 15). Second, he draws on truths that have come to light through the life, death, and resurrection of Jesus and our connection with these realities through faith, baptism, and membership in the Church. These realities have important implications for the way we live.

4:25   **Therefore, putting away falsehood**—since his readers have embraced the truth, Paul exhorts them to renounce lying (see Col 3:8–9) and encourages them to **speak the truth, each one to his neighbor**. This is a quotation from Zech 8:16, an instruction for a renewed Israel. Paul adds a new motive: **for we are members one of another**. Among members of the body of Christ,[13] telling the truth is only logical. Should one's ear deceive one's hand, or one's eye mislead one's foot?

4:26–27   Continuing to recall Old Testament teaching, Paul quotes Ps 4:5:[14] **Be angry but do not sin**. The Psalm continues, "commune with your own hearts on your beds, and be silent" (4:4 RSV).[15] This teaching recognizes a distinction between the emotion of anger, for which we may not be responsible, and what we do with it.[16] People may say and do things that make us angry, sometimes rightly angry, but the psalm Paul cites counsels restraint in our response. Paul goes further, advising, **do not let the sun set on your anger**. Keep short accounts. If at all possible (Rom 12:18), reconcile quickly with the person from whom you are estranged (Matt 5:25; 18:15; Luke 17:3–4). If that is not possible, as often it is not, do not hold on to your anger; surrender it to the Lord. Forgive and do your best to release from your anger the person who has offended you. Why? So that you may **not leave room for the devil**. Experience teaches that when people harbor anger, it festers, eating away at them; often this hostility spreads to infect other people as well. In the midst of these familiar human dynamics, Paul discerns the invisible activity of Satan. Paul says more about excessive and uncontrolled anger in 4:31.

4:28–29   The exhortation addressed to the **thief** risks going unheeded, since few people identify themselves as thieves. However, the Greek says literally, "let the one who steals, steal no longer." One does not have to be a professional thief to steal, whether it be by engaging in any form of fraud, taking things from one's

---

13. See Rom 12:5; 1 Cor 12:12–27.

14. See Ps 4:4 (RSV): "Be angry, but sin not." The NAB renders the Hebrew as "Tremble and do not sin" (Ps 4:5).

15. The NAB and the RSV follow different systems for numbering verses of the Psalms. Ps 4:5 in the NAB is Ps 4:4 in the RSV.

16. The Catechism lists anger among the passions and offers helpful insight about the morality of the passions (1762–75). It also lists anger among the capital sins (1866), since anger can be a sin (2302) that engenders other sins and vices.

Managing Anger

LIVING TRADITION

Saint John Chrysostom develops Paul's teaching on anger with keen and colorful observations about how people react:

I appeal to you to extinguish your anger before the sun sets. For if you fail to master it on the first day, both the next day and often even for a year you will prolong it and the enmity will increase from then on without any further help. For enmity causes us to suspect that words spoken in one sense were meant in another, the same with gestures, and these infuriate and exasperate us and make us more angry than madmen, not wanting to say a person's name or to hear it and speaking ourselves with invective and abuse.

How are we to quiet this passion? . . . By reflecting on our own sins, and how much we have to answer for to God. By remembering that we are bringing vengeance not on an enemy but on ourselves, by reflecting that we are delighting our real enemy, the devil, and that for his sake we are doing wrong to the members of our own body. If you want to be at enmity, be so with the devil. It is for this purpose that God has armed us with anger, not that we should thrust a sword against our own bodies but that we should plunge the whole blade in the devil's breast. And this we shall do by being merciful to ourselves, by being peaceably disposed towards one another. (*Homilies on Ephesians* 14)[a]

a. *Commentary on the Epistle to the Galatians and Homilies on the Epistle to the Ephesians*, trans. William John Copeland (Oxford: J. H. Parker, 1840), 255–56.

place of employment, not paying taxes that we owe, not paying for downloaded software or music, or cheating at school. Furthermore, it is not enough merely to avoid evil; a Christian should seek to do good. Not only should a Christian abandon a dishonest occupation, but he or she should **labor** to earn an honest living. The fact that Paul specifies **with his [own] hands** indicates that most of Paul's intended readers were slaves or the working poor and would have recalled his own example (Acts 20:34–35). The reason for working is not only to support one's own family but so **that he may have something to share with one in need**.[17] Sharing with the poor is not optional but essential to Christian life (Acts 20:35). The **foul** (*sapros*, literally, "rotten") **language** that Paul excludes does not merely refer to vulgarity but to any harmful speech, such as gossip or backbiting, that leaves a bad taste and poisons relationships. Instead, Christians should speak in a way that is constructive (**for . . . edification**), that responds to people's needs, and that allows the Lord to speak kind or wise words through them to **impart** †**grace**.

17. See Gal 6:10; 1 Thess 4:11; 2 Thess 3:8–13.

Imitators of God (4:30–5:2)

[30]And do not grieve the holy Spirit of God, with which you were sealed for the day of redemption. [31]All bitterness, fury, anger, shouting, and reviling must be removed from you, along with all malice. [32][And] be kind to one another, compassionate, forgiving one another as God has forgiven you in Christ.

[1]So be imitators of God, as beloved children, [2]and live in love, as Christ loved us and handed himself over for us as a sacrificial offering to God for a fragrant aroma.

NT: John 13:34; Gal 2:20; Col 3:12–15; Heb 10:10, 14

Catechism: anger, 2302–3; sealed with the Spirit, 1274, 1296; forgiveness, 2842–45; adoption as children transforms us, 1694, 1709; Christ's sacrifice effective through love, 616

Lectionary: 4:30–5:2: Unity of Christians, Peace and Justice in a Time of War or Civil Disturbance

In these verses Paul continues to identify right and wrong behaviors. What sets them apart is the way the Apostle links Christian conduct to our relationship with each person of the Trinity.

4:30   The first sentence somewhat abruptly raises the stakes. Perhaps reflecting on the destructive power of "rotten" talk leads Paul to urge his readers to **not grieve the holy Spirit of God**. Paul is quoting Isa 63:10, a text that recalls how Israel provoked the Spirit of the Lord who lived among them in the tabernacle and the temple. The Spirit of God who dwells in us is particularly sensitive to anything that harms relationships in his temple, the Church. This text helps us to see that the Holy Spirit is a person, as it is not possible to grieve an impersonal force. Paul recalls that his readers **were sealed** with the Spirit (see comment on 1:13 and sidebar on p. 42). The Spirit's presence protects us and indicates that we belong to God[18] until **the day of redemption**, when God takes possession of what is his. Although we have already been redeemed—have received forgiveness of our sins (1:7)—we still await a redemption "of our bodies" (Rom 8:23) at the second coming of Christ (see 1:13–14). This future redemption entails liberation from the tendency to sin, the resurrection and transformation of our bodies (1 Cor 15:51–53), and entry into the full "freedom of the children of God" (Rom 8:21). Meanwhile, our job is to cooperate with and not to grieve the indwelling Holy Spirit who is at work to bring all these things to pass.

4:31–32   Paul then returns to the topic of anger and hostility in relationships. Sometimes our anger requires repentance. The apostle insists on the complete removal

18. Acts indicates that receiving the Spirit is a distinguishing characteristic of Christians (Acts 2:38–39; 5:32; 8:14–17; 10:44–48; 19:2–6).

Paul and the Trinity

The term "Trinity" is not found in the Bible but is a term that arose later to describe the Church's faith in one God revealed in three persons as a response to heretical challenges. Although he did not know the term, Paul believed in the divinity of the Father, Son, and Holy Spirit, in their oneness, and in the distinctiveness of their relations with one another. In contrast to later theologians who sought to describe the relations of the divine persons philosophically, Paul was content to describe the diverse roles of the divine persons on the basis of the early Christian experience of God.

Paul began as a devout Jew who believed in one God as expressed in Israel's daily prayer, the Shema (Deut 6:4 RSV). He never diverged from that conviction, although later he understood the Shema to refer also to Jesus (1 Cor 8:6). After encountering the risen Jesus on the road to Damascus, Paul came to recognize him as God's divine Son and to understand God as his Father and ours (Gal 1:15–16; 4:4–6). Three days after encountering Christ, Paul was baptized and received the Holy Spirit (Acts 9:17–18), an event that affected him powerfully, as he immediately became a bold preacher of the Messiah and eventually a great theologian of the Spirit.

Rather than focus on what each of the divine persons *is* in himself and in relation to the others, Paul focuses on what each of the divine persons *does* in God's plan of salvation. Although he usually reserves the word "God" (*theos*) to speak of the Father, Paul clearly understands the Son and the Spirit to be fully divine and to fulfill divine roles in the work of salvation (such as ruling over all, giving life, sanctifying, and the like) and to cooperate in that work in distinctive ways. He regards the Father as the creator and author of the divine plan; the preexistent Son as the redeemer (through the paschal mystery) and exalted Lord who fulfills that plan (Gal 4:4–6; Phil 2:5–11); and the Spirit (who is both the Spirit of God and the Spirit of Christ) as the one who communicates the blessings of the divine plan to baptized believers, cleansing and sanctifying them, uniting them in one body, giving them access to God in worship, building them up through charisms, enabling moral conduct, and transforming them into God's image and likeness.[a]

Although Paul uses the name "Holy Spirit" to distinguish the Spirit from the Father and from Christ, the Spirit often functions as the means through whom the Father or Jesus communicates or operates in believers or in the Church. The personhood of the Spirit is indicated by the personal verbs used of him: the Spirit searches, knows, teaches, dwells, groans, cries out, intercedes, helps, and is grieved.[b]

Insight into Paul's rich Trinitarian theology may be attained by examining the many texts in which Paul refers to all three divine persons (1 Cor 12:4–6; 2 Cor 13:13), several of which are found in Ephesians (see index, "Trinity").[c]

a. Rom 8:4, 9, 13; 1 Cor 12:7–13; 2 Cor 3:18; 13:13; Gal 5:16; Eph 2:18; 5:18–20; 2 Thess 2:13.
b. Rom 8:26–27; 1 Cor 2:9–13; 3:16; Gal 4:6; Eph 4:30.
c. For more on the Trinity and Spirit in Paul, see Gordon D. Fee, *God's Empowering Presence: The Holy Spirit in the Letters of Paul* (Peabody, MA: Hendrickson, 1994), 827–45.

of a cluster of negative attitudes and the behaviors to which they lead: **bitterness**, an inner attitude of resentment; **fury**, passionate rage; **anger**, a settled attitude of hostility; **shouting**, loud quarreling; and **reviling**, abusive or slanderous speech. And **all malice** sums up these behaviors. Instead, Paul says, **be kind to one another** and **compassionate** (RSV "tenderhearted"; NJB "sympathetic"). There may be a play on words here: the Greek word for "kind" is *chrestos*, which some scholars think was pronounced at that time exactly like *christos*, "Christ." Thus "be Christ to one another." Rather than be angry or hostile at wrongs suffered, we are to forgive **one another as God has forgiven** us **in Christ**. The basis for Christians forgiving others is the fact that God has already forgiven us (see Matt 6:12, 14–15; 18:21–35) by coming to us in Jesus and showing us mercy. Our hearts are meant to be softened, overwhelmed by the kindness God has shown us, in a way that impacts all our relationships.

5:1–2   Recalling how God has forgiven us prompts Paul to urge his readers to imitate God **as beloved children** imitate their father. We cannot imitate God's omnipotence and omniscience, but we can imitate his forgiveness and generous love toward those who wrong us. Perhaps Paul is thinking of Jesus' exhortation in the Sermon on the Mount to show ourselves true children of our heavenly Father by loving even our enemies as God does (Matt 5:44–48). We are to †**live in love** (literally, "walk"). This is precisely how God's "beloved" Son lived: **Christ loved us and handed himself over for us**. The Messiah's death on the cross for us was voluntary, a free gift of himself, the absolutely indisputable sign of his committed self-giving love. This act had an incalculable effect on St. Paul, which he expresses in Gal 2:20 and refers to again in Eph 5:25. The Messiah's death was a **sacrificial offering to God**. The idea of Jesus' death as a sacrifice, as an act of worship, is explicit here. Paul uses an Old Testament phrase that describes a burnt offering whose smoke ascends and pleases God (Gen 8:20–22; Exod 29:18), **for a fragrant aroma**.[19]

Christ's sacrifice on the cross provides the pattern for how we are to offer ourselves to God, making our time, talents, and treasure available to God and others in self-giving love. The thought is the same as Rom 12:1: "I urge you therefore, brothers, by the mercies of God, to offer your bodies as a living sacrifice, holy and pleasing to God, your spiritual worship." In light of God's mercy revealed in Christ, we are to make our whole lives an act of worship. Our being "created in Christ Jesus for the good works God has prepared" (2:10) is so that we can live to "the praise of his glory" (1:12, 14).

---

19. Other versions translate this phrase as an adjective modifying the noun: "a fragrant offering" (RSV, NRSV, NIV) or "sweet-smelling sacrifice" (NJB).

Reflection and Application (4:24–5:2)

It is striking how much of Paul's practical instruction about our conduct is based on what God has done for us in Christ rather than on divine commands or ethical reasoning (as in ancient or modern moral philosophy). How we are to live derives from the fact that through faith and baptism we have acquired a "new self" that has been "created" (v. 24) to be like God, which unites us to Christ and to the other members of Christ's body.

More than that, this "new self" exists in a personal relationship with the three persons of the Trinity in a manner that profoundly shapes our actions. We try not to grieve the indwelling Holy Spirit by our words or deeds, not wanting to sadden the Spirit, whose nature is joy.[20] Rather than lose ourselves in destructive anger, as beloved children we aim to imitate the Father's love and forgiveness toward those who wrong us. That is what the one whom Christians can call "Abba" does (Matt 5:43–48; Rom 8:15; Gal 4:6). Finally, we seek to follow our Messiah Jesus in a way of life marked by self-sacrificing love: "The way we came to know love was that he laid down his life for us; so we ought to lay down our lives for our brothers" (1 John 3:16).

We are different from those who live around us because of the extraordinary †grace and blessings we have received (1:3–14; 2:1–22). Saint Paul summons us to live in a way that is consistent with the gifts we have received, the divine persons to whom we have been united, and the "new self" that is ours in Christ.

---

20. See Acts 13:52; Rom 14:17; 1 Thess 1:6. I owe this insight to Raniero Cantalamessa.

Children of Light

Ephesians 5:3–20

Having exhorted his readers to imitate God and to live in love like the Messiah who loved us and gave himself for us, Paul now returns to discussing concrete behavior, but the emphasis is different. Rather than contrasting the lifestyle of the old self and the new self, he contrasts the holiness of the Christian way of life to the darkness of the surrounding society. To imitate Jesus' love and sacrifice entails rejecting the impure and idolatrous conduct of the world and discerning what is pleasing to him (Rom 12:2). A holy way of life manifests God's light in the world. Living this way makes our lives an act of worship that culminates in Spirit-filled praise and thanks to God.

Avoiding Suggestive Speech (5:3–4)

---

³Immorality or any impurity or greed must not even be mentioned among you, as is fitting among holy ones, ⁴no obscenity or silly or suggestive talk, which is out of place, but instead, thanksgiving.

NT: Col 3:5, 8; Eph 4:29; Rom 1:28
Catechism: various kinds of sin, 1852; the pure in heart, 2518–19; greed, 2535–38; modesty, 2521–22

5:3   Here Paul returns to a subject he mentioned briefly at the beginning of the previous section (4:17–19). Sexual immorality characterized the pagan Gentile world to which his readers belonged, just as it does our world today. Paul takes a very strong stand: **Immorality or any impurity or greed must not even be mentioned among you, as is fitting among holy ones**. His reason is that this kind of conduct and speech is totally inappropriate among people set apart for a †holy God. God's people must completely avoid conduct that might compromise their holiness. "Immorality" (*porneia*) can refer to any form of sexual activity that occurs outside marriage: fornication, adultery, incest, prostitution, bestiality, and homosexual relations. "Impurity," literally, "uncleanness," describes the effect of immoral behavior on those who engage in them; they are rendered unclean, unfit for God's presence. Sexual immorality defiles the worship a Christian offers to God in the "temple of the holy Spirit," the Christian's body (1 Cor 6:18–19).

Finally, Paul mentions "greed" (*pleonexia*) or "covetousness" (RSV), which usually denotes an excessive desire to possess or consume material goods. However, this word sometimes also refers to sexual lust, as it may in this case.[1] Whichever meaning Paul had in mind (and interpreters are divided), both meanings are true: neither greed nor lust belongs in the lives of Christians.

Paul expands on the idea that **obscenity or silly or suggestive talk . . . is out of place** for God's holy people. What is wrong with sexual joking? First, it is incompatible with the "new self, created to be like God in true righteousness and holiness" (4:24 NIV). Second, it diminishes what sexual intimacy is all about: an expression of the mutual self-gift of a man and a woman in marriage, a sign of the relationship between Christ and the Church (5:25–32). Third, sexually suggestive speech and humor—common on television, in movies, and in many social settings—contributes to sexual misconduct because it coarsens us and gives immorality a false attractiveness. It desensitizes us to God's commandments, weakening inhibitions against wrongdoing, and conceals the ruin in families and the heartbreak in relationships that accompany adultery and other forms of sexual immorality.

Paul contrasts inappropriate speech with the kind of speech that ought to characterize a Christian: **thanksgiving**. The call to give voice to praise in all circumstances of life, whether prosperous or painful, is a frequent and consistent teaching of Paul that he practices himself.[2] Our parishes and Christian communities today would be rather refreshing if more of us observed the apostolic teaching about thankful speech! People whose conversation revolves around sex reveal an emptiness that they are seeking to fill. People whose conversation is full of thanksgiving show that God has already filled their hearts.

5:4

---

1. See 4:19, where *pleonexia* is translated "excess," and 5:5, where *pleonektēs* is translated "greedy person" in the NAB.

2. Paul teaches thankfulness in 5:20; Col 3:17; 1 Thess 5:18. He practices it in Acts 16:25; Rom 1:8; Phil 1:3; 1 Tim 1:12; 2 Tim 1:3.

The Bible on Wealth and Greed

BIBLICAL BACKGROUND

The Bible presents a nuanced position on the topic of material prosperity. On the one hand, wealth is recognized as something good, a blessing from God (Ps 112:1–3). It was bestowed on the patriarchs and was promised to Israel as a reward for covenant faithfulness (Deut 28). On the other hand, the Old Testament recognized that riches can lead people to self-reliance and forgetfulness of God (Deut 8:11–14). Often the poor, acutely conscious of their dependence on God, are just, while the rich become oppressors (Ps 5; 10; 49; 86).

In the Sermon on the Mount, Jesus declares that the kingdom of God belongs to the "poor in spirit" (Matt 5:3), those who know their need for God. In the New Testament, those who have wealth are summoned to radical detachment and generosity (Luke 12:33; 14:33) and to reliance on and thankfulness to God, "who richly provides us with all things for our enjoyment" (1 Tim 6:17; see also 1 Tim 4:4).

Jesus warns that a life of discipleship is incompatible with a life directed to acquiring things. "No one can serve two masters. . . . You cannot serve God and mammon" (Matt 6:24). "Mammon" is an Aramaic word meaning "that on which one relies" in reference to wealth or possessions. Often it is anxiety about future needs that tempts us to pursue wealth and material prosperity. Recognizing this problem, Jesus teaches his disciples to say "no" to anxiety and to trust in God for their material needs (Matt 6:25–34).

Paul counsels being content with the necessities of life and warns that "the love of money is the root of all evils, and some people in their desire for it have strayed from the faith and have pierced themselves with many pains" (1 Tim 6:10). Greed is a false and demanding idol. The pursuit of money has led not a few Christians to sacrifice their integrity, their families, and their faith.

Not Deceived about the Consequences of Immorality (5:5–6)

⁵Be sure of this, that no immoral or impure or greedy person, that is, an idolater, has any inheritance in the kingdom of Christ and of God.
⁶Let no one deceive you with empty arguments, for because of these things the wrath of God is coming upon the disobedient.

NT: 1 Cor 6:9–11; Gal 5:19–21; Col 3:5–6; 1 Thess 4:2–8; Rev 21:8

Catechism: covetousness as impurity and as greed, 2514–15, 2534–38; idolatry, 2113; mortal sin, 1861

5:5–6   The outcome of an immoral lifestyle is no laughing matter. The same three words used in 5:3 are used again, but this time in adjectival form. People who are **immoral or impure or greedy** have no †**inheritance**, or future share, in **the kingdom of Christ and of God**.[3] Those who live this way miss out on eternal life with God, the worst tragedy that can befall a human being. Paul does not say that this consequence comes to those who formerly lived this way (see 1 Cor 6:9–11) or to those who struggle and sometimes fall but repent (1 John 1:9) but rather to those who remain immoral, impure, or greedy.

As in 5:3, "greedy" (or "covetous," RSV) could mean either sexual lust or lust for material things. How is a person who is dominated by excessive desire an **idolater**? Jewish tradition had already recognized the connection between covetousness and idolatry. People who are greedy, whose desires are insatiable, have made a god of the object of their desire. Idolatry is one of the worst sins because it rejects God in order to worship something he created. The result is that God does not receive the honor and gratitude he deserves, and human beings, created in God's likeness, are reduced to adoring and becoming the slaves of lesser things intended to serve them. Auguste Rodin, the French sculptor best known for "The Thinker," sculpted a work he titled "The Eternal Idol." It depicts a naked man kneeling and kissing a naked woman on her heart, both figures completely absorbed in one another. Rodin understood the idolatrous potential of sexual desire.

Be sure of this. . . . Let no one deceive you with empty arguments. Paul is well aware that God's word forbidding sexual relations outside marriage is a hard teaching that people will try to deny or circumvent, so in the strongest terms he warns against being fooled. In 1 Cor 6:13–20, Paul refutes one such empty argument: the claim that sexual conduct is insignificant, merely a natural activity of the body similar to eating or sleeping. Twice elsewhere in his letters Paul warns of the eternal consequences of sexual immorality, along with the same warning not to be deceived (1 Cor 6:9–10; Gal 5:19–21). In those texts, sexual immorality is named among other behaviors that exclude a person from the kingdom of God. Other New Testament texts echo the same teaching (Mark 7:21–23; Rev 21:8; 22:15).

Paul reinforces his insistence that this kind of conduct is unacceptable for Christians by explaining that **because of these things**—sexually immoral lifestyles—**the wrath of God is coming upon the disobedient**.[4] In this last phrase Paul repeats two expressions that he used in 2:1–3 when he spoke of his readers' condition prior to their being saved through faith in Christ. The †wrath of God, a concept found in both the Old and the New Testaments,[5] does not refer to a divine outburst

3. This phrase reflects the divinity of Christ, since he and God the Father share the same kingdom.

4. The RSV translates the Greek literally, "sons of disobedience," which is a †Semitic way of describing people who are characterized by disobedience to God.

5. See, for instance, Exod 22:21–23; 32:10; Jer 7:20; Eph 2:3; Rom 5:9; 12:19.

of temper but rather to God's just punishment of serious wrongdoing. The Old Testament provides illustrations of God's judgment on sexual immorality, whether of Sodom and Gomorrah (Gen 19), the Canaanites who lived in the land before Israel (Lev 18:24–25), or Israel itself when its conduct resembled that of the men of Sodom or of the Canaanites (e.g., 1 Kings 14:24; Jer 23:14; Ezek 16:46–58). The term "disobedient" refers to all who do not obey God's law, whether written in the †Torah or written on the human heart (see Rom 2:5–16).

Reflection and Application (5:3–6)

Many people think that Christianity is negative toward sex, but just the opposite is true. Other biblical texts, such as the Song of Songs, depict the profound joy of love and sex. Within the context of marriage, sex is intended to renew and deepen the intimacy of a husband and wife and to be fruitful by bringing forth new life. In their sexual relationship they express with their bodies their total gift of self to each other. Precisely because of the lofty intention that God has in mind for sex, Christians from the first century to the present have sought to preserve its holiness (Heb 13:4). Rather than being inconsequential, sex is extraordinarily significant. Ephesians 5:23–32 depicts marriage, consummated in sexual union, as an image of the relationship between Christ and the Church. God does not object to sex itself but the abuse of this gift in adultery, fornication, and homosexual acts. When ripped from its proper context, sex often leads to deep pain in relationships and other harmful consequences. Addiction to pornography and other forms of sexual stimulation reveals lust as idolatry, a false god and cruel master to those who cannot escape its clutches. The gospel brings freedom from this slavery and makes it possible for us to experience in marriage the joy that God intended from the beginning when he designed sexual intimacy.

Living as Children of Light (5:7–10)

---

[7]So do not be associated with them. [8]For you were once darkness, but now you are light in the Lord. Live as children of light, [9]for light produces every kind of goodness and righteousness and truth. [10]Try to learn what is pleasing to the Lord.

NT: 1 Cor 5:9–12; 6:9–11; 2 Cor 6:14; Col 1:12–13; Matt 5:14–16; Phil 2:15; Rom 13:12–13

Catechism: baptism as enlightenment, 1216; "children of light" through the Holy Spirit, 1695; fruit of the Spirit, 736

Fig. 9. Ruins of the main agora (marketplace) of Ephesus, the commercial center of Asia.

In view of the consequences coming to people who live in rebellion against   **5:7**
God, Paul cautions his readers not to share in their fate. The translation **do not
be associated with them** is misleading, as it implies that one should have no
dealings with people who engage in evil conduct. The Greek, however, says "do
not be *partners* with them" (NIV, emphasis added).[6] In 1 Cor 5:9–11, Paul says
not to associate with *Christians* who are persisting in grave wrongdoing but
explicitly rejects avoiding sinners in society, because by doing so "you would
then have to leave the world." Here Paul recommends avoiding close relationships with evildoers that could lead his readers to share in the judgment that "the
disobedient" (v. 6) will experience. The NJB translates this verse, "Make sure you
do not throw in your lot with them." The partnering to avoid would presumably
include marrying someone who does not respect God's law, working at jobs or
entering into business relationships that involve one in what is morally wrong,
or spending time with people while they are doing or celebrating what is sinful.
Christians need to maintain some distance from the wrongdoing of the surrounding society so that they are not entangled or seduced by it (see Rev 18:4).

Paul explains why his readers should not be partners in evil—**For you were**   **5:8–10**
once darkness, but now you are light in the Lord. As in chapter 2 and in 4:17–24,
Paul recalls the stark contrast between his readers' past and present conditions.

6. Another form of the same Greek word is used in 3:6 to describe Gentile Christians as "copartners
in the promise" with Jewish Christians.

In Paul's letters, "darkness" usually refers to ignorance and spiritual or moral evil, and "light" refers to true †knowledge and spiritual and moral goodness. The Ephesians previously belonged to the darkness and were under Satan's rule (2:1–3), the kingdom opposed to God (Col 1:13). But now they have *become* light "in the Lord" because they are united to Jesus, in whom truth (4:21) and divine life are found.

The fact that they have become light has implications for their conduct: **Live as children of light.** He repeats the catchword "walk" (NAB: "†live") for the fourth time. "Children of light" is a †Semitic expression used by Jesus to refer to people who belong to God (Luke 16:8; John 12:36). Paul accents the fruit of their lives: **for light produces every kind of goodness and righteousness and truth.** Children of light manifest the kind of spiritual and moral goodness that everyone recognizes.

To clarify further how his readers should live, Paul adds, **Try to learn what is pleasing to the Lord.** Other versions catch the nuance of the Greek verb *dokimazō* better: "Try to discern" (ESV). Paul is encouraging them to reflect on what Jesus wants. Christian moral conduct is not merely spelled out for us in a set of instructions like the law of Moses. Yes, there are basic standards, like the Ten Commandments, the instructions of Eph 4:25–31 and 5:3–5, and the law of love (Rom 13:8–9; Gal 5:14). But in the many situations of life, we must discern what concretely is pleasing to the †Lord. Paul does not say it explicitly here, but the indwelling Spirit of Jesus makes this discernment possible (Rom 8:2–14; Gal 5:16–23).

Reflection and Application (5:7–10)

Martha, a friend of mine, was amazed when a lesbian friend for whom she had been praying for years announced that she had become a Christian. For some months Martha did not ask about her friend's lifestyle, afraid of how that conversation might go. Finally, she mustered the courage and asked. "Oh, that," her friend replied. "I figured out that Jesus didn't like it, so I quit." Becoming light and learning "what is pleasing to the Lord" changes everything, although not always so easily.

Shining Light on Wrongdoing (5:11–14)

¹¹**Take no part in the fruitless works of darkness; rather expose them,** ¹²**for it is shameful even to mention the things done by them in secret;** ¹³**but everything exposed by the light becomes visible,** ¹⁴**for everything that becomes visible is light. Therefore, it says:**

> "Awake, O sleeper,
> 　and arise from the dead,
> 　and Christ will give you light."

OT: Wis 2:12–16; Isa 26:19; 52:1; 60:1
NT: Matt 5:14–16; Rom 13:12–13; 1 Thess 5:5–8
Catechism: witnessing to the truth, 905, 909, 2044, 2471–73
Lectionary: 5:8–14: Fourth Sunday of Lent (Year A)

After criticizing the wrong kind of conduct (5:3–7) and commending the right kind of conduct (5:8–10), Paul repeats the cycle, but with a variation.

Take no part in the fruitless works of darkness repeats the idea of avoiding 　　5:11
inappropriate associations (5:7) but makes clear that this applies above all to evil deeds. Paul contrasts what "light produces" in 5:9 (literally, "the fruit of light") with the "fruitless works of darkness."[7] The new element here is an exhortation not simply to avoid evil behaviors but rather to **expose them**. In the New Testament the Greek verb *elenchō* usually means to reprove a wrongdoer and thus expose his or her fault (see Luke 3:19 and Matt 18:15), whether or not the reproof is accepted. The NJB captures the meaning: "show them up for what they are."[8] It is the "works of darkness" themselves rather than the wrongdoers that Paul tells us to "expose" or censure in some way. Ordinarily, the setting in which Christians are responsible to correct wrongdoing is *within* the community of faith (Matt 18:15–16; 1 Cor 5:12; Gal 6:1). But in this text Paul is referring to the conduct of the "sons of disobedience." How are Paul's readers to expose or reprove the sinful actions of the surrounding pagan society? Probably the primary means is by giving a shining example in their own conduct of "goodness and righteousness and truth" (5:9). Paul praises the Christians of Philippi for shining as lights "in the midst of a crooked and perverse generation" (Phil 2:15). Sometimes, however, exposing evil for what it is requires direct verbal testimony. When that is the case, Christians must be courageous and prepared to pay the price (Matt 14:3–4; Acts 24:25; Rev 11:3–12; 12:10–11).

Avoiding all participation in and exposing "the works of darkness" are neces-　　5:12
sary **for it is shameful even to mention the things done by them in secret**. It would be possible to misunderstand Paul as prudishly saying that this conduct

---

7. This terminology recalls Gal 5:19–23, where Paul contrasts Christian conduct, "the fruit of the Spirit," with "the works of the flesh."

8. To understand the meaning of *elenchō*, it helps to see the various ways it is translated (in this case by the RSV) in its seventeen New Testament occurrences: "reprove" (Luke 3:19; Titus 2:15; Rev 3:19), "convict" (John 8:46; 1 Cor 14:24; James 2:9; Jude 15), "rebuke" (1 Tim 5:20; Titus 1:13), "expose" (John 3:20; Eph 5:11, 13), "tell him his fault" (Matt 18:15), "convince" (John 16:8; 2 Tim 4:2), "punish" (Heb 12:5), and "confute" (Titus 1:9).

Fig. 10. The theatre of ancient Ephesus, where Demetrius and the silversmiths protested the commercial impact of Paul's successful evangelization (Acts 19:25–29).

is too shameful to bring up and address. Actually, he is repeating the point made in 5:3–4, where he says that immorality should not be casually discussed among Christians. The link is stronger in the Greek, since the word translated here as "shameful" has the same root as "obscenity" in 5:4. It is one thing to converse about immorality in a joking manner and quite another to seriously criticize it as Paul does here. The apostle refers to conduct done "in secret," since most wrongdoing takes place behind closed doors.

5:13–14   Paul expects that when Christians confront immorality, whether by shining the light of Christian witness before the world, by gently reproving a brother or sister, or by openly censuring public wrongdoing, the situation will change: **but everything exposed by the light becomes visible, for everything that becomes visible is light.** In other words, whatever light shines on becomes illuminated, enlightened. Paul hopes for the conversion of people who are in darkness as a result of the light of Christ shining through Christians.

Of course, things do not always work out this way. Jesus, the perfect light, let his light shine by word and example. Some people received the light and became light; others rejected the light (John 1:9–11; 3:19–21). As followers of Jesus, we can expect the same mixed response to our testimony. However, we can be sure that if we want to overcome darkness, we need to turn on a light. It has been said that evil flourishes when good people do nothing. Once the

---

Correction and Friendship

John Chrysostom recommends that we act as true friends:

> Reprove your brother, accept his anger for the love that you owe to Christ and for the love which you owe to your brother. Stop him as he heads down the road to destruction. . . . There is no evidence of friendship as certain as to tell someone their wrongs. It is for this we are friends, that we may be able to help one another. A man will listen in a different spirit to a friend than to any other person. Therefore I urge you to never hold back from reproving, nor be displeased at being reproved. (*Homilies on Ephesians* 18)[a]

a. *Commentary on the Epistle to the Galatians and Homilies on the Epistle to the Ephesians*, trans. William John Copeland (Oxford: J. H. Parker, 1840), 296–97.

---

encounter between light and darkness occurs and the darkness is revealed, the outcome for which we hope and pray is conversion.

To explain how this transformation occurs, Paul recalls his readers' experience of the transformation Christ accomplished in their lives. **Therefore, it says: / "Awake, O sleeper, / and arise from the dead, / and Christ will give you light."** Paul may be quoting an early Christian baptismal hymn based on such Old Testament texts as Isa 60:1–2 and Isa 26:19. The hymn addresses the person to be baptized as one who is morally asleep (Rom 13:11–14; 1 Thess 5:5–8) and dead in sin (Eph 2:1) and invites him or her to receive the light and life of Christ. For the Christian who has fallen into serious wrongdoing, these words are an invitation to repent and receive Christ's grace again.

Reflection and Application (5:11–14)

This passage is very relevant in a culture whose mass media encourage sexual immorality for everyone. As a consequence of this barrage, many are tempted to complacency or hopelessness. How can we "expose" or "reprove" the wrongdoing that surrounds us?

First, we Catholics can seek to set an example of holiness in sexual conduct. This is a hard battle, but we can prevail because of the "new self" created in us through our union with Christ and the gift of the Holy Spirit (4:20–24). If we fall into sexual sin, we can repent quickly, making use of the sacrament of reconciliation to be restored by God's grace. A friend of mine who struggled with lust resolved, "If I can't excel in resisting temptation, I will excel in repenting." Eventually he overcame his weakness and today he is a faithful priest. Prayer, Scripture reading, and the counsel and encouragement of other Christians can make the freedom Christ won for us effective in our lives if we persevere in faith and hope.

Second, all who have pastoral or teaching roles in the Church can teach regularly about sexual morality, resisting the societal pressure to be silent on this topic. We can explain God's gracious purpose for sex in the context of Christian marriage and family life, avoiding the tone of shame or fear that has sometimes characterized Christian discussion about sex. At the same time, clergy, catechists, and youth ministers can teach against sexual wrongdoing in all its forms, especially the most common ones: internet pornography, masturbation, sex between single people, cohabitation, homosexual relations, contraception,and adultery.[9] Pastors can pray for, counsel, and recommend resources to those who desire to escape from sexual addiction.

Third, we can confront sexual immorality within the Christian community. This is not easy and requires much gentleness and sensitivity. It does not mean becoming a busybody and looking into the business of others, nor does it legitimate gossip. Those who have pastoral responsibility or those who are mature in the faith are to take the lead (Gal 6:1). People whose immoral lifestyles are known in the community should not receive communion[10] or exercise leadership roles in the Church, both for their own good and in order not to give an example that could lead others to sin (Matt 18:6–7; Luke 17:1–2; 1 Cor 11:27–31).

Finally, we can speak the truth about what is right and wrong not only to one another but to our non-Christian friends and neighbors. We will want to speak humbly, since we know our failings and those of other Christians. Many non-Christians, though not all, will respect and admire our ideals even if they are not yet ready to be chaste themselves. We can also work in the public arena in favor of policies and laws that promote sexual morality, preserve family life, and protect people from sexual exploitation.

Living Wisely (5:15–17)

[15]Watch carefully then how you live, not as foolish persons but as wise, [16]making the most of the opportunity, because the days are evil. [17]Therefore, do not continue in ignorance, but try to understand what is the will of the Lord.

9. See Catechism 2351–72, 2380–81, 2390–91. For a brief analysis of contraception in light of John Paul II's theology of the body, see Mary Healy, *Men and Women Are from Eden* (Cincinnati: Servant, 2005), 91–102; for the early Christian understanding, see Michael J. Gorman, *Abortion and the Early Church* (Downers Grove, IL: InterVarsity, 1982), 70–71, 78–82.

10. *Code of Canon Law*, canon 915.

NT: Col 1:9; 4:5; Rom 12:2; Phil 2:15
Catechism: discerning and doing God's will, 2824–26, 2847–49

Having reminded his readers of their baptism (5:14) by which they are now   **5:15–17**
"light in the Lord" (5:8), Paul returns to exhorting them to proper Christian conduct. In these verses, he uses vocabulary common to the wisdom literature of the Old Testament, especially Psalms, Proverbs, and Sirach—words such as †**live** (literally, "walk"), **foolish, wise, ignorance,** and **understand.** The early Church relied on Old Testament wisdom literature to teach catechumens how to live, so much so that the book of Sirach came to be called Ecclesiasticus, the "church book."

Biblical wisdom is not theoretical or scientific knowledge but rather inspired practical understanding about how to live that comes from reflecting on human experience and God's word (Ps 1:2). Wise conduct proceeds from the fear of the Lord, which is a reverent obedience toward God and his commands. Foolish conduct is the exact opposite: conduct that is not well considered, conduct that goes against God's commands and characterizes the life of those who do not know God. "Fools say in their hearts, / 'There is no God'" (Ps 14:1; 53:1). Conduct that is truly wise is moral conduct, and it leads to true success in life. Thus "wisdom" is a concise way to describe the Christian way of life.

Paul's wisdom exhortation, however, differs from the timeless wisdom teaching of the Old Testament in two respects. First, Paul highlights the critical period in which his readers are living: **the days are evil.** Christians live within the overlap of two ages, namely, the present rule of darkness (6:12) and the future kingdom of Christ that was inaugurated by Jesus' resurrection. So Paul exhorts his readers to take advantage of the time they have, **making the most of the opportunity,** literally, "redeeming," or "liberating," the present moment by doing good. Second, Paul proposes a criterion that is uniquely Christian. Continuing in the language of wisdom, he says, "Do not be foolish"—the literal meaning of verse 17a—**but try to understand what is the will of the Lord.** As in 5:10, Paul asks his readers to reflect on what Jesus wants. Christian wisdom is based not on human experience or on the †Torah alone but on a relationship with the risen Lord, from whom Christians gain the ability to discern and do what is pleasing to him by means of his indwelling Spirit (Rom 8:3–14).

Being Filled with the Spirit (5:18–20)

¹⁸And do not get drunk on wine, in which lies debauchery, but be filled with the Spirit, ¹⁹addressing one another [in] psalms and hymns and spiritual

songs, singing and playing to the Lord in your hearts, **²⁰giving thanks always**
and for everything in the name of our Lord Jesus Christ to God the Father.

OT: Prov 20:1; 23:31-35

NT: 1 Pet 4:3-4; Rom 13:13-14; Col 3:16-17; 1 Cor 14:26

Catechism: drunkenness, 2290; the Holy Spirit in liturgical celebrations, 1104-9; singing, 1156-58; praise, 2641; giving thanks always, 2637-38

Having exhorted his readers not to be foolish like the society that surrounds them, Paul applies this general principle to another kind of unbecoming conduct that typified pagan society: drinking parties. The alternative "intoxication" that Paul recommends is to be filled with the Spirit. He then describes the Spirit-filled behaviors that Christians should seek to manifest (5:19-21).

5:18   The first phrase of verse 18 quotes an Old Testament wisdom text that warns against being enamored of wine.[11] Paul is objecting to getting drunk and losing control of one's speech and actions, whatever the alcoholic beverage or drug of choice may be. Paul criticizes drunkenness on the basis of what it leads to: **debauchery**, the ruin that comes from excess or throwing off restraint, and the opposite of the wise conduct recommended in 5:15. Saint John Chrysostom comments, "Immoderate indulgence makes one rash, passionate, prone to stumbling, anger and severity. Wine was given to gladden us, not for intoxication."[12]

In a surprising contrast, Paul tells his readers to **be filled with the Spirit** rather than to be filled with wine. Why would Paul view being filled with the Spirit as an alternative to intoxication? At Pentecost, skeptical bystanders accused the Spirit-filled apostles of being "drunk with new wine" because of their joyful praise of God (Acts 2:13). It seems likely that both Paul and Luke understand the gift of the Spirit as fulfilling the messianic promises of superabundant "wine" (Isa 25:6; 55:1-2; Joel 2:24-26; Amos 9:13-14) that symbolize the fullness of life and joy God promised his people. In the New Testament the Spirit brings joy and exultation.[13]

Although Paul understands his readers to have been already sealed with the Holy Spirit, he nevertheless instructs them to "be filled" with the Spirit. The †passive form of the verb indicates that it is God who does the filling while the use of the present †imperative indicates that Paul wants his readers to make a habit of being filled with the Spirit. The Acts of the Apostles repeatedly describes the post-Pentecost Christians as filled with the Spirit when they were

---

11. The phrase "do not get drunk on wine" is from the †Septuagint version of Prov 23:30 and is not found in the Hebrew Bible, on which modern translations are primarily based.

12. *Homilies on Ephesians* 19.5.18, in Mark J. Edwards, ed., *Galatians, Ephesians, Philippians*, ACCS (Downers Grove, IL: InterVarsity, 1999), 191.

13. See Acts 13:52; Rom 14:17; Gal 5:22; 1 Thess 1:6.

faced with trials, testified on behalf of their Lord, worked miracles, or endured persecution with joy (Acts 4:8, 31; 7:55; 13:9, 52). Other Pauline texts exhort Christians to "be aglow with the Spirit" (Rom 12:11 RSV) and to "live by the Spirit" (Gal 5:16–25; see Rom 8:3–14).

In this instance, the purpose of being filled with the Spirit is worship and the **5:19** mutual upbuilding of the community. Following the command to "be filled with the Spirit" in verse 18, five Greek participles in verses 19–21 identify activities that manifest the presence of the Spirit. The first four of these characterize Christian worship; the fifth, "be subordinate to one another" (v. 21), characterizes Christian relationships and will be discussed in the next two chapters.

The first activity that corresponds to being filled with the Holy Spirit is **addressing one another [in] psalms and hymns and spiritual songs**. This sounds slightly odd. Are Christians to behave like characters in an opera or musical, singing speeches to one another? But if one considers biblical psalms such as Ps 95, 100, and 105–7 and classic hymns like "O Come, All Ye Faithful," one discovers that religious songs often address the faithful, summoning them to worship or to recount God's great deeds to one another. "Psalms," "hymns," and "spiritual songs" similarly mean religious singing, although the last of these indicates songs inspired by the Spirit. "Psalms" could refer to singing or chanting from the book of Psalms, or it could refer to Christian canticles, like the Song of Zechariah and the Song of Mary found in Luke 1.

The second and third participles describe a single activity. The phrase **singing and playing to the Lord in your hearts** makes clear that Christians are to sing to Jesus (in the New Testament, "the Lord" usually refers to Christ) not merely with words but by raising their innermost selves to him. The Greek verb translated "playing" hints at the use of stringed instruments in worship on these occasions. Although this kind of singing could happen at any time, this takes place especially at the liturgical gatherings of the community. Besides various New Testament texts that may have originated as hymns (Phil 2:6–11; Col 1:15–20; Rev 4:8, 11; 5:9–10, 12–13), we have extrabiblical evidence that early Christians sang worship songs to Jesus. Around AD 112, Pliny the Younger, the Roman governor of Bithynia, in present-day Turkey, wrote to the emperor Trajan that in their meetings the Christians "sing responsively a hymn to Christ as to a god."[14]

The fourth participle refers to yet another behavior that manifests the **5:20** Spirit—**giving thanks always and for everything**. Although the verb for "giving thanks" is *eucharisteō*, it does not refer exclusively to celebrating the Lord's Supper but rather refers to all praise and thanks to God for his gifts, whether

---

14. Pliny the Younger, *Letters* 10.96.

as individuals or in gatherings for prayer in households and families, as well as in eucharistic celebrations. In the first-century Church, congregations had to be small enough to meet in homes, and the Eucharist was celebrated in the context of a meal (1 Cor 11:17–21). To new Gentile Christians, those joyful celebrations may well have seemed comparable to the eating and drinking that accompanied pagan sacrifices,[15] which could account for Paul's striking contrast between getting drunk and being filled by the Spirit.

As in the Catholic Church's liturgical prayers, Paul teaches that this praise should be offered **in the name of our Lord Jesus Christ to God the Father**. This does not primarily mean concluding prayers by saying "in Jesus' name" or "through Christ our Lord," although that is a fine practice. The "name" represents the person, so to give thanks "in the name of our Lord Jesus Christ" means praising and thanking God *in union with Jesus*, aware that our relationship with the Father is in and through his beloved Son.

The unifying thread that runs through 5:3–20 is the liturgy of life (Rom 12:1–2), offering God acceptable worship as Jesus did by his sacrifice (Eph 5:2). The way that we do this is by abstaining from the impure speech and conduct of people around us who do not obey God (vv. 3–7), by letting our light—expressed in words and deeds that are good, right, and true—shine in the world (vv. 8–14), by discerning what is truly wise (vv. 15–16) and what Jesus wants us to do (v. 17), and by celebrating with others in Spirit-filled praise and thanks to God through Jesus Christ (vv. 18–20).

Reflection and Application (5:18–20)

People "party" today in the same way they always have. Alcohol and other intoxicants still fuel many celebrations and can lead to wild conduct and immorality. Although the temptation to abuse alcohol and the presence of people with problems of alcoholism should make us careful, the moderate use of alcohol still has a place among Christians and a basis in Scripture (Ps 104:15; Sir 31:27–28; John 2:3–10; 1 Tim 5:23).

Paul's main interest in this text is not to address drunkenness but to exhort Christians to "be filled with the Spirit" and to manifest the Spirit-filled behavior he describes. This command may sound strange to Catholics who believe correctly that they received the Holy Spirit at baptism and confirmation. However,

15. Some immature Christians in Corinth seem not to have appreciated the difference (see 1 Cor 11:20–22).

Acts describes postbaptismal fillings of the Spirit, and the liturgy contains prayers such as this:

> Grant that we, who are nourished by his body and blood,
> may be filled with his Holy Spirit,
> and become one body, one spirit in Christ. (Third Eucharistic Prayer)

Why do we need to be filled again? David du Plessis, a famous Pentecostal preacher, offered one good reason: "Because we leak!" Between our initial experience of salvation and our ultimate salvation at the second coming of Christ, Christians constantly need to be renewed in the grace of the Spirit. Moreover, God is so great that we never reach the end of being filled with his fullness (3:19).

By urging his readers to "be filled with the Spirit," Paul indicates that this is something we must choose, even though it is plain that it is God who does the filling. So what is our part? Besides welcoming the Spirit by worshiping God in song and giving thanks always, two Gospel texts are particularly instructive. In John 7:37–39, Jesus says, "Let anyone who thirsts come to me and drink. Whoever believes in me, as scripture says: / 'Rivers of living water will flow from within him.' / He said this in reference to the Spirit that those who came to believe in him were to receive." In this passage, three verbs describe those to whom the "rivers of living water" are given: those who *thirst*, those who *come* to Jesus, and those who *believe* in him. In Luke 11:9–13 Jesus urges his disciples to ask, seek, and knock, assuring them that there is nothing the Father desires more to grant his children than the Holy Spirit.

Once we have asked expectantly for the grace of the Holy Spirit and have opened ourselves like Mary to whatever God wills (Luke 1:38), it makes sense to give ourselves to the activities that characterize Spirit-filled people: singing together, worshiping the Lord in our hearts, and "giving thanks always and for everything in the name of our Lord Jesus Christ to God the Father." By doing this, we invite the Spirit—like someone who raises a sail to catch the wind.

Many saints have emphasized praying for the Spirit. Saint Seraphim of Sarov (1759–1833) taught that the goal of every devout practice and of life itself is to acquire the Holy Spirit. Every day Pope John Paul II prayed a prayer for the Holy Spirit that his father gave him when he was a boy.[16] Whether in our personal or communal prayer, if we keep asking God to fill and guide us with his Spirit, he will.

16. John Paul II, *Crossing the Threshold of Hope*, paperback ed. (New York: Knopf, 1995), 141.

Wives and Husbands, Christ and the Church

Ephesians 5:21–33

The mountains that are hardest to climb often afford the most spectacular vistas. This passage on Christian marriage is like that. It is difficult for several reasons. Probably no element of human life arouses more longing and hope for happiness, yet yields as much pain and disappointment, as marriage. Even the happiest couples admit that marriage is not as easy as it may appear—and in our culture, marriage is in crisis. Divorce is more common than at any previous time in our history. People are confused about what marriage entails and about who can enter into marriage: only a man and a woman. We live in an age that has seen great progress in the status of women yet is confused regarding the differences between men and women. Besides raising these difficult issues, Eph 5:21–33 contains an instruction that sounds strange and offensive to people today: "Wives should be subordinate to their husbands."

Yet Eph 5:21–33 contains rich teaching about Christian marriage. It provides the biblical basis of the Church's understanding of marriage as a sacrament, and it gives us a breathtaking glimpse of Jesus' spousal love for the Church, his bride. For these reasons, Pope John Paul II devoted considerable attention to this text in his theology of the body and in his apostolic letter *On the Dignity and Vocation of Women*.[1] It is worth our while to study and pray over this clas-

---

1. See paragraphs 23–25 of this document (*Mulieris Dignitatem*, 1988). John Paul also treated Eph 5:21–33 in detail in his Wednesday audiences from July 28, 1982, through December 15, 1982, and returned to it several times in the subsequent audiences through July 4, 1984. A revised translation by Michael Waldstein may be found in John Paul II, *Man and Woman He Created Them: A Theology of the Body* (Boston: Pauline, 2006), 465–515 (abbreviated hereafter as *TOB*). See Mary Healy, *Men and*

sic text on marriage and to seek the mind of the Lord. Ephesians 5:21–33 is a mountain worth climbing, despite the challenges.

The text we are examining is part of a larger unit (5:21–6:9) that belongs to a literary genre known as "household code." Aristotle and other Greek and Jewish writers wrote guidelines for the management of the ancient household (see sidebar on p. 156). Although this section of Ephesians resembles other household codes, its teaching differs in crucial ways from Greek and Jewish advice of its day.

In this chapter we will study Paul's opening exhortation to everyone (5:21) and his teaching about wives and husbands (5:22–33), reserving a fuller discussion of household codes for the next chapter. The passage has four parts:

5:21   An exhortation to all members of the community
5:22–24   An exhortation to wives
5:25–32   An exhortation to husbands (in three parts)
5:33   A concluding exhortation to husbands and wives

An Exhortation to Everyone (5:21)

---

²¹**Be subordinate to one another out of reverence for Christ.**

OT: Sir 3:17
NT: John 13:1–17; Gal 5:13; Phil 2:3; 1 Pet 5:5
Catechism: for the baptized, 1269; for the sacramentally married, 1642; voluntary humility, 2546; family members equal in dignity, 2203

Grammatically, this phrase is part of the sentence that begins in 5:18, and   **5:21** it provides the final instance of the activities that characterize people who are filled with the Spirit (5:18–20). It functions as a hinge that joins that exhortation to Paul's teaching about household relationships (5:22–6:9) and indicates the fundamental attitude that must shape all relationships within the Christian household.

What does it mean to **Be subordinate**? The Greek verb is *hypotassō*, which literally means "to place or arrange under." Here it occurs in the †middle voice (*hypotassomai*) with the meaning "to place oneself under," or more simply, "submit oneself to" or "defer to."[2] It is clear from the context that *voluntary*

Women Are from Eden (Cincinnati: Servant, 2005), for a helpful introduction, and Christopher West, *Theology of the Body Explained* (Boston: Pauline, 2003), for an accessible commentary.

2. It is difficult to find a single English word to translate *hypotassomai* in all instances, so I will use a variety of terms. "Be subject to," the translation given in the RSV, NRSV, and NJB, does not do justice to the voluntary nature of what Paul is teaching. "Submit" and "submission" imply passivity and have

Household Life in the First Century

In Ephesus and other Greco-Roman towns and cities of Paul's day, the basic social unit was the household rather than the nuclear family. In a household, a family spanning multiple generations might live together with slaves, servants, laborers, business partners, and sometimes tenants. If circumstances did not allow the members to reside in the same building, they nevertheless understood themselves as belonging to the same house. The household was an economic unit as well, functioning as the hub of a farm or business. Family life afforded little scope for individual decision making. On some occasions whole households embraced Christianity with the head of the household (Acts 16:15, 31–34; 18:8; 1 Cor 1:16). Although heads of households were usually men, some well-to-do women functioned as heads of households, perhaps after inheriting the family property (Acts 16:14–15; 1 Cor 1:11; Col 4:15).

---

subordination is intended, like the other voluntary expressions of Spirit-filled life mentioned in 5:19–20 (singing hymns, giving thanks, etc.).

The motive for mutual subordination is indicated by the words **out of reverence for Christ**. The Greek word translated "reverence" is *phobos*, literally, "fear." Here it refers to the attitude esteemed so highly in Scripture, "the fear of the Lord" that "is the beginning of wisdom" (Ps 111:10 RSV), one of the seven gifts of the Spirit (Isa 11:2–3). It describes the loving reverence of a human being toward God—and in this case of a Christian toward Jesus—that motivates doing his will, knowing that we are accountable to him. Remembering that our brothers and sisters are members of Christ's body (4:25; 5:30) increases our reverence, because as our Lord has said, "whatever you did to one of the least of my brothers, you did to me" (Matt 25:40, my translation).

The truly unusual nature of this instruction is that Paul tells his readers to submit themselves **to one another**, still addressing all the members of the community. At first this seems contradictory. How can two individuals place themselves "under" each other? Some people conclude that the radical instruction to "subordinate yourselves to one another" democratizes all relationships in the household, nullifying the instructions in 5:22–6:9 that support the traditional order in household relationships. But if Paul wanted to eliminate relationships

---

other negative associations except when speaking of a mutual relationship. The NAB translation, "be subordinate," has other problems (see footnote 10 on p. 163).

of authority in 5:21, he would not use the words "respect," "obey," and "be obedient" in the verses that follow (5:33; 6:1, 5).[3]

The meaning of this unusual instruction becomes clearer in the light of similar texts that teach about relationships in the church. In Gal 5:13 Paul says, "serve one another through love" (literally, "be slaves to one another") and in Phil 2:3, "humbly regard others as more important than yourselves." In other words, each person is to treat others with humility and love, deferring to others rather than seeking his or her own interests or will (1 Cor 13:5; Phil 2:4).

Reciprocal humility and love determine even the relationships that entail authority. An analogous exhortation to be humble toward one another combined with an exhortation to defer (*hypotassomai*) to those in authority occurs in 1 Pet 5:5: "Likewise, you younger members, be subject to the presbyters. And all of you, clothe yourselves with humility in your dealings with one another, for 'God opposes the proud but bestows favor on the humble.'" Undoubtedly, behind this teaching stands Jesus' own teaching about leadership as service (Luke 22:25–27), which was demonstrated and explained when he washed the feet of his disciples (John 13:13–15), foreshadowing his humbling himself for our sake on the cross. The specific instructions that Paul gives to wives and husbands, children and parents, slaves and masters in 5:22–6:9 put flesh on the meaning of "be subordinate to one another out of reverence for Christ."

Reflection and Application (5:21)

I got a glimpse of how radical this teaching must have originally sounded when I explained this verse to a parish Bible study that included parents and children. "Parents," I said, "Paul is telling you to submit to your children." I paused, and all of the children in the room suddenly woke up and paid attention. I then explained that Paul was not really overturning biblical teaching on children obeying parents and honoring their fathers and mothers. But he *was* saying that parents should also defer to their children by respecting their needs and desires, rather than acting solely for their own convenience. Whenever Christians are called to exercise authority or leadership in relation to one another, they are to do so with humility, knowing they are serving people of the highest status, namely, members of Christ's own body.

3. Other commentators deny that Paul's exhortation here means that everyone should be mutually subordinate and suggest that Paul means each should submit to his or her respective authorities in the first-century household: wives to husbands, children to parents, and slaves to masters. But this interpretation does not do justice to Paul's consistent use of "one another" to refer to reciprocal relationships (e.g., 4:2, 25, 32).

An Exhortation to Wives (5:22–24)

[22]Wives should be subordinate to their husbands as to the Lord. [23]For the husband is head of his wife just as Christ is head of the church, he himself the savior of the body. [24]As the church is subordinate to Christ, so wives should be subordinate to their husbands in everything.

NT: 1 Cor 11:3; Eph 1:22; 4:15–16; Col 3:18; 1 Pet 3:1–6

Catechism: husband and wife as equals, 369, 1605; the Church as bride of Christ, 773, 796; Christian marriage, 1602, 1612–17, 1624; sin and domination in marriage, 1606–8; self-denial in marriage, 1615

These verses are the hardest to understand in the Letter to the Ephesians and cause many people to cringe. In this section we will consider only what Paul was saying to his first-century readers. At the end of the chapter, we will take up the question of how to interpret this text in today's very different cultural setting.

5:22   In Greek this verse is compact because the verb "be subordinate" is carried over from 5:21 rather than restated: literally, it reads, "the wives to their husbands as to the Lord." The previous verse speaks paradoxically of deference that operates in two directions, but here it is unidirectional, from wives to husbands. While mutual submission was a radically new idea, the subordination of wives to their husbands was the social norm and even a matter of law in the first-century Roman Empire (see sidebar on p. 162). Two things, however, are striking about Paul's instruction. First, Greco-Roman and Jewish household teaching invariably addressed the head of the household, who was expected to impose this order on the members of his household. But Paul addresses married women as free persons who can choose. He summons them to willingly **be subordinate to their husbands**. Other New Testament texts contain similar exhortations (Col 3:18; Titus 2:5; 1 Pet 3:1–6). Second, Paul exhorts wives to do so **as to the Lord**, that is, to yield to their husbands sincerely as an expression of their submission to Jesus.

Paul is saying to the wives in his first-century audience that to defer to their husbands in the ordinary give-and-take of family life is a way of following Christ. It is worth noting that Paul says "subordinate yourselves" rather than "obey," the word he uses in his instruction to children and slaves in 6:1, 5. Other ancient Greek and Jewish writers routinely use the word "obey" for the relationship of wife to husband.[4] Paul's word choice indicates that he views the relationship

4. Andrew T. Lincoln, *Ephesians*, Word Biblical Commentary (Waco: Word, 1990), 367–68. According to Lincoln, the difference of meaning in the two words should not be exaggerated.

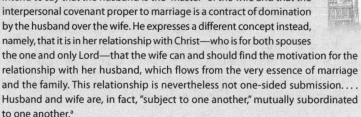

John Paul II on "Wives Should Be Subordinate to Their Husbands"

The author speaks about the mutual submission of the spouses [Eph 5:21], husband and wife, and in this way shows also how to understand *the words* he writes afterward *about the submission of the wife to the husband*. . . . When he expresses himself this way, the author does not intend to say that the husband is the "master" of the wife and that the interpersonal covenant proper to marriage is a contract of domination by the husband over the wife. He expresses a different concept instead, namely, that it is in her relationship with Christ—who is for both spouses the one and only Lord—that the wife can and should find the motivation for the relationship with her husband, which flows from the very essence of marriage and the family. This relationship is nevertheless not one-sided submission. . . . Husband and wife are, in fact, "subject to one another," mutually subordinated to one another.[a]

a. John Paul II, *TOB*, August 11, 1982, 473; emphasis original.

---

of wives to husbands to be different from that of children to parents or slaves to masters. The voluntary subordination Paul envisions is familial rather than military or task oriented. It would not have meant wives passively waiting for orders from their husbands but rather wives fulfilling their family and household responsibilities with all the personal initiative that these entail and in a manner that defers to the husband's leadership. Nor should we imagine that this excluded wives from exercising considerable influence as some of the famous women of the Bible clearly did (e.g., Gen 21:10–12; 1 Kings 1) or respectfully admonishing a husband when necessary (Matt 18:15–18; Luke 17:3–4; Col 3:16).

Paul now presents a reason for this instruction to wives: **For the husband is head of his wife**. In the context of discussing order in first-century household relationships (5:21–6:9), Paul indicates that the husband is placed "over" his wife as the metaphor of "head" suggests (see sidebar on p. 160). It is on that basis that Paul has exhorted wives "to place themselves under" (the literal meaning of *hypotassomai*) their husbands in the previous verses. Although Paul is clearly affirming an order of precedence in the husband-wife relationship, it is not correct to reduce the meaning of "head" to "authority over," as 5:28–31 will make clear. In keeping with the Jewish tradition of interpretation, Paul derives this order from the second biblical story of creation in Gen 2, where the man is created first and the woman is taken from man's side (1 Cor 11:3, 8–9; 1 Tim 2:12–13). Paul saw no contradiction between this social order and the

5:23–24

What Does "Head" Mean?

BIBLICAL
BACKGROUND

In Greek the metaphor "head" (*kephalē*) builds on the physiologi-
cal relationship of head to body and usually means what is above,
preeminent, first, or foremost, as in the "head of the corner," "top of
a mountain," or "capital city." In describing persons, it can indicate
prominence or precedence with or without signifying "authority
over," although the meaning "authority over" is sometimes included
(Col 2:10). Occasionally, "head" can convey the meaning of "source,"
as in the headwaters of a river, but that use is not common. When
"head" is associated with a "body" to which it belongs, other metaphorical associations come into play, as in 4:15–16 and 5:28–31. In every case,
the precise meaning of the metaphor is determined by its context (see commentary on the meaning of "head" in 1:22 and 4:15).

first story of creation, which teaches that men and women were both created
in the divine image and are of equal dignity (Gen 1:27). In 1 Cor 11:11–12 he
affirms the interdependence of woman and man.

After affirming that the husband is head of the wife, Paul adds a comparison
that probably surprised his first readers and that certainly startles us: **just as Christ
is head of the church**. It is not surprising that Paul refers to Christ as "head of the
church," since he said this in 4:15. What is surprising is that Paul would compare
Christ's transcendent headship of the Church to the ordinary human relationship
of husband and wife. Paul indicates his awareness of the difference, distinguishing Christ's more extensive role by adding, **he himself the savior of the body**,
with "himself" signalling what is unique to Christ. Every analogy is imperfect,
containing points of correspondence and points of dissimilarity, above all when
human and divine realities are compared.[5] While in Paul's view a husband has
precedence over his wife in some way analogous to Christ's sovereignty over the
Church, Christ's role in relationship to his "body," the Church, is infinitely greater
as he is her †Lord and savior as well. The Greek text signals that unlike things
are being compared by including a "yet" or "nonetheless" (*alla*) that the NAB
and most translations omit at the beginning of the next clause: **As the church is
subordinate to Christ, so wives should be subordinate to their husbands in
everything**. The verb *hypotassomai*, to subordinate oneself or to defer (as in 5:21),

5. Along these lines, John Paul II says, "The language of the Bible is sufficiently precise to indicate
the limits of the 'likeness,' the limits of the 'analogy.' For biblical Revelation says that, while man's 'likeness' to God is true, the '*non-likeness*' which separates the whole of creation from the Creator is *still
more essentially true*" (*On the Dignity and Vocation of Women* 8).

is repeated in this verse. Some people have joked that the Church's subordination to Christ sets a rather low standard for wives! But Paul is pointing to the ideal responsiveness of the Church to her head when she is true to her identity, the loving surrender of a bride to her bridegroom, anticipating the marriage imagery that unfolds in the following verses. Even though Paul exhorts them to act "out of reverence for Christ," the self-subordination to which he summons wives is neither compulsory nor passive. "Considering the 'subordination of the Church' to Christ, it would not occur to anyone to think of 'compulsory' subordination. . . . No one would consider the Church as passive. . . . Her love consists, among others, in that she moves in her own accord to place herself in the position where He can embrace her. Her subordination is answer to His love."[6]

The words "in everything" need to be understood as a statement of principle rather than a norm that allows no exception.[7] For instance, Paul would not say that a wife should cooperate with her husband in what she knows to be sin, nor should he be interpreted as enjoining acquiescence to abuse.[8] Another reason not to interpret "be subordinate . . . in everything" in an absolute sense is that in another text Paul himself speaks of a husband's responsibility to his wife in regard to her conjugal rights: "a husband does not have authority over his own body, but rather his wife" (1 Cor 7:4). Although Paul upholds a traditional order between husband and wife, his approach to marriage differs markedly from that of the surrounding society.

Reflection and Application (5:22–24)

Unity, diversity, and equality in Christ. Is Paul's exhortation to wives to defer to their husbands compatible with his radical affirmation in Gal 3:28 that "There is neither Jew nor Greek, there is neither slave nor free person, there is not male and female; for you are all one in Christ Jesus"? What does Paul's denial of ethnic, social, and gender distinctions among those who are "one in Christ"

---

6. E. Kahler as quoted by E. Rivera, "'Wives, Be Subject to Your Husbands,'" *Philippiana Sacra* 3 (1968): 243.

7. In 1 Cor 7:10–11 Paul acknowledges that marital separation, while undesirable, is sometimes unavoidable. Paul's letters, like other parts of Scripture, include both unqualified statements of principle that require discernment in the way they are applied and other texts that apply principles to particular circumstances (e.g., 1 Cor 10:14, 25–28).

8. Pope Pius XI spoke of limits to a wife's subordination in his encyclical "On Christian Marriage" (*Casti connubii* 27): "This subjection, however, does not deny or take away the liberty which fully belongs to the woman both in view of her dignity as a human person, and in view of her most noble office as wife and mother and companion; nor does it bid her obey her husband's every request if not in harmony with right reason or with the dignity due to a wife; nor, in fine, does it imply that the wife should be put on a level with those persons who in law are called minors."

Women in the First Century

In the Jewish and Greco-Roman culture of the Mediterranean world, women were not equal to men. "To some early Jewish teachers, women were inherently evil . . . ; Josephus claimed that the Law prescribed their subordination for their own good. . . . Philo complains that women have little sense."[a] Plato regarded the soul as sexless but considered souls inhabiting female bodies as thereby handicapped at attaining wisdom or virtue. Aristotle regarded women as inferior by nature.

Although Luke (Acts 13:50; 17:4, 12) and Greco-Roman authors depict some women as occupying roles of influence, Roman law gave complete authority to the head of the household, the *paterfamilias*, over his wife and children.[b] Wives were generally less educated and typically fifteen years younger than their husbands.

Marriage in Greco-Roman society was less oriented to establishing a loving family than to producing legal heirs to receive, preserve, and transmit property. Although some Stoics, such as Musonius (AD 30–101), advocated marital fidelity and mutual love, the typical †Hellenistic view is represented by Pseudo-Demosthenes (fourth century BC): "We have wives to bear us children, concubines for the daily care of our persons, mistresses we keep for the sake of our pleasure" (*Against Neaera* 122).[c]

a. C. S. Keener, "Man and Woman," in *Dictionary of Paul and His Letters*, ed. Gerald F. Hawthorne et al. (Downers Grove, IL: InterVarsity, 1993), 586.

b. Some wives were exempt because they remained legally part of their fathers' households to avoid the loss of family property through marriage.

c. A. Murray, trans., *Private Orations III*, Loeb Classical Library (Boston: Harvard, 1939), 445–46.

mean? Obviously, he is not saying that the institution of slavery had ceased to exist or that gender differences disappear at baptism. Rather, Galatians was written to affirm that †Gentiles obtain a right relationship with God (justification) and full membership in the people of God through faith in Christ apart from circumcision and observance of the law of Moses. Here Paul insists on the oneness and equality before God of Jews and Gentiles "baptized into" and "clothed" with Christ (Gal 3:27); he defies cultural norms in Greco-Roman society by asserting that this equality grounded in union with Christ extends to slaves and women.[9] Furthermore, Paul teaches that a shared relationship with Christ must radically change the dynamics of relationships among believers. The exhortation to "Be subordinate to one another out of reverence for Christ"

9. Aristotle and some other Greek authors regarded slaves and women as intrinsically inferior.

(5:21) is only the first of a number of changes in relationship dynamics taught in 5:21–6:9.

Paul's understanding of oneness and equal dignity in Christ, however, does not eliminate diversity. In a passage that contains the closest parallel to Gal 3:28 in the †undisputed letters (1 Cor 12:13; see vv. 12–28), Paul addresses the issue of unity and diversity. He compares the Church to the human body to affirm the importance and necessity of each of the Church's members, despite the fact that some members "seem" to be "weaker," "less honorable," or "less presentable." Which part is greater, the ear or the eye, the hand or the foot? Since we are one body, the different roles we fulfill are of secondary importance and do not determine our worth. In Paul's view, differences in honor, function, or even authority in the Church do not contradict or negate a fundamental equality in Christ. "Some people God has designated in the church to be, first, apostles; second, prophets; third, teachers . . . then gifts of healing, assistance, administration" (1 Cor 12:28)—and all are equally members of Christ's body. All have "the same concern for one another" because they are united to one another; all share the same suffering, honor, and joy (1 Cor 12:25–26).

Unity, diversity, and equality in the Trinity. Earlier in 1 Corinthians, Paul uses both "head" and "be subordinate" to describe relationships among the persons of the Trinity. In 1 Cor 11:3 he writes, "I want you to know that Christ is the head of every man, and a husband the head of his wife, and God the head of Christ." By the use of "head," Paul indicates an order between husband and wife that is in some way analogous to the order between God the Father and Christ. The fact that one is called "head" does not indicate that the other has a lesser status or value. Later in the same letter, Paul says, "When everything is subjected to him, then the Son himself will [also] be subjected to the one who subjected everything to him, so that God may be all in all" (1 Cor 15:28). The word translated "subjected" is *hypotassomai*. Early church councils affirmed the fundamental equality of the three persons of the Trinity.[10] The Christian tradition has interpreted these texts as manifesting a diversity of relations within the Trinity, an order that does not compromise their equality: the Father begets the Son, and the Holy Spirit proceeds from the Father and is sent by the Son

---

10. Against Arianism, the full equality of the Son to the Father was confirmed at the Council of Nicaea in 325. The full equality of the Holy Spirit to the Father and the Son was confirmed by the First Council of Constantinople in 381, which declared that the Spirit is of equal dignity and worthy of the same worship as the Father and the Son. Because the name of the heresy rejected in both cases was "subordinationism"—assigning an inferior status to the Son and to the Spirit—translating *hypotassomai* as "be subordinate" (5:21, 24), as the NAB does, can be confusing. However, all the alternative translations have other problems.

(John 5:26).[11] Although all three persons fulfill distinctive roles in the work of salvation, their unity is not impaired. The equality of the three divine persons is based in their oneness. The communion of persons within the Trinity is a model for the communion of all members of the Church and especially of the communion between a man and a woman in marriage.

Sarah Sumner, an evangelical theologian, explains the relationship of husband and wife in light of the New Testament statements in the previous paragraph about the relationship between God the Father and Jesus. God puts all things under Christ (Eph 1:22; Heb 2:8) and then Christ places himself in subjection to the Father (1 Cor 15:27–28). But the Father also exalts Christ to the right hand of God so that ultimately Christ shares one throne with the Father (Rev 5:12–13; 22:1–3). "The Father delights to share his seat of power with the Son. . . . There is trust within the Trinity, not competition. Therefore Christ is not unwilling to be subject to God (1 Cor 11:3). Nor is God unwilling to share his seat of power with him. . . . The Father exalts the Son to the highest place (Phil 2:9–10) 'so that all may honor the Son even as they honor the Father' (John 5:23)."[12] Christ, in turn, exalts his bride, the Church, giving her a share in his ministry and in his reign (Eph 2:6; 2 Tim 2:12; Rev 22:5). Sumner sees God's headship of Christ as the key to understanding how the husband and wife can be equals even though the husband is designated the head. "It's the husband's responsibility to exalt his wife as God exalts Christ and Christ exalts the church. It's up to the husband to ensure that his wife is honored no less than he."[13]

Love Your Wives as Christ Loved the Church (5:25–27)

---

[25]**Husbands, love your wives, even as Christ loved the church and handed himself over for her** [26]**to sanctify her, cleansing her by the bath of water with the word,** [27]**that he might present to himself the church in splendor, without spot or wrinkle or any such thing, that she might be holy and without blemish.**

OT: Isa 54:4–8; 62:4–5; Ezek 16; Hos 2:16–20
NT: John 15:3; 17:17; Col 3:19; Titus 3:5; 1 Pet 3:7

11. The creed of the Western Church affirms that the Spirit "proceeds from the Father and the Son" in keeping with Rev 22:1, where "the river of life-giving water . . . flowing from the throne of God and of the Lamb" represents the Spirit and "flowing" is the identical verb rendered as "proceeds" in John 15:26. Both ways of describing relations within the Trinity are true.

12. Sarah Sumner, *Men and Women in the Church* (Downers Grove, IL: InterVarsity, 2003), 176.

13. Ibid., 180–81.

Catechism: marriage in the Lord, 1612, 1615–17; the Church as the bride of Christ, 757, 772–73, 796
Lectionary: 5:2a, 21–33: Sacrament of Marriage

In his instruction to husbands (5:25–32), Paul exhorts them to love their wives, giving them two models to illustrate how they are to love: first, Christ's love for the Church expressed in his sacrificial gift of himself (vv. 25–27), and second, the care that husbands take for their own bodies (vv. 28–31). In a startling conclusion (v. 32), however, Paul quotes a text from Genesis to reveal a profound relationship between these two models based in the meaning of marriage. In the course of these verses, he sheds new light on Christ's death on the cross as an act of spousal love.

I once heard a married man describe Eph 5:25 as "the hardest verse in the   **5:25**
Bible," not because he does not love his wife, but because of the extraordinary standard for husbandly love presented here. It is important to understand that Paul is not speaking of romantic or sexual love (*eros*), the kind of love celebrated in popular music and film. *Eros* is a wonderful gift created by God; it is a love based in desire that arises naturally and is appropriately expressed in marital intimacy. Here, however, the Apostle speaks of *agapē*,[14] the "great love" attributed to God in 2:4, a love that arises from a choice of the will and that does not depend on the worthiness or response of the person beloved. Although this love is grounded in a decision, it involves the entirety of the one who loves, including the emotions.[15] This is another innovation of the gospel: "This exhortation to husbands to love their wives is unique. It is not found in the Old Testament, rabbinic literature, or in the household codes of the Greco-Roman era."[16] **Husbands, love your wives** could be paraphrased, "Husbands, set your heart on your wives: prize, cherish, and care for them. Be affectionate toward them and seek their good."

Rather than explain in detailed, practical terms how husbands should treat their wives, Paul presents a model: **even as Christ loved the church and handed himself over for her**. The two Greek verbs (*agapaō*, "loved," and *paradidōmi*, "handed over") are the same as those used in 5:2 and Gal 2:20 to refer to the moment when the Messiah manifested his love by voluntarily surrendering his life on the cross.[17] The final words, "for her," literally "on her behalf," continue

14. *Agapē* is the noun corresponding to the verb for love, *agapaō*, used here in the Greek.
15. 1 Cor 13:4–7 offers Paul's classic description of this love. Pope Benedict XVI discusses the relationship of *eros* and *agapē* in *Deus caritas est* 2–8 and states that *eros* between a man and a woman finds its fulfillment in the *agapē* of married love.
16. Harold W. Hoehner, *Ephesians: An Exegetical Commentary* (Grand Rapids: Baker Academic, 2002), 748.
17. Other biblical texts that explain why Christ died point to God's love for the world (John 3:16), Jesus' love for the Father (John 14:31), or Jesus' love for his disciples (John 13:1; 15:13). This is the only instance that explains the cross as expressing Christ's love for "the church."

the language of sacrifice. By invoking Jesus' death on the cross as the model for husbands, Paul summons men to lay down their lives for their wives. While on rare occasions dying for one's wife may be literally necessary, he means it in the everyday sense of husbands dying to self by prioritizing their wives' needs and wants before their own. Essentially Paul is saying, "Husbands, seek the good of your wives regardless of the cost to you." With these words Paul instructs husbands to deny themselves as completely as he has instructed wives to deny themselves by subordinating themselves to their husbands (5:22, 24).

The Old Testament †prophets often compared God's relationship with his people Israel to a marriage.[18] John the Baptist refers to Jesus as the "bridegroom" (John 3:29) and describes himself as the bridegroom's friend. Jesus alludes to himself as "the bridegroom" in the Gospels (Matt 22:1–14; 25:1–13; Mark 2:19), hinting at his divine identity. The book of Revelation looks forward to "the wedding day of the Lamb" as the goal of history (Rev 19:7–8; 21:2, 9–11). Nevertheless, in these verses, Paul plumbs new depths in the early Church's understanding of Jesus' spousal relationship with the Church.

5:26   The Apostle explains why the heavenly bridegroom sacrificed himself for the Church in terms of three overlapping purposes.[19] First, he did so **to sanctify her, cleansing her by the bath of water with the word**. To sanctify means to make †holy, to set someone or something apart from what is profane and to qualify that person or object for God's presence. The means Jesus uses to cleanse and sanctify the members of the Church is baptism, "the bath of water" (see Acts 22:16; 1 Cor 6:11; Titus 3:5). The last phrase, "with the word" ("by the word," NRSV), might refer to the gospel message (Eph 1:13; John 15:3; 17:17), the profession of faith made by the newly baptized (Rom 10:9–10), or the formula used in baptism. Paul is saying Jesus offered his life as a sacrifice so that through the word of God and baptism we could become the kind of people fit for God's presence.

In both the Jewish and Greek cultures of that time, the immediate cosmetic preparation of the bride included a bath with fragrant oils so that she could be as clean and beautiful as possible. Baptism, Paul is saying, is the Church's bridal bath that prepares her to be united to her bridegroom. That it is Christ who bathes his bride is unique, because washing the bride is the job not of the bridegroom but of female servants or family members. It recalls Jesus' humility and love expressed in his washing the feet of his

18. See Isa 54:4–8; 62:4–5; Ezek 16; Hosea 2:16–20.
19. The Greek text of 5:26–27 consists of three clauses beginning with *hina*, which means "so that." This parallel structure is preserved in the ESV as "that he might sanctify her, . . . that he might present the church to himself in splendor, . . . that she might be holy."

disciples (John 13:1–17). By cleansing his bride through his death on the cross, Jesus placed himself in a lower position (Phil 2:6–8) and served her; in doing so he provided an example for husbands of how to "be subordinate" (5:21) and serve their wives.

The second purpose of Jesus' death on the cross was to **present to himself**   5:27
the church in splendor, without spot or wrinkle or any such thing. According to ancient custom in the Near East, still practiced in some places, marriage is a two-step process. First comes betrothal, or engagement, when the contract is signed. From that point on the man and woman are legally husband and wife. The second step occurs when the bride is brought to the home of the groom and presented to him, and they begin to live together as man and wife. Then the major celebration occurs. For the Church, this will occur in the future, when Christ returns to claim his bride and his people will share in the "wedding feast of the Lamb" (Rev 19:9).[20] Although the fullness lies in the future, Christ already cares for his bride by means of the sacraments and the gift of the Spirit (5:29). Jesus' sacrifice on the cross, whose benefits we receive through baptism, cleanses us, and his gift of the Spirit adorns us with his own splendor: "You were renowned among the nations for your beauty, perfect as it was, because of my splendor which I had bestowed on you, says the Lord GOD" (Ezek 16:14).[21]

The third purpose of Christ's sacrifice for his bride was **that she might be holy and without blemish** (see 1:4). This repeats the idea of the first purpose, to sanctify the Church, but here the emphasis is on holiness as the Church's special privilege. Every bride aspires to make herself as lovely as she can be on her wedding day. Jesus has arranged for his bride to be able to adorn herself with the beauty of holiness, with conduct and character that is becoming (see Rev 19:7–8).

The New Testament speaks about the holiness of the Church and of individual Christians in two ways: as a present reality already received by faith and baptism (e.g., the frequent references to all Christians as "holy ones" or as "saints") and as transformation that occurs as Christians cooperate with †grace (e.g., 1 Pet 1:15). Jesus gave himself as a sacrifice both to cleanse us and to empower us to live lives of holiness.

20. Because of Ephesians' emphasis on a realized †eschatology, some scholars think that v. 27 refers to the present state of Christians as cleansed and sanctified by Christ (1 Cor 6:11). However, other Pauline texts that speak of the Church being "presented" to Christ (2 Cor 11:2; Col 1:22–23, 28) refer to this as a future event.

21. The image of washing recalls a poignant story from Ezek 16:1–14 describing how the Lord originally found Israel, under the image of an abandoned newborn baby girl. God nurtured her, and, when she reached maturity, bathed her, adorned her, and married her by entering into a covenant with her.

Reflection and Application (5:25–27)

In 5:25–27 Paul retells the story he told in Eph 2 of our former helplessness and of how God saved us by his grace. This time Paul focuses on Christ's motive for surrendering himself to death on the cross, namely, love for the Church, his bride. While Eph 2:8 spoke of faith as the means by which we receive the grace of salvation, the present verses show that the way Christ cleanses us from sin and makes us holy is through baptism. Our part is faith, made possible by grace; his part is baptism. In the sacrament, Christ himself baptizes through the hands of the minister and communicates to us the purifying power of his sacrificial death through water and words.

Jesus wed the Church when he died for her, rose for her, ascended, and poured out his Spirit on her. He pronounced his solemn vows when he took bread and wine and said, "This is my body, which will be given for you. . . . This cup is the new covenant in my blood, which will be shed for you" (Luke 22:20). In the Eucharist, Jesus makes a total gift of himself to us; it is the expression, par excellence, of our marriage covenant with him. When we partake of it, he unites us to himself in a foretaste of the wedding feast of the Lamb.

Love Your Wives in the Way You Care for Your Own Bodies (5:28–30)

---

²⁸So [also] husbands should love their wives as their own bodies. He who loves his wife loves himself. ²⁹For no one hates his own flesh but rather nourishes and cherishes it, even as Christ does the church, ³⁰because we are members of his body.

NT: 1 Cor 12:27; Eph 1:23; 1 Pet 3:7
Catechism: conjugal love, 2360–65; respect for one's own body and that of others, 1004

5:28–29a   Paul follows up with a very practical model of the way **husbands should love their wives**—they should care for their wives in the same way as they care for **their own bodies**. This is simpler to understand and implement. It is obvious that among normal people **no one hates his own flesh**—here "†flesh" refers to a person's body—**but rather nourishes and cherishes it**. In other words, people naturally feed and clothe their bodies; they do good to their bodies because their bodies are the physical expression of themselves. Paul is urging husbands to take as much thought for the well-being of their wives as they do for their own well-being. Paul then reinforces this exhortation with what appears at first to be no more than a pragmatic insight that many married men acquire by experience: **He who loves his wife loves himself.** In other words, "Do good to your wife and you'll be glad you did. What you do for her comes back to you." However, in the next three verses Paul will show that he has something deeper in mind.

Paul's return to the example of Jesus makes clear that he has more in mind than enlightened self-interest: **even as Christ does the church.** Just as husbands care for their physical bodies, Jesus likewise looks after the Church, **because we are members of his body**, the physical expression of Christ on earth. This recalls what we noted earlier about Jesus' identification of the Church as an extension of himself (1:23). Note that Paul substitutes himself and his readers ("we") for "the church." The Church is not a building, not merely an institution, not primarily the clergy, the hierarchy, or the Vatican; rather, it is all of us, the people of God who compose the body Christ nourishes and cherishes.

5:29b–30

How does Jesus do this? The word translated "nourishes" means "to feed." Christ feeds us on the word of God and on his own flesh in the Eucharist (Matt 4:4; John 6:51–58; Catechism 103). The word translated "cherishes" literally means "to warm," and here figuratively, "to care for tenderly." (Paul also uses it in 1 Thess 2:7.) Christ cares for us by providing for our needs, hearing our prayers, and remaining close to us (Matt 28:20). Although Jesus alone can do what he does for the members of his body, his loyal care provides an example for husbands of how to treat their wives.

Reflection and Application (5:25–30)

Pondering Paul. After exhorting everyone to subordinate themselves to one another, Paul tells wives to subordinate themselves to their husbands as to the Lord and husbands to love their wives as Christ loved and gave his life for the Church. Both instructions entail a kind of absolute self-gift. But why the difference between them—defer and respect (5:33) versus nourish and cherish? Clearly, Paul is seeking to reform long-established social patterns marred by sin and to introduce gospel values. However, is it possible that these contrasting exhortations reflect a more profound insight? Do they correspond to something rooted in the psychology of men and women that moves their hearts toward their spouses when they give or receive this kind of treatment? In fact, some studies report that men express a greater need for respect, and women for love.[22]

22. For a popular account that reports the evidence and applies it to married life, see Emerson Eggerichs, *Love and Respect* (Nashville: Thomas Nelson, 2004).

Many marriage books counsel husbands and wives to relate to each other in ways that bear some analogy to this teaching. In my own marriage I have seen my love increase and my wife's heart grow tender when I place her needs and concerns before my own. Likewise, when my wife speaks and acts in a way that indicates her respect and reliance on me, it draws me to her and makes me want to be a responsible man who deserves her confidence.

It also is worth observing that Paul speaks to both partners about their responsibilities rather than their rights. He does not tell husbands to love their wives *if* their wives are respectful and defer to them. Nor does he tell wives to subordinate themselves *if* their husbands are loving and self-sacrificing. Both are called to do their own part rather than focus on getting the spouse to change.

Finally, although Paul recognizes an order in family relationships, he does not focus on husbands exercising authority but rather on husbands adopting a humble attitude (5:21), giving their lives sacrificially by nourishing, cherishing, and loving. His teaching resembles that of Jesus, who appoints the apostles to lead the Church but instructs them about humility, love, and service rather than about asserting their authority.

Loving Jesus. Although the experience of sinful male domination has led some feminists to reject the marriage imagery of the Old and New Testaments, this imagery corresponds to a deeply seated intuition of what it means to be male and female reflected in many stories and poems that conclude with a marriage. The bride is beautiful and her bridegroom delights in her; he has gone to extraordinary lengths to win her as his wife. According to John Paul II, the image of Christ the bridegroom means that *"all human beings—both women and men—are called* through the Church, *to be the 'Bride' of Christ, the Redeemer of the world.* In this way 'being the bride,' and thus the 'feminine' element, becomes a symbol of all that is 'human.'"[23] The Divine Lover is the hero, the one who initiates, who sacrifices himself to rescue the one he loves—we are the beloved, the one who returns his love.

If we accept our identity as belonging to his beloved bride, some wonderful love poetry in the Old Testament, such as Ps 45 and the Song of Songs, is available to express our love for Christ. Throughout the history of the Church, these texts and others, such as Bernard of Clairvaux's marvelous commentary on the Song, have expressed and nurtured the Church's bridal love for her Lord.[24]

---

23. *On the Dignity and Vocation of Women* 25; emphasis original.

24. Traditionally, the title "bride of Christ" has been used for consecrated women, since their lives express this marital symbolism with particular clarity. According to Raniero Cantalamessa, "They are like an epiphany of the Church as bride" (*Loving the Church* [Cincinnati: St. Anthony Messenger, 2005], 43).

Loving the Church. A simple corollary follows from Eph 5:25–30: if Christ loves his bride the Church so much, so should we. Christ is fully aware of the many shortcomings of every Christian and of every institutional expression of the Church's life, yet he "nourishes and cherishes" each member of his body and the Church as a whole. Insofar as we are sinners, Christ has compassion on us. Insofar as we are justified and sanctified through baptism, Christ sees us in light of the †holy new creation he has made us. Finally, insofar as we are seeking holiness, Christ sees in us the beauty of holiness that shall one day be ours, that he is forming in us even now. We can look at our brothers and sisters in this same light.

The Oneness of Husband and Wife, Christ and the Church (5:31–32)

---

[31]"For this reason a man shall leave [his] father and [his] mother
   and be joined to his wife,
and the two shall become one flesh."
   [32]This is a great mystery, but I speak in reference to Christ and the church.

OT: Gen 2:18–24
NT: Mark 10:2–12; Eph 3:3–9; Col 1:26–27; 2:2–3
Catechism: marriage as a great mystery, 772, 1602, 1613–16; one flesh, 1605; sacramental marriage, the Eucharist, and the Holy Spirit, 1621–24, 1627

In these two verses it is as if Paul fits the final piece in the jigsaw puzzle and reveals a picture that is different from the one we thought we were looking at. He shows us that the two models for husbands loving their wives that he has just proposed—that is, loving their wives as Christ loved the Church and loving their wives as they care for their own bodies—are really one model after all.   **5:31–32**

Paul quotes Gen 2:24, a verse that explains the origin and meaning of marriage. In the second story of creation, after God takes a rib from the man and fashions the first woman, God presents her to the first man. Adam responds enthusiastically, "This one, at last, is bone of my bones / and flesh of my flesh; / This one shall be called 'woman,' / for out of 'her man' this one has been taken" (Gen 2:23). The narrator of the story in Genesis explains that this original oneness is the basis of marriage in the words that Paul now quotes: **For this reason a man shall leave [his] father and [his] mother / and be joined to his wife, / and the two shall become one flesh**. In this context (as in 5:29), the word "†flesh" means "body."[25] Thus Gen 2:24 and Eph 5:31 teach that marriage, consummated in sexual intercourse, unites the husband and wife as one entity, one body. Although they remain distinct persons, the two now share one life, they form one family, their interests and future well-being are profoundly intertwined; God has made them one (Mark 10:9).

This explains what Paul was really saying when he exhorted husbands to love their wives "as their own bodies." The two have become one. Just as Christ is the head of the Church, his body, so also the husband is the head of the wife, who is, metaphorically speaking, the "body" of her husband. Just as Christ "nourishes and cherishes" the Church (5:29) because "we are members of his body" (5:30), husbands should care for their wives in like manner, since "he who loves his wife loves himself" (5:28).

The meaning of Paul's statement that the husband is "head of the wife" in 5:23 becomes clearer in this light. The term "head" cannot be reduced to "authority over" in the way one might speak of the "head" of a government or department. Instead, when "head" is used with its metaphorical counterpart, "body," the emphasis shifts to the unity and complete community of interest of the two. What benefits the one benefits the other. What harms the one harms the other. Paul depicts the communion of persons of husband and wife "as if spouses also formed an organic union."[26] Paul does not say so explicitly, but a practical interdependence of husband and wife in marriage also follows from the head-body metaphor. The head cannot function without the body, nor the body without the head; dialogue and cooperation are their natural modes of being. The indissolubility of the marriage bond is likewise implicit: to separate head and body is to put an end to something living.[27] "Therefore, what God has joined together, no human being must separate" (Matt 19:6).

Paul explains that Gen 2:24 has always had a deeper meaning: **This is a great mystery, but I speak in reference to Christ and the church**. As mentioned above (see 3:3–5), †mystery refers to the once hidden plan of God that has now been revealed in Christ. Paul is saying that human marriage instituted at creation points to a reality greater than itself, namely, the marriage of Christ

25. Hebrew—the original language of Genesis—does not have a distinct word for "body," so it often uses the word for "flesh" when it means "body" (e.g., Lev 6:3; Num 19:7). This is why the NAB translates the Hebrew for "one flesh" in Gen 2:24 as "one body" whereas other translations provide the more literal rendering "one flesh." First Corinthians 6:16 confirms this, since Paul quotes Gen 2:24 to warn of the danger of becoming "one body" with a prostitute through sexual intercourse.

26. John Paul II in *TOB*, August 25, 1982, 479. In this section the pope describes the head-body metaphor as "*a supplementary analogy*" to that of bridegroom and bride for the relationship of Christ and the Church and husband and wife.

27. See Sumner, *Men and Women in the Church*, 164–67.

and the Church. What Gen 2:24 and marriage itself reveal to us about Christ and the Church is that the two become one, an indissoluble union of head and body, bridegroom and bride.

Paul's readers already know that the Church is the body of Christ and that all of them are members of his body (4:25; 5:30). The *way* they became members of Christ's body was sacramentally, by being baptized (1 Cor 12:12–13).[28] The *basis* for their being members of Christ's body was the Spirit of Christ living in them (see also Rom 8:9; 1 Cor 6:17, 19), consecrating them, and making their bodies an extension of his own. But in Eph 5:31 Paul reveals another, closely related basis on which the Church is the body of Christ—by being married to Jesus! Marriage brings about a one-body relationship. The Church is the body of Christ by virtue of being the Bride of Christ.

Finally, if we read Paul's exhortation to wives and husbands again, after the final piece has been inserted in the puzzle, we can also see that the loving spousal union of Christ and the Church in turn sheds light on the new reality of marriage in the Lord. Christian marriage derives its spiritual power from the act of sacrificial love by which Jesus redeemed, cleansed, and adorned his Bride. By living "in Christ" and being "filled with the Spirit," husbands and wives draw on the power of Christ's sacrifice to love and to subordinate themselves to each other.

Reflection and Application (5:23–32)

Marriage, a sacrament. Although the New Testament teaches about marriage in a variety of places, Eph 5:32 is the primary basis of the Church's recognition of Christian marriage as a sacrament.[29] Sacraments are "efficacious signs of grace, instituted by Christ and entrusted to the Church, by which divine life is dispensed to us" (Catechism 1131). How then is marriage "efficacious" and how does it dispense divine life?

Before the coming of Christ, God's purpose for marriage was often thwarted due to the hardness in human hearts (Mark 10:5), and for this reason the law of Moses permitted divorce (Deut 24:1). The good news is that in the New Covenant through the gift of the Spirit, Jesus removes our "stony hearts" (Ezek 36:25–27) and makes us capable of fulfilling God's will (Rom 8:4), including lifelong marriage. "By coming to restore the original order of creation disturbed

28. Paul also links being one body with receiving the Eucharist: 1 Cor 10:17.

29. The Vulgate translates *mysterion* ("mystery") in 5:32 as *sacramentum*: "this is a great sacrament." What the Western Church calls "sacraments," the Eastern churches call "mysteries" (see Catechism 774).

by sin, [Jesus] himself gives the strength and grace to live marriage in the new dimension of the Reign of God" (Catechism 1615).

How is this accomplished? When a woman and a man give their consent before the Church, when the Holy Spirit is invoked on the couple through prayers and blessings, "the spouses receive the Holy Spirit as the communion of love of Christ and the Church. The Holy Spirit is the seal of their covenant, the ever-available source of their love and the strength to renew their fidelity" (Catechism 1624, citing Eph 5:32). In other words, the husband and wife become participants in the love between Christ and the Church—they become capable in a new way of drawing on that powerful divine love that surpasses human strength.

The grace of the sacrament. If Christian marriage is a sacrament and communicates [†]grace, why do so many Christians divorce? As with all the sacraments, the efficacy and fruitfulness of the sacrament of matrimony depends on the dispositions of those who receive them. Christ always gives grace through the sacraments, but all too often we present obstacles to that grace.

For the grace of matrimony to be fully effective, we need the dispositions of a disciple: faith and obedience to the word of God. Both the husband and the wife need to live in a state of grace and to understand and follow the Lord's teaching about family life contained in Scripture and taught by the Church. Failing to grasp the oneness to which couples are called can contribute to divorce, especially if couples perceive Christ's teaching about the permanence of marriage merely as law. But when the eyes of their hearts are enlightened to recognize that God has united spouses to one another in a union like the oneness of Christ and the Church, the beauty and dignity of their calling can inspire courage and hope. In the context of Eph 5:18–20, being "subordinate to one another out of reverence for Christ" (5:21) is linked to being continually filled by the Spirit. For this reason, regular prayer, Scripture reading, and reception of the sacraments can help Christians persevere in the grace of matrimony. The maxim is true: "the family that prays together, stays together." The Catechism invites married people to discipleship: "It is by following Christ, renouncing themselves, and taking up their crosses that spouses will be able to 'receive' the original meaning of marriage and live it with the help of Christ" (1615, citing Matt 19:11). Christian marriage challenges both husband and wife to die to self.

Although Christ has made it possible to live the grace of lifelong marriage in this world, all too often Christian marriages fail. Our brothers and sisters in this situation deserve our compassion and love. Their suffering can spur us to do everything in our power to strengthen marriage and family life in the Church and in society.

Concluding Exhortation (5:33)

[33]In any case, each one of you should love his wife as himself, and the wife should respect her husband.

OT: Lev 19:18
NT: Matt 22:39; Eph 5:25, 28; 1 Pet 3:2, 7
Catechism: male and female equal in dignity, 369, 2203

In this verse Paul returns from his explanation about the spousal relation-   **5:33**
ship of Christ and the Church and resumes his original practical topic of how
Christian wives and husbands should relate to each other. Since he has been
addressing husbands in the previous section (5:25–32), he summarizes his
instruction first to them, and then to wives. Paul personalizes his instruction
to husbands—**each one of you**—and expresses their responsibility to care for
their wives in yet a third formulation. Having said that husbands are to love
their wives as Christ loved the Church (v. 25) and as they love their own bodies
(v. 28), Paul now says that every husband **should love his wife as himself**. This
follows logically from the fact that husband and wife are one. At the same time,
this guideline echoes Jesus' commandment to love one's neighbor as oneself
(Matt 22:39, based on Lev 19:18) and applies it to marriage. Like the gospel
instruction, this teaching does not command loving oneself but rather presupposes that people do so. It summons husbands to seek the same good for their
wives that they seek for themselves. A husband's love for his wife certainly differs
from the love he should show toward his neighbors, yet there is an underlying
similarity, namely, seeking the good of another as much as one's own.

Likewise, Paul varies his instruction to the wives slightly. Instead of urging
them to "be subordinate," he says that **the wife should respect her husband**.
The Greek word translated "respect" literally means to "fear," but in contexts
like this one it describes an attitude of respect toward someone over us (Luke
1:50; Rom 13:7; 1 Pet 2:17). The noun form of this word was used in reference
to Christ in 5:21 and was translated as "reverence."

Paul's summary repeats in slightly different words the ideas set forward in 5:22–
32: husbands are to love their wives; wives are to respect their husbands.

Reflection and Application (5:21–33)

Insights from Pope John Paul II. The pope teaches that the innovation the
gospel brings to the relationship of husbands and wives is the teaching of mutual

subordination, which introduces a new dynamic. Just as Paul's teaching that in Christ there is "neither slave nor free" eventually resulted in the abolition of slavery, so must the truth of mutual subordination of spouses, "and not just that of the wife to the husband[,] . . . gradually establish itself in hearts, consciences, behaviors and customs."[30] To be subject to one's spouse means to be completely given to her or to him. Mutual subordination entails a reciprocal gift of self that is sincere, unconditional, and lifelong.

According to John Paul II, the "essence of the love of a husband is to lay down his life for his bride." This kind of "love excludes every kind of submission by which the wife would become a servant or slave of the husband, an object of one-sided submission. Love makes the *husband simultaneously subject* to the wife, and *subject* in this *to the Lord himself,* as the wife is to the husband."[31] Ephesians 5:21–33 can be summed up as follows: "the Bridegroom is the one who loves. The Bride is loved: it is she who receives love, so as to love in return."[32] While both are called to love and to subordinate themselves to the other, the meaning imprinted in their bodies is for the husband to initiate the gift, and for the wife to receive the gift. Her subordinating herself means "the experiencing of love."[33] Both fundamental equality and the difference between men and women are grounded in God's creation of humanity in his image as male and female (Gen 1:27), a divinely intended complementarity. This human and embodied love of husband and wife reveals the divine love of God for the human race and of Christ for his Church.

Applying Paul's teaching today. Relations between men and women through-out history have been marred by a harmful dynamic that Gen 3:16 attributes to the Fall. Often men have used their power and position for their own benefit rather than for the good of those whose well-being was entrusted to them. Among Christians, a one-sided interpretation of Eph 5:22–24 that stressed the submission of wives but neglected mutual subordination and the sacrificial love of husbands has sometimes served to legitimate this sinful pattern. But Jesus' teaching about leadership turns the pyramid of power upside down: "Whoever wishes to be great among you shall be your servant; whoever wishes to be first among you shall be your slave. Just so, the Son of Man did not come to be served but to serve and to give his life as a ransom for many" (Matt 20:26–28).

In Eph 5:21–33 Paul applies Jesus' example to the role of the husband in marriage. The husband as head is to adopt an attitude of humble service and

30. *On the Dignity and Vocation of Women* 24.
31. *TOB*, August 11, 1982, 473–74.
32. *On the Dignity and Vocation of Women* 29.
33. *TOB*, September 1, 1982, 485.

to love his wife sacrificially. Nearly everyone agrees that this is how husbands should conduct themselves, even if practice falls far short of this ideal. Nearly everyone also agrees that Paul's teaching that wives should subordinate themselves to their husbands means something different in societies that have come to recognize the equality of men and women. Does it have any continuing relevance? Catholics hold a variety of opinions.

Some Catholics hold that Eph 5:22–24 no longer applies and adopt (often unwittingly) a secular feminist perspective that upholds the equality of women by denying or minimizing all but the most obvious physical differences between the sexes.[34] Couples influenced by this approach seek to divide parenting responsibilities, household tasks, and the world of work outside the home on a utilitarian basis without regard for gender differences.

Other Catholics emphasize that Paul's exhortation must be reinterpreted in the light of a deeper understanding of the equality of men and women, entailing a recognition that decision making needs to be by mutual agreement. Nevertheless, the creation of humanity in God's image as male and female (Gen 1:27) means that the distinction between the sexes has permanent significance. Although husband and wife are equal, their roles in the family are not identical. Those who take this approach maintain that family life and especially raising children are best served by complementary but flexible gender roles.

A third group considers Christlike servant leadership on the part of husbands and voluntary deference on the part of wives to be part of God's enduring plan for marriage.[35] While proponents of this view uphold the equality of women and reject the dependent status of women in the Greco-Roman world and the oppression of women in traditional societies, they believe that this pattern better reflects the sacrament of matrimony in which the husband symbolizes Christ and the wife symbolizes the Church in the mystery of redemption. At the same time, the analogy of head and body in "one flesh" underscores a profound union in marriage that expresses itself in mutual subordination and in decision making that is marked by respectful dialogue. Husbands view their role of presiding in

34. Some feminists take a more radical approach, viewing 5:22–24 and similar texts as patriarchal reassertions of the logic of power by later authors, subverting Paul's teaching in Gal 3:28. However, to reduce biblical texts to the will to power is to attribute to them an inspiration that is sinful rather than holy and is hard to reconcile with what the Catholic Church believes about the divine inspiration, unity, and trustworthiness of Sacred Scripture (see *Dei Verbum* 11 or Catechism 105–7).

35. In contrast to biblical teaching about slavery that offers no theological justification for the institution, biblical texts explain the order between husband and wife by reference to creation and the spousal imagery of God and Israel and Christ and the Church (see comments on 5:23–24). For a contemporary effort to retrieve traditional teaching, see St. John Chrysostom, *On Marriage and Family Life*, trans. Catherine Roth and David Anderson (Crestwood, NY: St. Vladimir's Seminary Press, 1997).

a relationship of equals as love and responsibility, not privilege and entitlement. Wives defer to their husbands with dignity, not servility; actively, not passively; thoughtfully, not blindly. Proponents of this view believe the positive experience of contemporary families seeking to implement Eph 5:21–33 in a holistic manner confirms the continuing validity of this teaching.[36]

Catholics who hold to both the second and third positions described above understand their approaches to be consistent with the teaching of Pope John Paul. Prior to the Second Vatican Council, church teaching on family life simply restated Paul's instruction regarding the responsibility of husbands to love their wives and wives to be subordinate to their husbands.[37] Since then, however, the Church's magisterium has approached this subject with sensitivity to the historic oppression of women, neither repeating nor retracting previous teaching, while expressing support for the positive points brought forth by the women's movement. Pope John Paul's extensive treatment of Eph 5:21–33 emphasizes the equal dignity of women, the mutual subordination of husband and wife, and the responsibility of husbands to love their wives sacrificially and to relate to them with respect. The pope clearly sees that traditional patterns need to be reformed, and he emphasizes this side of the issue. However, the pope insists on the irreducible differences between men and women and stresses the complementarity of male and female. Rather than reject the metaphor of the husband as head or the instruction that wives should be subordinate to their husbands, he interprets each in a way that prioritizes mutual submission, love, and oneness in marriage.

Immense changes have taken place in the roles of women and men in society and in the family over the last few decades, and the way Christians should respond is not always easy to discern. In the end, every married person needs to prayerfully consider what the Spirit is saying to him or her through Eph 5:21–33. Whatever one thinks about the contemporary relevance of the exhortation to wives to be subordinate to their husbands, wives and husbands alike are called to understand their respective roles in light of their oneness in Christ and the exemplary love of our heavenly bridegroom.

36. Catholic sociologist W. Bradford Wilcox reports and evaluates the outcomes of various approaches to this issue among Protestants in his book *Soft Patriarchs, New Men: How Christianity Shapes Fathers and Husbands* (Chicago: University of Chicago Press, 2004).
37. See Pope Pius XI's encyclical *Casti Connubi* (*On Christian Marriage*) par. 23, 26–28.

Children and Parents, Slaves and Masters

Ephesians 6:1–9

Paul continues his teaching about household relationships with exhortations to children, parents, slaves, and masters. His inspired counsel speaks to Christians today despite the immense distance in time and cultural setting.

I explained at the beginning of the previous chapter that scholars refer to Eph 5:21–6:9 as a "household code" because it resembles other ancient writings that offer guidelines for household relationships (see sidebar on p. 156). Nevertheless, this household code (like its close parallel in Col 3:18–4:1) differs from other examples in Greco-Roman and Jewish literature. First, as was noted, Paul introduces the entire section with the exhortation, "Be subordinate to one another out of reverence for Christ" (5:21), a teaching that radically alters the manner in which authority is to be exercised. Second, rather than address only heads of households like other household codes do, Paul speaks directly to wives, children, and slaves as free persons whom he invites to willingly subordinate themselves. He honors them by speaking to them *first*, before addressing those over them. Third, other household codes do not tell heads of households to be considerate toward those in their charge, as Paul does consistently. Finally, Paul's instructions to each of the six groups—wives, husbands, children, parents, slaves, and masters—make explicit reference to Christ, directing all parties to relate to one another in light of their relationship with Jesus.

Some scholars suggest that Paul is responding to pressure from women and slaves when he reasserts the traditional hierarchy in household relationships (albeit with some radical modifications). If this is true, Paul's matter-of-fact tone indicates that the problem was not severe. Others suggest that Paul's concern is public relations, namely, to show that Christians are orderly citizens and to avoid scandalizing the surrounding society. While a motive like this is mentioned in other passages (1 Tim 6:1–2; Titus 2:5–10; see 1 Pet 2:12–3:2), it is not evident in the household codes of Ephesians and Colossians.

Children and Parents (6:1–4)

[1]Children, obey your parents [in the Lord], for this is right. [2]"Honor your father and mother." This is the first commandment with a promise, [3]"that it may go well with you and that you may have a long life on earth." [4]Fathers, do not provoke your children to anger, but bring them up with the training and instruction of the Lord.

OT: Gen 18:19; Exod 20:12; Deut 5:16; 6:6–9, 20–25; Prov 6:20; 23:22; Sir 3:1–16
NT: Col 3:20–21; 2 Tim 3:15
Catechism: duties of children, 2214–20; duties of parents, 2221–30

6:1–3　　　Paul tells children to **obey** (*hypakouō*, literally, "hear under") their parents, an unqualified form of submission that entails both listening to teaching and following commands. By adding **in the Lord**,[1] Paul indicates that obedience to parents is a responsibility that children fulfill as an expression of their relationship with Jesus. Greco-Roman society also held that children owed obedience to parents. However, when Paul writes, **for this is right**, he was not merely saying this is fitting because it accords with conventional morality. The word he uses for "right," *dikaios*, means "righteous" or "just," which for Paul means conduct that conforms to God's will. He supports what he is saying by citing the law of Moses (Exod 20:12; Deut 5:16), **Honor your father and mother.** The early Christians, like the Jews, understood this fourth commandment to oblige children to remain under their parents' authority at least as long as they lived with them and to care for and respect parents in their old age (Sir 3:12–13; 1 Tim 5:8).[2]

Like any skilled Bible teacher, Paul calls his readers' attention to something in the text that they may not have noticed: **This is the first commandment with a promise.** For Paul, the Ten Commandments stood at the head of the

1. The NAB places these words in brackets because some ancient manuscripts do not include them. It is likely that these words were omitted from some manuscripts because their location in the sentence might leave the mistaken impression that only Christian parents were to be obeyed.
2. Peter T. O'Brien, *The Letter to the Ephesians*, Pillar New Testament Commentary (Grand Rapids: Eerdmans, 1999), 443.

Paul and the Law

Ephesians 6:2 is an example of how Paul assumes the continuing validity of the law of Moses as a guide to Christian conduct, provided that it is properly applied. Some people think Paul regarded the Old Testament law as obsolete because of his reference to Christ "abolishing the law with its commandments and legal claims" (2:15) or his firm insistence that we are justified by faith in Christ and not by "works of the law" (Rom 3:28; Gal 2:16). But Paul's position is more nuanced than that. In Romans he emphatically denies "annulling the law" (Rom 3:31) and says rather that the purpose of Jesus' death on the cross for sin and the gift of the Spirit is so "that the just requirement of the law might be fulfilled in us, who walk not according to the flesh but according to the Spirit" (Rom 8:4 RSV). The whole of the law is summed up in the commandment to love, which the Spirit enables us to fulfill (Rom 13:8; Gal 5:13–23).

In Paul, the law functions in several ways, including (1) to indicate the kind of conduct God approves, as in 6:2–3; (2) to identify patterns of conduct that God rejects (1 Tim 1:8–10); (3) to bring awareness of sin (Rom 7:7–9); and (4) to foreshadow things about Christ and Christian life (1 Cor 10:1–11).

---

many commandments (later numbered at six hundred thirteen) in the law of Moses. While many of these commandments and the law itself are accompanied by promises of God's blessing (Deut 28:1–14), there is obviously something special about the *first* promise: **that it may go well with you and that you may have a long life on earth.** The words "on earth" can be translated as "in the land" (NJB). Like Jesus (e.g., Luke 6:38), Paul does not hesitate to motivate his readers with the promise of a reward: a long and blessed life. Experience confirms that obeying parents and respectfully caring for them in their old age contributes to the well-being of families and even to the health and longevity of individuals. Experience also teaches, though, that not all who honor their parents live to a ripe old age, the martyrs being the clearest counter-examples. Nevertheless, Paul's restatement of this Old Testament promise encourages the hope of reward for right conduct.

All the promises of God find their "Yes" in Jesus (2 Cor 1:20). Those who honor their parents "in the Lord," in union with Christ, but who die early or suffer greatly in this life will not fail to receive "long life in the land," understood as a †type of eternal life in the kingdom of God (Matt 5:5; Rom 4:13; see sidebar on p. 43). God's promises of blessing for covenant faithfulness like this one and Jesus' promises of reward for disciples are certain and will not fail. But only God knows which promises and rewards will be granted to an individual in this life and which will come to pass in his eternal kingdom (see Mark 10:29–30).

6:4   As Paul turns his attention to the responsibilities of parents, he focuses on **Fathers**. Fathers, according to Roman law, had virtually absolute power over their children and very few obligations. But "in the Lord" both parents and children have responsibilities. Paul instructs fathers about what they should do and what they should not do. He begins by saying, **do not provoke your children to anger**. Some fathers may have been tempted to exercise authority over their children in a manner that was inconsiderate, disrespectful, or self-serving. Or perhaps Paul aims to restrain the tendency of some fathers to place excessive demands on their children out of a desire to help them achieve. Earlier, Paul warns about the danger of holding on to anger (4:26–27) and of venting it unrestrainedly (4:31). Here he warns against *provoking* anger, perhaps concerned that fathers not exasperate their children by unreasonable discipline or restraint.

Positively, Paul instructs fathers (and we should include mothers as well), **bring them up with the training and instruction of the Lord.**[3] The phrase "of the Lord" means "of Jesus." Parents' greatest responsibility is to form their children as disciples of Jesus. "Training," *paideia*, refers to the whole process of education and formation in life, including "discipline," the word used here by most English translations.[4] "Instruction," however, refers more to admonition or correction.[5] Here Paul is saying that parents are responsible to correct and discipline their children, a consistent theme of the wisdom literature (e.g., Prov 13:24; 19:18).

Paul presupposes that his readers, whether Jewish or †Gentile, are familiar with the Old Testament teaching about the obligation of parents to speak the word of God to their children. It is found in the Shema (Deut 6:4–9), a prayer that includes the great commandment about loving God that devout Jews pray daily. After enjoining Israelites to love God "with all your heart, and with all your soul, and with all your strength" (Deut 6:5), Moses tells parents to drill these words of God's law into their children. "Speak of them at home and abroad, whether you are busy or at rest" (Deut 6:7). The end of Deut 6 elaborates on this instruction, directing parents to explain to their children that the

---

3. The NJB paraphrases: "correction and advice inspired by the Lord." The JB is similar: "correct them and guide them as the Lord does."

4. Some typical texts that speak of "training" include Prov 1:7–8; Wis 1:5; Heb 12:7–11.

5. Other texts that use this term include Wis 16:6; 1 Cor 10:11; Titus 3:10.

commandments were given them by God after he saved them from slavery in Egypt and that they hold out the promise of a "prosperous and happy . . . life" (Deut 6:24) if Israel continues to keep them. The Ephesian Christians, whom God saved from slavery to sin, Satan, and death (see 2:1–7), would have understood that the Old Testament commandments and promises, interpreted in the light of the Christ, applied also to them as they do to us.

Reflection and Application (6:1–4)

Although the relationship between children and parents has shifted considerably in the modern world, children still have an obligation to obey their parents, at least as long as they are minors, and to care for them in their old age. Parents still need to be careful not to place unreasonable demands on their children.

For Catholic parents in the twenty-first century the crucial point here is the responsibility to raise their children in the Lord and to discipline them when they need it. Strong cultural pressures oppose fulfillment of these basic responsibilities, and Christians need to avail themselves of all the resources available to hold their ground. Secular experts seek to dissuade Christian parents from "imposing" their values on their children. The mass media and public education often aggressively promote a rival worldview to that of Scripture and inculcate an approach to morality deeply at odds with that of the Church. Catholic schools and parish programs that catechize children can play an important role, but parents remain the primary religious educators of their children. Parents will find much that is useful for their parenting by reading Proverbs and Sirach alongside the Gospels and Epistles.

Many Catholic parents understand the value of introducing their children to the liturgy, the sacraments, the Catechism, the saints, and the rosary. Far fewer understand the importance of introducing children to the Bible. Deuteronomy 6 presents a program for raising children in "the training and instruction of the Lord." First, parents themselves are to love God with their whole hearts and to cherish the word of God (Deut 6:5–6). Second, parents can learn to talk about God's word with their children and to establish family customs that underscore the importance and holiness of Scripture. Deuteronomy recommends writing it "on the doorposts of your houses" and wrapping it around "your wrist" and "your forehead" (Deut 6:6–9), practices that devout Jews observe literally. Third, parents can find ways to train ("drill," Deut 6:7) their children in God's word, for example, reading them Bible stories, teaching them to memorize verses, and, when they are old enough, reading and discussing Scripture as a family.

Finally, parents can make use of the annual feasts that celebrate our salvation—especially Christmas, Easter, and Pentecost—and the occasions when family members receive the sacraments as teachable moments to explain Catholic faith from the Bible (Deut 6:20–25; see Exod 13:14–15).

Slaves and Masters (6:5–9)

⁵**Slaves, be obedient to your human masters with fear and trembling, in sincerity of heart, as to Christ, ⁶not only when being watched, as currying favor, but as slaves of Christ, doing the will of God from the heart, ⁷willingly serving the Lord and not human beings, ⁸knowing that each will be requited from the Lord for whatever good he does, whether he is slave or free. ⁹Masters, act in the same way towards them, and stop bullying, knowing that both they and you have a Master in heaven and that with him there is no partiality.**

OT: Lev 25:38–55; Job 31:13–15
NT: 2 Cor 5:10; Col 3:22–4:1; 1 Tim 6:1–2; Titus 2:9–10; Philem 1:15–16
Catechism: value of work, 2427; equal dignity, 1934; human solidarity, 1939–42; slavery prohibited, 2414, 2424

Slavery was a fact of life in the Roman Empire of Paul's day. Although there was debate about how slaves ought to be treated, no one questioned whether slavery should exist, and even the occasional slave insurrections were not aimed at abolishing slavery. Paul and other New Testament authors were not in a position to eradicate this institution, although their teaching eventually led to its undoing (see sidebar on p. 186). The Reflection and Application section will consider an analogous application of this text to Christian life today.

6:5–6   Slaves are instructed to **be obedient**—the same strong word used in the instruction for children—to their **human masters . . . as to Christ**. To obey "as to Christ" is a very high standard, and Paul will repeat this idea three times in as many verses (vv. 6, 7, 8). In addition, he describes this obedience in few vivid phrases. First, he says **with fear and trembling**, a biblical expression that refers to reverence before God or to humans whom God has placed in authority (see 2 Cor 7:15; Phil 2:12). In addition, the service of slaves should be offered not merely in a way that only appears to be good—**not only when being watched, as currying favor**. Rather, their service should be well-motivated **in sincerity of heart** and **from the heart**. This is extraordinary. Why should slaves, obliged to serve against their will, give their masters whole-hearted service? Paul gives a

Slavery in the Roman Empire

BIBLICAL BACKGROUND

The economy of the Roman Empire was based on slave labor. About one third of the people living in the empire at that time were slaves. Slavery was not based on race. Rather, people became slaves by owing debts they were unable to repay, by being captured as prisoners of war, or, most commonly in the first century, by being born slaves. The status and living conditions of slaves varied depending on their work and the status of their masters. Some slaves mainly did manual work, especially farm labor; others were trained for responsible roles as craftsmen, physicians, architects, scribes, and teachers.

Slaves were considered the personal property of their owners and were thus subject to beatings and even death at the hands of their masters. Slaves had some rights. They could marry, but their offspring belonged to their masters. They could also acquire money or property and even buy their own freedom. It was the ordinary practice for masters to free slaves after some years of service, although these freed persons usually retained some obligations of service to their masters. Slavery in the Roman Empire was not a benign institution, but it was nevertheless more humane than the European and American enslavement of Africans from the fifteenth to the nineteenth centuries.

remarkable answer, indicating that the Christian slaves in Ephesus were **slaves of Christ**. To be a slave of God or of Christ is not a matter of shame but of honor. Scripture refers to Moses as a slave of God (1 Kings 8:53; Neh 10:30; Dan 9:11), Paul describes himself as a slave of Christ (Rom 1:1; Gal 1:10; Titus 1:1), and Revelation refers to †prophets, martyrs, and all Christians this way (Rev 2:20; 10:7; 19:2; 22:6).[6] Christians can be called slaves of Christ because we were purchased by his blood (1 Cor 6:19–20; 7:22; Rev 5:9) and belong to him. Furthermore, the slaves Paul addresses are **doing the will of God**. In other words, Christian slaves fulfill God's will and serve Christ by serving their masters, even though their work has no explicit Christian or ministerial dimension and even though they did not choose this service. Identifying oneself as a slave of Christ, called to whole-hearted service, is a spiritual attitude that can benefit any Christian bound to a task he or she did not choose.

Paul indicates the attitude slaves should take: **willingly serving the Lord and not human beings**. They are to do their work voluntarily, offering it as service

6:7–8

---

6. Most translations say "servant" rather than "slave," but it is the same Greek word used in 6:6, *doulos*.

The Bible on Slavery

Although slaveholders in the United States used biblical texts to defend the institution of slavery, this was an abuse of Scripture. The Old Testament presupposes slavery as a fact of life in the ancient Near East and regulates it in Israel to render it more humane. The law of Moses commands that slaves be given the sabbath as a day of rest and explains to owners, "Remember that you too were once slaves in Egypt" (Deut 5:14–15), helping them to identify with their slaves. Israelite slaves received special protections: their servitude was limited to six years, after which they were to be set free and provided means to live (Deut 15:12–15). In contrast to the worldviews of other ancient religions, the Old Testament does not depict slaves as inferior to free persons in God's eyes.

Paul's direction for slaves was to render faithful service to their masters in accord with the norms of the day. Although he generally recommends that "everyone should remain in the state in which he was called," on one occasion he suggests that slaves avail themselves of the opportunity for freedom if it should come their way (1 Cor 7:20–21). In another instance, Paul urges Philemon, a church leader, to welcome his runaway slave, Onesimus, "no longer as a slave but more than a slave, a brother," perhaps hinting at emancipation (Philem 15–17, 21). Although in society the difference between a slave and a free person was great, in the Church both were of equal standing, full members of the body of Christ (Gal 3:28; Col 3:11). Although the early Church was in no position to change such a fundamental structure of society, key Christian teachings had the long-term effect of revealing what was wrong with slavery. Christian teaching about the creation of human beings in God's image, the oneness and equality of all in Christ, the commandment regarding love of neighbor (Lev 19:18; Luke 10:27), and the Golden Rule (Luke 6:31; also Matt 7:12) inevitably undermined slavery's foundations.

to the †Lord Jesus and not merely to human masters. The result is that they will be rewarded as servants of Christ for what they are doing: **knowing that each will be requited from the Lord for whatever good he does**. "Requited" has a negative connotation that is not intended here. The RSV is clearer: "knowing that whatever good any one does, he will receive the same again from the Lord." No good deed will go unrewarded. The slave owner may not notice or compensate the slave, but Jesus is going to pay back the slave in full. Paul's assurance builds on a basic point of the kerygma, the proclamation of the gospel: Jesus will one day judge every human (Acts 10:42; 17:31; John 5:22), **whether he is slave or free**. The basis of that judgment will be what people have done, their works, as

Paul and the rest of the New Testament teach (John 5:29; Rom 2:6; 2 Cor 5:10). He will reward slaves who have done their work well for his sake.

Then Paul says something very counter-cultural: **Masters, act in the same**   **6:9** **way towards them**. This recalls the exhortation to mutual subordination in 5:21, "Be subordinate to one another out of reverence for Christ." Paul does not literally mean that masters are to obey their slaves. But the Apostle is saying that Christian slave owners should treat their slaves in a considerate manner that Jesus will find acceptable. Specifically this means they are to **stop bullying**, literally, "refrain from threats." In the Greco-Roman world masters often controlled their slaves through fear: "Owners were known to threaten beatings, sexual harassment, or selling male slaves away from the households with the result that they would be parted forever from their loved ones."[7] Paul reminds slave owners of the fundamentally equal status they share with their slaves: **knowing that both they and you have a Master in heaven and that with him there is no partiality**. In other words, masters will themselves be judged by their master Christ on the basis of their conduct, and this judge treats masters and slaves the same.

Reflection and Application (6:5–9)

Employees and employers. While the economic system of the Roman Empire was very different from that of our world, today as then, some people work for other people.

Paul's essential message to slaves was to do a good and conscientious job out of love for Christ, since Jesus will compensate them for whatever they do. If this is true of slaves who did not agree to their servitude, how much more ought employees to do good work for those whom they have agreed to serve? If a slave plowing the ground was serving Christ through his labor, is not the same true for teachers, computer programmers, and secretaries who work for secular employers? How much more for those of us who work for the Church! Employers can be unfair or make poor decisions. Yet the Christian employee's responsibility is to do what the boss says (provided it is not morally wrong), offering whatever feedback is allowed, and to render faithful service as long as he or she remains at that job.

Paul's exhortation to slave owners applies also to employers. They are to act considerately toward their employees and pay an adequate wage. They also must not bully their subordinates or otherwise use their authority as if it were their

7. O'Brien, *Ephesians*, 454.

John Paul II on Slavery

LIVING
TRADITION

On February 22, 1992, Pope John Paul visited a former holding place for slaves on Gorée, an island off the coast of Senegal, from which thousands of Africans were transported to the Americas under appalling conditions. The pope offered this reflection:

> The visit to the "slave house" recalls to mind that enslavement of black people which in 1462 Pius II . . . described as the "enormous crime," the "magnum scelus." Throughout a whole period of the history of the African continent, black men, women, and children were brought to this cramped space, uprooted from their land and separated from their loved ones to be sold as goods . . . [as] victims of a disgraceful trade in which people who were baptized, but who did not live their faith, took part. How can we forget the enormous suffering inflicted, the violation of the most basic human rights, on those people deported from the African continent? How can we forget the human lives destroyed by slavery?
>
> This sin of man against man, this sin of man against God, must be confessed. How far the human family still has to go until its members learn to look at and respect one another as God's image, in order to love one another as sons and daughters of their common heavenly Father![a]

a. Joel S. Panzer, *The Popes and Slavery* (New York: Alba House, 1996), 118–19.

personal prerogative. Those who are owners, chief executives, or managers must not consider themselves superior but conduct themselves as servant leaders, knowing that the position they hold was given them by God for the common good. They must not forget that they too have a "boss" to whom they will one day give an account for how they treated the people who worked for them.

A Summons to Spiritual Battle

Ephesians 6:10–24

The letter to the Ephesians is a very polished piece of writing and closes with a powerful conclusion. In classical †rhetoric the end of a speech, called the *peroratio*, has the goal of summing up what has gone before and summoning the listeners to act on what they have heard. Ephesians 6:10–20 is exactly that kind of conclusion. Paul's farewell greetings follow in 6:21–24.

The topic of Paul's concluding remarks is spiritual warfare, the Christian struggle against the work of the devil. This conflict is an important theme in the New Testament (see sidebar on p. 191) that appears in Jesus' temptation by the devil, his ministry of casting out demons, the final petition of the Lord's Prayer, and Satan's activity in Jesus' death (Luke 22:3; John 13:2, 27). Paul's letters and Acts are sprinkled with numerous references to Satan's opposition to Christians and to the spread of the gospel.[1] James 4:7 and 1 Pet 5:8–9 exhort Christians to resist the devil. Likewise the book of Revelation gives special emphasis to the conflict between Christians and the agents of the devil. Although it could seem to be a new theme in this epistle, the conflict with evil spiritual forces has been touched on in nearly every chapter of Ephesians.[2]

Saint Paul's words here should be read like those of a general to his troops before a battle: the purpose of his words is to inspire, strengthen, and guide the attitudes and actions of his soldiers for what lies immediately ahead. Or to use a more familiar comparison, Paul's words are like those of a football coach at halftime whose team is ahead by a large margin (because of Christ's victory).

---

1. E.g., Acts 13:10; 16:16–18; 26:18; Rom 16:20; 1 Cor 7:5; 2 Cor 2:11; 11:14; 12:7; 1 Thess 2:18; 2 Thess 2:9; 1 Tim 3:6–7; 5:15; 2 Tim 2:26.
2. Eph 1:21; 2:2; 3:10; 4:27; and possibly 5:16.

Nevertheless, each player must play hard and remain vigilant because the game is not over yet and the opposing side is crafty and capable.

The Enemy, the Objective, the Strategy (6:10–12)

[10]Finally, draw your strength from the Lord and from his mighty power. [11]Put on the armor of God so that you may be able to stand firm against the tactics of the devil. [12]For our struggle is not with flesh and blood but with the principalities, with the powers, with the world rulers of this present darkness, with the evil spirits in the heavens.

NT: John 12:31; Rom 13:11–14; 1 Cor 16:13; Eph 1:19–22; Col 1:13; 2 Tim 2:1
Catechism: diabolical activity, 395; Jesus defeats Satan, 550; battle with the powers of evil, 409, 1707, 2015
Lectionary: 6:10–13, 18: Common of Holy Men and Women

As in any good motivational speech, Paul's concluding exhortation is full of verbs in the †imperative—it is a call to action. In the opening section, he makes clear that our *opponents* are the devil and the evil spiritual forces under his authority, that the *objective* is to stand firm, and that the *strategy* is to get the power we need from Jesus by putting on God's armor.

6:10–11   Paul signals that he is concluding: **Finally**, he exhorts his readers, **draw your strength from the Lord**. Paul's wording in Greek expresses this command with a †passive verb (literally, "be strengthened in the Lord")[3] to indicate that it is not a matter of the readers exercising their own strength but a matter of relying on Christ to strengthen them. The way we do this has been stated many times in this letter: by knowing that we are "in Christ" (1:3–14), by growing up "in every way into him who is the head" (4:15), and by putting on "the new self" (4:24), which is Christ. This unites us to **his mighty power**, the same words used in 1:19 to refer to God's power that raised Jesus from the dead and exalted him above all other powers. To do this requires a deliberate choice to **Put on**, to clothe oneself with, Christlike attitudes and actions that Paul now describes as **the armor of God**. Other translations catch the nuance of the Greek for "armor" (*panoplia*) by describing it as the "full," "complete," or "whole armor of God." Christians are to be fully armed with both defensive and offensive equipment.

Paul now explains the first strategic objective in this conflict—**so that you may be able to stand firm**. We do not put the devil to flight or crush demonic

3. Most translations say simply, "Be strong in the Lord."

Christians and the Devil

While the Old Testament depiction of spiritual evil is somewhat vague, the New Testament presents a clearer picture. As in Judaism, there is no question of dualism—the erroneous view that God and the evil power are equal. God is absolutely supreme. However, Satan has gained power over the human race (Gen 3:15; John 12:31; Eph 2:2; 1 John 5:19) because of sin. Jesus defeated Satan by his victory over temptation in the wilderness, by his ministry of healing and exorcism, and above all by his death on the cross (John 12:31; Col 2:15). The Church functions as the vanguard of the kingdom of God and a protected zone where Christians live in union with Christ and with one another. To be outside Christ's Church is to be vulnerable to Satan's power (1 Cor 5:4–5; Col 1:13; 1 Tim 1:20). Christians are capable of living free from the domination of Satan and his demonic agents, although this freedom is not automatic or uncontested. It depends on Christians maintaining their union with Christ and resisting the devil (James 4:7; 1 Pet 5:8–9).

Jesus describes Satan as having malice against the human race and seeking to destroy it (John 8:44; 10:10). The devil is "the father of lies" (John 8:44), the source of false teaching (2 Cor 11:3–4; 1 Tim 4:1), and the deceiver of the world (Rev 12:9). The New Testament portrays the devil as not only tempting people to sin but opposing God's people in other ways. The Gospels portray demons as the cause of some physical (Luke 13:11) and mental illnesses (Mark 5:2–5). In other biblical books, Satan is the accuser of God's people and charges humans with sin in the presence of God (Job 1:8–11; 2:3–5; Rev 12:10). He works to undermine solidarity among humans through slander, gossip, and anger (2 Cor 2:11; 1 Tim 3:7) and to hinder evangelization (Acts 13:10; 2 Cor 4:3–4; 1 Thess 2:18). The devil is closely associated with death and is responsible for holding humans in bondage through the fear of death (Heb 2:14–15). Satan was at work in Judas and the others who conspired to bring about Jesus' death (John 13:2, 27; 1 Cor 2:8), and he continues to inspire the persecution of Christians (Rev 12:17). Satan will be active in the final assault against Christians by the antichrist, who will combine oppressive political power with religious deception (2 Thess 2:3–12; Rev 13:1–8). (See sidebar on p. 93.)

powers underfoot. Defeating Satan is God's work and has been accomplished through the death and resurrection of Christ. Our first concern must be to defend the territory that Christ has won in our lives. To do so we must be on guard **against the tactics of the devil**, his "wiles" (NRSV and RSV) or "schemes" (NIV). The danger is not that Satan will overwhelm us with his power but that we will be deceived or tricked by him.

6:12   The reason we need divine power and divine equipment is that **our struggle is not with flesh and blood**. The Greek word for "struggle" here is a wrestling term, indicating the up-close and personal nature of the conflict. Yet this struggle is not primarily against human opponents or even our own human weakness but against the demonic ranks that exercise power in the †world (2:2). Paul has already mentioned **the principalities** and **the powers** in Ephesians (1:21), and now he adds **the world rulers**—this is either a description of what these powers do or another rank not mentioned elsewhere in the Bible. Scripture gives only a little information and is not systematic in classifying demonic ranks (see sidebar on p. 93). Paul considered it sufficient to affirm that these beings are under the power of the devil and serving his purposes. They exercise power in this world in the **present** age, characterized by moral and spiritual **darkness**.[4] The nature of all these beings is indicated by the final phrase, **the evil spirits in the heavens**.[5] They are aligned with evil; their power and influence over earthly events is indicated spatially by their location "in the †heavens."

Reflection and Application (6:10–12)

The idea of spiritual warfare is at odds with the secular worldview that denies the existence of supernatural beings and therefore their involvement in human affairs. While this denial sometimes claims to be scientific, science is incapable of offering evidence against the existence of spiritual beings, since the scientific method considers only physical, material, and social causes. The discovery of a biological cause of an illness, for example, does not exclude the possibility that the devil could also be at work, just as the use of medicine does not exclude that God is at work in the cure (Sir 38:1–14). Psychological and social disorders can likewise have both natural and spiritual causes. A holistic Christian outlook can both recognize the genuine contributions of science in understanding physical causes and, by the light of divine revelation and Christian experience, can discern and overcome evil spiritual forces at work in our world.

The experience of evil leads even many secular people to suspect that there is something wrong with the world that is bigger than the sum total of human failures. Sometimes this comes through personal experiences of spiritual evil or sometimes through reflecting on history and current events. After the senseless mass murder of thirty-two students at Virginia Tech University in 2007,

---

4. It is not clear why the JB offers the following: "the Powers who originate the darkness in this world."

5. The RSV adds "hosts," not found in the Greek: "the spiritual hosts of wickedness in the heavenly places."

Newsweek journalists commented, "Somehow, somewhere, someone planted an evil seed in Cho [the perpetrator]—if not the Devil himself."[6] Or to take another example, how else could Nazism have arisen and the horrors of the Holocaust occurred in one of the most educated and cultured nations of the twentieth century?

The opposite error to denying the existence of spiritual evil is superstition and fear that sees the devil everywhere. The correct path is to be guided by Scripture's sober and modest presentation, interpreted in the light of the Church's experience over the centuries.

Some people object to Scripture's warfare imagery in these verses because it seems inconsistent with the "peace" Christ preached (2:17). Paul, however, makes very clear that the enemy is demonic, not human. The New Testament provides ample guidance about the Christian attitude toward human adversaries: "Love your enemies, and pray for those who persecute you" (Matt 5:44; see also Rom 12:14–21). No biblical warrant exists for Christian violence against persecutors. Rather, the human capacity for warfare finds its truly appropriate object in the devil and evil spirits. The Christian tradition gives this spiritual interpretation to the fiercest of the Psalms and other Old Testament warfare texts.

The Armor of God (6:13–17)

> [13]Therefore, put on the armor of God, that you may be able to resist on the evil day and, having done everything, to hold your ground. [14]So stand fast with your loins girded in truth, clothed with righteousness as a breastplate, [15]and your feet shod in readiness for the gospel of peace. [16]In all circumstances, hold faith as a shield, to quench all [the] flaming arrows of the evil one. [17]And take the helmet of salvation and the sword of the Spirit, which is the word of God.

OT: Wis 5:17–20; Isa 11:4–5; 49:2; 52:7; 59:17
NT: 2 Cor 10:3–5; 1 Thess 5:8; Heb 4:12; 1 Pet 1:13
Catechism: deliver us from evil, 2850–54; faith, 1814–16; Scripture as strength for our faith, 131–33

In this section Paul exhorts his readers to stand firm and to arm themselves with the proper equipment, namely, the armor of God. Then he singles out six pieces of a soldier's equipment and makes each represent an attitude or practice that will enable Christians to prevail in the spiritual battle.

---

6. Evan Thomas et al., "Making of a Massacre," *Newsweek*, April 30, 2007, 24.

6:13   In light of the powerful enemy that stands against us and the need to hold our ground, Paul repeats his exhortation: **put on the armor of God**. As a prisoner in chains, Paul would have been familiar with the armaments of the Roman soldiers, and his audience would have also pictured the gear of Roman soldiers. The term "armor" includes not only protective gear that shields the soldier from harm but also offensive weapons.[7] The "armor of God" recalls two passages from Isaiah. The first (Isa 11:1–10) depicts the †Messiah clothed with God's attributes of justice and faithfulness, acting to rescue God's beleaguered people (see Isa 10:24–34), to destroy the wicked, to gather Israel, to draw the †Gentiles, and to establish the reign of God in a renewed creation. The second (Isa 59:14–21) depicts God himself armed as a warrior fighting on behalf of his people.[8]

To clothe oneself with God's armor means to embrace attitudes and actions that unite Christians with the victorious Messiah. The goal is **to resist** Satan's attacks—the same word found in James 4:7 and 1 Pet 5:9—and **to hold your ground** (literally, "to stand") when all is said and done. The **evil day** is any occasion in which the devil comes to tempt or to try Christians, whether in the present or at the final time of trial[9] that will precede Christ's return.

6:14–15   In detailing the equipment that he exhorts his readers to put on, Paul reinforces teaching given earlier in the letter regarding attitudes and conduct that are fitting for Christians. Scholarly interpretations of what Paul intends by each piece of equipment vary. Rather than discuss all the possibilities, I will interpret each piece of armor in a manner that is both grounded in the text and practical for Christian life.

Paul again says, **stand fast**. The Greek verb "to stand," used four times in various forms in 6:11–14, is an important word in Paul for describing what Christians are called to do.[10] The first three pieces of equipment cover parts of the body: from the waist down, from the waist up, and the feet. Paul exhorts his readers to have their **loins girded in truth**, alluding to a leather apron sol-

7. Paul often uses images of weapons or armor to describe Christian life or the ministry of apostles: Rom 13:12–14; 2 Cor 6:7; 10:3–5; 1 Thess 5:8. In his use of this metaphor, Paul does not aim at completeness or precision regarding a Roman soldier's equipment.

8. Although Isa 59:15–17 describes "the LORD" (i.e., God) as the one who takes up arms, it is likely that Paul understands this to refer to Jesus, since he interprets Isa 59:20 this way in Rom 11:26. Another Old Testament text that speaks of the Lord arming himself as a warrior is Wis 5:17–22.

9. See Matt 24:9–25; Luke 21:12; 2 Thess 2:3–12; 1 John 2:18; Catechism 675–77.

10. Here translated "stand firm" (v. 11), "resist" (v. 13), "hold your ground" (v. 13), and "stand fast" (v. 14). Other Pauline references to standing include Rom 5:2; 11:20; 1 Cor 10:12; 15:1; Gal 5:1; Phil 1:27–28; 4:1; Col 4:12; 1 Thess 3:8; 2 Thess 2:15. Andrew T. Lincoln, *Ephesians*, Word Biblical Commentary (Waco: Word, 1990), 447, lists these and others.

diers wrapped around their waist to protect their midsection and thighs.[11] The wording is very close to the †Septuagint of Isa 11:5, which describes how the Messiah dresses himself as he prepares for war: "His loins will be girded with righteousness and his sides clothed with truth" (my translation). In the Bible the same word can be translated either faithfulness or truth.[12] This is the fifth time that Paul has mentioned truth in Ephesians (1:13; 4:15, 21, 25), referring both to the truth of the †gospel and to truthful conduct. The first step in arming ourselves for spiritual combat is to wrap ourselves in the truth of the gospel and to be truthful in all we say and do.

Next, Christians are to put on **righteousness as a breastplate**. The Roman breastplate was a piece of metal armor that protected the heart and lungs from arrows, spears, knives, and swords. Isaiah 59:17 describes the †Lord putting on a breastplate of righteousness when he comes to judge wickedness and save those who turn from evil.[13] God metaphorically dons the breastplate of righteousness to reveal that his saving action reflects his justice. Christians, however, are **clothed with** (literally, have "put on") "righteousness" to protect their chests, metaphorically speaking, from being pierced by the devil. Although Paul sometimes uses "righteousness" to refer to the right standing with God that is ours through faith (especially in Romans), here he uses it to mean "upright conduct." In 4:20–24 Paul reminded his readers they were taught to "put on the new self, created in God's way in righteousness." To put on the breastplate of righteousness is to conduct oneself justly in a manner consistent with the new self.

Third, Paul tells Christians to have **your feet shod in readiness for the gospel of peace**. Roman soldiers sometimes wore military sandals and sometimes a half-boot, not to shield their feet from blows but to equip them for traveling great distances. Rather than identify a specific kind of footwear, Paul wants his readers to recall Isa 52:7:

> How beautiful upon the mountains
>> are the feet of him who brings glad tidings,
>> Announcing peace, bearing good news,
>>> announcing salvation, and saying to Zion,
>>> "Your God is King!"

11. Some English translations use the word "belt" in their translation of 6:14, but no such word is present in the Greek text.

12. The Hebrew word is *emet*; the Greek word is *alētheia*. Both can be used either for the accuracy of a statement or for reliability in a relationship.

13. See also Wis 5:18; Isa 11:5.

Just as the Messiah came proclaiming good news of peace (2:14–18), all Christians are also called to evangelize, whether at home, at school, at work, or traveling on mission. First Peter 3:15 places the same accent on "readiness": "Always be ready to give an explanation to anyone who asks you for a reason for your †hope." Speaking the gospel to others is an important part of the spiritual warfare that has both defensive and offensive aspects. Sharing the good news strengthens our own faith, while simultaneously shining the light of God's truth in the darkness (5:13–14).

Fig. 11. Stone relief from Ephesus of a gladiator fully armed as a soldier.

6:16–17   Next comes one of the most important items of defensive armor: **In all circumstances, hold faith as a shield, to quench all [the] flaming arrows of the evil one**. Roman soldiers carried a large shield, four feet tall and two and a half feet wide, to protect the whole body against arrows and spears. This shield was made of wood covered with thick leather. The leather was sometimes soaked in water to quench arrows tipped with flaming pitch. In the Bible, God is often described as the shield of his people (Gen 15:1; Ps 5:13; 18:3, 31, 36), and in Ps 91:4 God's faithfulness is described as a shield. In urging his readers to take up the shield of faith, Paul is summoning Christians to believe firmly in God and in his word, especially when under attack. The "flaming arrows of the evil one" refer to all the devil's assaults, whether external (persecution or trial) or internal (e.g., temptations to doubt, despair, or fear). This is the same counsel given in 1 Pet 5:8–9—to resist the devil, "steadfast in faith."

Paul next exhorts his readers to **take the helmet of salvation**. Roman soldiers wore a helmet of bronze to protect their heads from fatal blows. In Isa 59:17 the Lord wears "salvation, as the helmet on his head." In God's case, the helmet of "salvation" is not needed for protection but to reveal his identity: he is the one who brings salvation. The Greek verb translated "take" (*dechomai*) may also be rendered "receive." For Paul's readers, receiving this piece of armor means putting their hope in God to save them, to don "the helmet that is hope for salvation" (1 Thess 5:8).[14] That a helmet protects the head is perhaps intended

---

14. The following Old Testament texts describe the attitude Paul is recommending: Ps 25:5; 42:6, 12; 43:5; 119:81; Isa 33:2; Mic 7:7.

The Word of God Drives Out Sin and Demons

St. Thomas Aquinas explains "the sword of the Spirit" as follows:

The third function of weapons is for attacking. For not only must one defend oneself, but it is also necessary to attack the enemy. Just as in bodily warfare this is accomplished by a sword, so also is this accomplished by the word of God, which is, spiritually, the sword of the Spirit which you must take up. As it says in Hebrews 4:12, "For the word of God is living and active, sharper than any two-edged sword, and piercing through to the division between soul and spirit, joints and marrow; discerning the purposes and thoughts of the heart." Thus preaching is called the sword of the Spirit because it cannot reach the human spirit unless it is wielded by the Holy Spirit: "It will not be you speaking but the Spirit of your Father who is speaking in you" (Matt 10:20). . . .

Thus we have weapons for fighting the demons themselves, namely, the sword of the Spirit which is the word of God. This happens frequently in sermons in which the word of God, penetrating the hearts of sinners, drives out the tangled mass of sins and demons.[a]

a. *Commentary on Ephesians*, excerpt on Eph 6:13–17; trans. Francis Martin, unpublished manuscript.

---

as an encouragement to guard our minds with hope for the future, confident that God will act to save us.

Christians must also take **the sword of the Spirit, which is the word of God**. This is the first and only mention of an offensive weapon on this list. Roman soldiers used a short sword for hand-to-hand combat. In Isa 11:4 we are told that the Spirit-filled Messiah "shall strike the ruthless with the rod of his mouth, / and with the breath of his lips he shall slay the wicked"—in other words, he overcomes his enemies simply by speaking a word of power. Paul alludes to this text in 2 Thess 2:8 in describing Jesus' victory over the antichrist, "the lawless one." Revelation 19:15 describes Jesus' victory over evil at his second coming with similar imagery: "Out of his mouth came a sharp sword to strike the nations."

But what does it mean for Christians to "receive" (*dechomai*, as above) the sword of the Spirit? Paul's wording suggests it has two aspects: receiving God's word by listening to it[15] and wielding it as a sword by speaking it. The word of God to be received includes the gospel message (1 Thess 1:5–6) and "the teach-

15. New Testament writers commend a wholehearted reception of the word of God (Matt 13:18–23; Acts 17:11; 1 Thess 2:13; James 1:21–25).

ing of the apostles" (Acts 2:42) as it comes to us through Scripture and in the Church (1 Tim 3:15; 2 Tim 3:16). Reading, meditating on, and studying the word of God strengthens us by the power of the Spirit present in God's word. Once we have received the word, we are able to speak it by the power of the Spirit who lives in us. The sword of the word is a powerful defense, as Jesus showed in the wilderness when he quoted Scripture to turn aside the devil's temptations (Matt 4:3–10; Luke 4:3–12). At the same time "the sword of the Spirit" is an offensive weapon, enabling Christians to advance the kingdom of God by proclaiming the good news. Paul describes the gospel as "enormously powerful, capable of destroying . . . every pretension raising itself against the knowledge of God" (2 Cor 10:4–5; see also Rom 1:16; Heb 4:12). Perhaps Paul is also encouraging his readers to speak Spirit-inspired words of prophecy, teaching, preaching, and testimony within the community as he does in 1 Cor 14:26 and Col 3:16.

The six practices or attitudes that Paul has named with which Christians should arm themselves for spiritual battle are as follows:

1. The belt: base all you say and do on the gospel truth.
2. The breastplate: conduct yourself righteously, united to Christ.
3. The footwear: always be ready to share the gospel.
4. The shield: when troubles come, put your faith in God and his word.
5. The helmet: hope in God's salvation, no matter what.
6. The sword of the Spirit: listen to the word of God and proclaim it to advance Christ's kingdom.

Reflection and Application (6:13–17)

Practically speaking, how does this armor provide us with spiritual protection? If I wrap God's truthfulness around me, being honest and keeping my word even when it is to my disadvantage to do so (Ps 15:4), I gain the trust of others and protection from Satan's attacks on relationships. If I clothe myself with God's righteousness, I do not go to internet sites that feed my lust, nor do I engage in dishonest business practices. I avoid gossiping or criticizing others behind their backs. When I fail to do what is right, I repent quickly, trusting that the Lord will forgive me and "cleanse [me] from all unrighteousness" (1 John 1:9 RSV). When a catastrophe occurs, whether personal or national, I keep my head covered with the helmet of salvation, hoping in God's goodness and trusting in his power to work everything out for the good (Rom 8:28). When doubts or fears arise, I hold up the shield of faith, determined to trust in God's revealed word (Ps 56:4–5).

The strategy of putting on the armor of God has two basic results. First, I give the devil much less to work with! Second, if I keep myself close to the Lord, as Ps 91 says many times over, ultimately nothing can harm me.

People who have seen movies that sensationalize the devil's work might be disappointed by the rather ordinary practices that follow from Paul's teaching about spiritual warfare—pray, read Scripture, tell the truth, conduct oneself righteously, maintain attitudes of faith and hope. How is that conquering the devil? The fact is that 95 percent of overcoming evil spirits is basic Christian attitudes and conduct. This is why the Christian tradition, rather than focusing on the demonic, emphasizes repenting of sin, forgiving others, and practicing the virtues. These practices deny the devil points of entry.

Nevertheless, at times there is a need to directly confront demons with the power of Christ and free people from the devil's malice. The liturgical rites that lead up to baptism include exorcisms. The Church also has a Rite of Exorcism for people subject to demonic possession, an extreme form of Satanic domination. To avoid potential abuses, canon law restricts the use of this rite to priests specially designated by their bishops.

Far more common than cases of demonic possession is demonic oppression, a kind of spiritual bondage that afflicts people, often without their realizing it. Strange impulses, sinful habits that resist normal means of overcoming them, weird temptations, and significant emotional disorders *can* indicate demonic oppression, often in combination with psychological causes. Oppression of this kind can result from being the victim of abuse or some other trauma or from wrongdoing on the part of the person that opened the door to demonic activity. Common sins that have this effect include participating in occult practices, non-Christian religions, abortion, sexual perversions, or surrendering oneself to unrestrained lust, fury, or bitterness. In these cases what is needed is forgiveness toward those who wronged us, repentance of our sins with explicit renunciation of the wrong attitudes and behaviors, prayer for healing and the grace of the Spirit, and a renewed decision to "put on the armor of God." It helps to explicitly renounce any evil spirit associated with the problem and command it to leave in Jesus' name, exercising Christian freedom and authority over evil (Mark 16:17; Luke 10:19; James 4:7). Either clergy or lay people who have been trained can help others through this kind of prayer of "spiritual liberation" or "deliverance."[16] Counseling may also play an important role in the healing of the whole person.

16. Helpful resources include Neal Lozano, *Unbound: A Practical Guide to Deliverance from Evil Spirits* (Grand Rapids: Chosen, 2003).

The Priority of Prayer (6:18–20)

---

[18]With all prayer and supplication, pray at every opportunity in the Spirit. To that end, be watchful with all perseverance and supplication for all the holy ones [19]and also for me, that speech may be given me to open my mouth, to make known with boldness the mystery of the gospel [20]for which I am an ambassador in chains, so that I may have the courage to speak as I must.

OT: Exod 17:8–12; Isa 62:6–7
NT: Luke 18:1; Acts 28:20; 2 Cor 5:20; Phil 4:6–7; Col 4:2–6; 1 Thess 4:16–18
Catechism: Holy Spirit as master of prayer, 2623, 2652, 2672; unceasing prayer, 2742–45; intercession, 2634–36

Now Paul turns his attention to prayer, although it is presupposed in the instructions to "draw your strength from the Lord" and to "put on the armor of God" (vv. 10–11). Paul seems to envision prayer as the seventh and final piece of equipment (in the Bible, seven is a number that symbolizes completeness). Like "the sword of the Spirit," prayer functions both defensively and offensively.

6:18   Paul begins by urging his readers to **pray at every opportunity**—not just once a week or once a day, but whenever we can. This is essentially the same message found in 1 Thess 5:17, "pray without ceasing." Elsewhere Paul recommends praise and thanksgiving, but here he urges **all prayer and supplication**, that is, prayers of petition, entreating God for the help we need. We are instructed to pray **in the Spirit**. Prayer "in the Spirit" is prayer that relies on the help of the Holy Spirit.[17] The person who prays in the Spirit is conscious that prayer is not something we do on our own but that "the Spirit . . . comes to the aid of our weakness; for we do not know how to pray as we ought" (Rom 8:26). A person who prays "in the Spirit" asks for the Spirit's help and tries to surrender to God praying in and through him or her. To pray in the Spirit means much the same thing as to ask in Jesus' name, to seek to pray in union with Jesus and according to his will (John 14:13–14; 16:23–24; 1 John 5:14). Every form of Christian prayer can and should be offered "in the Spirit"—liturgical prayer, prayers like the Our Father or Hail Mary, silent prayer, conversational prayer, and prayer in tongues.[18]

---

17. Other texts that speak of the Spirit's role in prayer include 1 Cor 14:2, 14–16; Jude 20.

18. According to Gordon Fee, it is likely that by prayer "in the Spirit" Paul is referring especially, though not exclusively, to praying in tongues, since he uses nearly the identical expression in 1 Cor 14:14–15. "What Pauls says about this kind of praying in 1 Cor 14:1–5 and 14–19 demonstrates that he engaged in it regularly and encouraged the believers in Corinth to do so as well." Interpreting "pray . . . in the Spirit" this way means one needs to understand prayer in tongues not only as "speaking mysteries

Next Paul adds, **be watchful with all perseverance.** The verb "be watchful" literally means "stay awake." Often people's best "opportunity" to pray is early in the morning or late at night, so the encouragement to stay awake is quite appropriate. Being watchful also implies staying spiritually alert, like soldiers on guard duty. Jesus' words to his disciples in the garden of Gethsemane come to mind: "Could you not watch with me one hour? . . . The spirit indeed is willing, but the flesh is weak" (Matt 26:40–41 RSV). It is persevering prayer that obtains what it seeks (Luke 11:5–11; 18:1–8; see also 2 Cor 12:7–10). Using the verb form of the word translated here as "perseverance," Luke tells us four times in Acts that after the resurrection the apostles and the church "devoted themselves" to prayer.[19]

What should we pray for? Paul first urges his readers to entreat God **for all the holy ones,** all Christians. Although elsewhere Paul urges that prayers be offered "for everyone" and "for kings and for all in authority" (1 Tim 2:1–2), it is clear from his own practice reported at the beginning of his letters (e.g., Eph 1:15–19; Phil 1:3–11; Col 1:3–11) that Paul's first priority was to pray for strength, †knowledge, endurance, and love for fellow Christians. The Mass reflects this priority by summoning us to pray for the needs of the entire Church in the prayer of the faithful and as the first petition in the extended intercessions of the Good Friday liturgy.

Paul then asks for prayers for himself. Rather than ask for acquittal by the court or for comfort and strength in his imprisonment, the Apostle asks for prayers that he may proclaim the †gospel right where he is.[20] With a touch of irony, he describes himself as **an ambassador in chains.** An ambassador is a duly authorized representative of a government; Paul represents the kingdom of God and its sovereign, the †Messiah Jesus. While an ambassador might wear a gold chain to indicate the dignity of his office, Paul's chains indicate he is not being treated with the honor that an ambassador deserves. He pays no attention to this but asks prayers that he might be effective in delivering the message entrusted to him, namely, **the mystery of the gospel** (3:1–9). First, he prays **that speech may be given me.** Other translations say "a message" or "words." It is not that St. Paul is at a loss for words! Rather, Paul depends on God inspiring him with the appropriate words on each occasion when he speaks. Second, he depends on God to strengthen him **with boldness** when he evangelizes. This is so important that Paul repeats this idea in the next

6:19–20

---

to God, or praising and blessing God . . . but [as] a way of engaging the enemy in the ongoing conflict" (*God's Empowering Presence* [Peabody, MA: Hendrickson, 1994], 730–31).

19. Acts 1:14; 2:42, 46; 6:4.

20. See the introduction for more on Paul's apostolate while in prison.

phrase, **so that I may have the courage to speak as I must**. The same Greek root (*parrēsia-*), meaning "boldness" or "fearlessness" in speech, is used in both phrases. Evangelization is never merely a human act; it always depends on God's active involvement for the right words and for spiritual courage to be effective. Prayer makes this possible.

Paul believes that prayer is powerful in its effects. Prayer is not simply to make us feel better but rather to bring about God's intervention in history. God has chosen to honor his people by making us partners in accomplishing his will not only by doing good and proclaiming the gospel but also by praying for the spread of the gospel and the needs of our brothers and sisters. God waits on the prayer of his people.

Closing Greetings (6:21–24)

> [21]**So that you also may have news of me and of what I am doing, Tychicus, my beloved brother and trustworthy minister in the Lord, will tell you everything.** [22]**I am sending him to you for this very purpose, so that you may know about us and that he may encourage your hearts.**
>
> [23]**Peace be to the brothers, and love with faith, from God the Father and the Lord Jesus Christ.** [24]**Grace be with all who love our Lord Jesus Christ in immortality.**

NT: Col 4:7–9; 2 Thess 3:16

Catechism: communion of the saints in charity, 953, 959; charity as friendship and communion, 1829; solidarity and Christian brotherhood, 1939

Paul concludes his letter to the Ephesians and to the others to whom this letter is sent with a brief introduction of the bearer of the letter and a greeting that amounts to a final blessing.

6:21–22   There was no public postal service in the Roman Empire, so letters were entrusted to a reliable person to deliver by hand. Paul's practice was to send his letters by someone on his missionary team, in this case Tychicus. The messenger would serve the community in other ways, by giving them news of Paul and perhaps relaying additional instructions and exhortation (like Judas and Silas in Acts 15:32). Upon returning to Paul, the messenger would be in a position to report about the community's progress. In the case of a circular letter, intended for more than one community, the messenger might visit and read the letter in each place.

Tychicus is mentioned several other times in the New Testament. He was a trusted colleague of Paul's from the Roman province of Asia (whose capital

John Paul II's Life of Prayer

LIVING TRADITION

Those who were close to Pope John Paul II testify that prayer "at every opportunity in the Spirit" was at the center of his spiritual life. Besides his daily routine of Mass, the Liturgy of the Hours, the rosary, and an hour or two of silent prayer, the pope would often study or write in the presence of the Holy Eucharist. Those who joined him for liturgy in his private chapel often heard him pray before Mass and after communion with deep sighs reminiscent of Rom 8:26. Often as Pope John Paul II rode in his Popemobile, smiling and waving to the people, he would pray in the Spirit for the crowds that came out to greet him. During televised liturgies, the countless millions who watched close-ups of his face were fascinated by what they saw. "Even during the lengthy Masses, his face was not the face of someone presiding over a great public ceremony. It was the face of a man lost in prayer, living in a dimension beyond words."[a]

a. George Weigel, *Witness to Hope* (New York: HarperCollins, 1999), 364.

was Ephesus) who accompanied Paul to Jerusalem at the end of his third missionary journey with the financial gift he brought from the †Gentile churches (Acts 20:4). Elsewhere Paul speaks of possibly sending Tychicus to Crete (Titus 3:12) and of having sent him to Ephesus on another occasion (2 Tim 4:12). Paul describes Tychicus as a **beloved brother and trustworthy minister in the Lord.**

This text provides one of the strongest links between this letter and the letter to the Colossians, since Eph 6:21–22 is nearly identical to Col 4:7–8. Thirty-two words are exactly the same. The simplest explanation is that Ephesians and Colossians were written and sent close to the same time, with Paul or a secretary tacking on the same commendation of the bearer of the letter.[21]

6:23–24 It was common in Greco-Roman letters of the first century to conclude with a prayer-wish for the recipients of the letter. Paul also concludes this way but uses language that is distinctively Christian and reflects the content of his letter. If Ephesians was read to its original recipients during the liturgy, as seems likely, these final words would have been heard as a blessing from Paul at the end of the "sermon." The **peace** that comes from God the Father and †Messiah Jesus has been an important theme of this letter (2:14–18); so have God's **love**

21. Some scholars interpret this as an indication that Ephesians was written later by a disciple of Paul's in imitation of Colossians (see the introduction and "Who Wrote Ephesians?" on www.Catholic ScriptureCommentary.com).

and **grace** and the response of **faith**.[22] This prayer-wish is not directed exclusively "to you," the original recipients of the letter, but **to the brothers**, that is, to fellow Christians (male and female) and to **all who love our Lord Jesus Christ**. Paul anticipates his letter will reach a wider circle of readers who share a personal relationship with Jesus—they love *our* †Lord. The concluding words **in immortality** may refer to the eternal future of those who belong to Jesus or to the way his true disciples cling to him "with love undying" (RSV).

22. Examining Paul's use of these terms in Ephesians is instructive: peace (1:2; 2:14–18; 4:3; 6:15); God's love (1:4; 2:4; 3:17, 19; 5:2, 25); Christian love (1:15; 4:2, 15–16; 5:2, 25, 28, 33); grace (1:6–7; 2:5, 7–8; 4:7); and faith (1:15; 2:8; 3:12, 17).

Suggested Resources

From the Christian Tradition

Aquinas, St. Thomas. *Commentary on Saint Paul's Epistle to the Ephesians*. Translated by Matthew L. Lamb. Aquinas Scripture Series 2. Albany, NY: Magi, 1966. Careful exposition in light of the whole of Scripture and the questions of classical theology.

Edwards, Mark J., ed. *Galatians, Ephesians, Philippians*. ACCS. Downers Grove, IL: InterVarsity, 1999. Selections from patristic writings on every passage of the biblical text.

St. John Chrysostom. *Homilies on the Epistle to the Ephesians*. Twenty-four sermons that provide a fascinating example of pastoral preaching and teaching on the Bible. Each sermon includes exposition followed by exhortation. Available online or in print. See volume 13 of *A Select Library of the Nicene and Post-Nicene Fathers of the Christian Church*, Series 1. Edited by Philip Schaff et al. 1889. Reprinted Peabody, MA: Hendrickson, 1994.

Scholarly Commentaries

Lincoln, Andrew T. *Ephesians*. Word Biblical Commentary. Waco: Word, 1990. A carefully researched study by an Anglican scholar that interprets Ephesians as authored by a follower of Paul who adapted material from Colossians and Romans to speak to a later generation.

MacDonald, Margaret Y. *Colossians and Ephesians*. Sacra Pagina. Collegeville, MN: Liturgical Press, 2000. A social-scientific analysis to understand what might be happening in the communities addressed by the letter.

O'Brien, Peter T. *The Letter to the Ephesians*. Pillar New Testament Commentary. Grand Rapids: Eerdmans, 1999. A balanced and readable commentary by a Protestant scholar that gathers the best from twentieth-century Ephesians scholarship; offers strong arguments in favor of Paul's authorship.

Schnackenburg, Rudolf. *The Epistle to the Ephesians*. Edinburgh: T&T Clark, 1991; originally published in German in 1982. Solid commentary that includes a study of the influence of Ephesians through history (thirty-two pages) and an excursus on the Church in Ephesians (seventeen pages).

Midlevel Commentaries

Casciaro, Jose Maria, et al., eds. *The Navarre Bible: The Captivity Epistles*. Dublin: Four Courts, 1992; originally published in Spanish in 1981. Commentary with quotations from Church documents and the writings of popes and saints, especially St. Josemaria Escrivá, founder of Opus Dei (seventy-eight pages on Ephesians, including the English and Latin text).

Stott, John R. W. *The Message of Ephesians: God's New Society*. The Bible Speaks Today. Downers Grove, IL: InterVarsity, 1986. A well-written, pastoral exposition by a prominent evangelical Anglican with rich insight into the meaning of Ephesians for Christian faith and life.

Popular Works

Hahn, Scott, and Curtis Mitch. *The Letters of St. Paul to the Galatians and Ephesians*. Ignatius Study Bible. San Francisco: Ignatius, 2005. Twelve pages on Ephesians, including text, notes, and study questions.

Smiles, Vincent M. *First Thessalonians, Philippians, Second Thessalonians, Colossians, Ephesians*. New Collegeville Bible Commentary. Collegeville, MN: Liturgical Press, 2005. Twenty-six pages on Ephesians.

Wright, Tom. *Paul for Everyone: The Prison Letters—Ephesians, Philippians, Colossians, Philemon*. 2nd ed. Louisville: Westminster John Knox, 2004. A highly readable commentary by a prominent evangelical Anglican biblical scholar and bishop; a helpful glossary and seventy-three pages on Ephesians.

Theology of Ephesians

Lincoln, Andrew T., and A. J. M. Wedderburn. *The Theology of the Later Pauline Letters*. New Testament Theology. Cambridge: Cambridge University Press, 1993. Theological summary of Lincoln's lengthy commentary (see above) in ninety rich and readable pages.

Pastoral Resources

Cantalamessa, Raniero. *Loving the Church*. Cincinnati: St. Anthony Messenger, 2005. Meditations on Ephesians originally given to the papal household.

Paul and Pauline Theology

Fitzmyer, Joseph A. "Paul," in *New Jerome Biblical Commentary*, edited by Raymond Brown et al., 1329–37. Englewood Cliffs, NJ: Prentice Hall, 1990.

Fitzmyer, Joseph A. "Pauline Theology," in *New Jerome Biblical Commentary*, edited by Raymond Brown et al., 1382–1416. Englewood Cliffs, NJ: Prentice Hall, 1990.

Gorman, Michael J. *Apostle of the Crucified Lord: A Theological Introduction to Paul and His Letters*. Grand Rapids: Eerdmans, 2004. Helpful overview by a Methodist biblical scholar.

Hawthorne, Gerald F., Ralph P. Martin, and Daniel G. Reid, eds. *Dictionary of Paul and His Letters*. Downers Grove, IL: InterVarsity, 1993. Competent articles from an evangelical Protestant perspective on a broad range of Pauline topics including historical background and key theological ideas.

Matera, Frank J. *New Testament Theology: Exploring Unity and Diversity*. Louisville: Westminster John Knox, 2007. Exposition of the theology of each Pauline letter in relation to the other theological traditions in the New Testament.

Glossary

The glossary explains key terms used in Ephesians as well as grammatical, literary, theological, or other technical terms used in the commentary. Words can be used in a variety of ways. The precise meaning (or meanings) in each instance is ascertained by considering both a word's possible meanings and the context in which it occurs.

Christology: theological understanding of Christ, especially of his being both divine and human.

disputed letters: six New Testament letters that bear Paul's name but whose authorship has been questioned by scholars: Ephesians, Colossians, 2 Thessalonians, 1 and 2 Timothy, and Titus.

ecclesiology: theological understanding of the Church.

eschatology, eschatological (from Greek *eschata*, "last things"): theological understanding of all that concerns the end of human history, the glorious return of the Christ, the resurrection of the dead, the last judgment, and eternal life in the kingdom. According to the New Testament, the end begins with Jesus' passion and resurrection, which is the transition from the former age to the new and final age of salvation history. Ephesians is often described as having a *realized eschatology* because it focuses on the blessings of the new age that Christians already enjoy (that is, are already realized; 1:3–14; 2:6). Nevertheless, the letter also points to a *future eschatology* (1:18; 2:7; 5:5).

faith (Greek *pistis*): (1) the response to the gospel that brings salvation and a right relationship with God (Eph 2:8; 3:17); in Paul, faith is a relationship term that entails belief in the truth about Jesus (his having risen from the dead, his being **Messiah, Lord**, and Son of God) and faithfulness, characterized by trust, surrender, and obedience (Rom 1:5; 10:8–10; Gal 2:20); (2) the content of the gospel the Church believes, Christian doctrine (Eph 4:5, 13); (3) confidence in God and in his word (2 Cor 5:7; Eph 6:16).

favor: *see* **grace**.

first installment (Greek *arrabōn*): a business term that refers to the down payment guaranteeing payment of a future sum. Paul refers to the Holy Spirit as the Christian's first installment on an eternal inheritance (1:13–14; 2 Cor 1:22; 5:5).

flesh (Greek *sarx*): (1) the body (2:14; 5:29, 31); (2) fallen human nature characterized by sinful inclinations and disordered desires (2:3; 1 Cor 3:1–3; Gal 5:19–21); (3) biological descent or relationship (2:11); (4) what is merely human (6:5) as in the phrase "flesh and blood" (6:12). Elsewhere in Scripture "flesh" has the normal anatomical meaning of muscle or soft tissue (Luke 24:39).

Gentiles (Greek *ethnē*), also translated as "nations": (1) people of non-Jewish descent; (2) people who are not a part of God's people, who do not know God, and who live immorally and unjustly ("pagans"). In Ephesians, Paul addresses his readers as Gentiles in the first sense (3:1) and exhorts them not to act like Gentiles in the second sense (4:17).

glory (Greek *doxa*): (1) honor; (2) majesty or greatness that is manifest; (3) splendor or brilliance. Ephesians speaks of God's glory (1:12, 14; 3:16), of the "glory," or excellence, of his grace (1:6), and of the glory of his inheritance shared with his people (1:18). (4) To ascribe glory to God (3:21) is to acknowledge his greatness.

gospel: (1) the good news of salvation through the death and resurrection of Jesus Christ that calls for a response of faith and repentance; (2) the Christian message in its entirety. "Gospel" later came to refer to one of the four canonical narratives of the life of Jesus.

grace (Greek *charis*): (1) an attitude of favor, generosity, or magnanimity, especially on the part of God (2:7); (2) a gift, benefit, or other consequence of this attitude, such as forgiveness of sins, the ability to act rightly, etc. (1:2, 6); (3) a gift of the Spirit to a person for the benefit of the Church, a charism (3:7; 4:7). The distinguishing character of "grace" is that it is freely given, not earned.

guarantee: *see* **first installment**.

heaven, heavenly realm, heavens (Greek *ouranos, epouranioi*): (1) the dwelling place of God, the risen Christ, and the holy angels; the invisible realm located metaphorically above creation (1:3, 20; 2:6) to which Christians ultimately belong (2 Cor 5:1–2; Phil 3:20); (2) a way of describing the totality of the created universe when combined with the word "earth" (1:10); (3) a middle zone between God's dwelling and the material universe in which the angelic **principalities and authorities**—both good and evil—exercise power over the world (3:10; 6:12). Elsewhere in the New Testament "heaven" is sometimes used as a reverent circumlocution for "God" (especially in Matthew in the phrase "kingdom of heaven"; also Luke 15:18; John 3:27).

Hellenistic: adjective referring to (1) the period of Greek political dominance of the eastern Mediterranean between the conquest of Alexander the Great (325 BC) and the consolidation of Roman power (148–30 BC); (2) Greek cultural influence (language, education, arts, religion, and political ideals) beginning in the Hellenistic period and continuing in the Roman Empire.

holy (Greek *hagios*): (1) in God, the quality of being completely other, transcendent; (2) in humans, the quality of being set apart for God, of belonging to him. Although the word primarily refers to one's relationship with God rather than to moral virtue, Scripture teaches that only a righteous way of living corresponds to God's holiness. In Ephesians, "holy" is used often to refer to God's people ("holy ones" or "saints").

hope: (1) a confident expectation (not merely a wish) regarding God's promised future blessings, in particular, eternal life (2:12; 1 Thess 4:13); (2) the eternal future itself (1:18).

imperative: a grammatical term referring to verbs that convey a command or instruction, for example, "do not get drunk on wine . . . but be filled with the Spirit" (5:18). In the last three chapters of Ephesians, thirty-six verbs in the imperative instruct readers about how they are to live their new identity in Christ.

indicative: a grammatical term referring to verbs that describe matters of fact— what happens or happened, what was, is, or will be. In the first three chapters of Ephesians, verbs in the indicative recount what God has done in Christ and the change that it has brought about for believers.

inheritance (also **heritage**): a share in the land that God promised to Abraham and his descendents (Deut 4:21; see sidebar on p. 43). As the story of salvation progressed, the understanding of this inheritance deepened, so that in the New Testament it represents eternal life with God (Col 1:12). "Inheritance" is also used to refer to Israel as God's special possession among all the peoples of the earth (Deut 32:9; Ps 79:1).

knowledge: understanding of God, Christ, or the truth that is more than knowledge of concepts or words, but is rather understanding that grows out of relationship with God and interior experience of the persons or things that are known (see sidebars on p. 49 and p. 100). To "make known" is to disclose or reveal and refers to divine revelation (e.g., 1:9; 3:3–5), the preaching of the gospel (6:19), as well as ordinary matters.

live (Greek *peripateō*, "walk"): to conduct oneself in a particular manner. In Ephesians, Paul uses this word five times to refer to following the Christian way of life.

Lord (Greek *kyrios*): (1) in secular usage, a term of respectful address (like "sir"), a title of a slave's master, of a man of high social standing, or of the Roman emperor; (2) in the **Septuagint**, *kyrios* (Lord) translates the divine name **YHWH** and refers to God; (3) in the New Testament "Lord" is used as a title of Jesus indicating his divine sovereignty (Phil 2:11). The Church uses this title in the liturgy when it says, "*Kyrie, eleison*" ("Lord, have mercy").

LORD (small caps): the way that most English Bibles translate the divine name **YHWH** in the Old Testament. Sometimes YHWH is represented by "GOD" with small caps, as in the phrase "Lord GOD" (Lord YHWH).

Messiah (from Hebrew *mashiah*, "anointed one"; Greek *Christos*): the descendant of King David promised by God, whom many Jews of Jesus' day hoped would come to restore the kingdom to Israel. The early Christians recognized Jesus as the Christ, the Messiah promised in the Jewish Scriptures, whose kingdom is universal. (See sidebar on p. 29.)

middle voice: a verb form in Greek between the active and the passive voice in which the subject acts either on him- or herself (reflexive: "I wash myself") or for him- or herself.

mystery (Greek *mystērion*, "secret"): God's saving plan kept secret for ages but now revealed by the Holy Spirit to the apostles and prophets for the Church (3:3–9). The content of the mystery is the gospel and the revelation of Christ himself (6:19); it includes God's intention to save Gentiles as well as Jews. The biblical use of the term should be distinguished from related theological uses: the "paschal mystery" in reference to the saving death and resurrection of Jesus; the mystery of God who surpasses human comprehension; events in the life of Jesus that disclose his identity and mission; the term for sacraments ("mysteries") in the Eastern churches.

nations: *see* **Gentiles**.

passive voice: a verb form in which the subject is acted on ("you were saved"). Sometimes Scripture uses the passive voice to indicate that God is the one who does the acting. In his prayer in 3:14–19 Paul employs five verbs in the "divine passive."

perfect tense: a Greek tense that is used to indicate an action completed in the past whose results continue into the present. For example, "I have been crucified with Christ; it is no longer I who live, but Christ who lives in me" (Gal 2:20 RSV).

present tense: usually indicates a habitual, continuous, or repeated action in Greek.

principalities and authorities (also powers, dominions, rulers, etc.): spiritual beings created by God who exercise power and influence in the world, some of whom are hostile to God and oppose his people and the spread of the gospel. Nevertheless, Christ has triumphed over them by means of the cross (Col 2:15) and has been exalted over them (Eph 1:21). Christians are called to stand firm against them by drawing strength from Christ and putting on the armor of God (6:10–19; see sidebar on p. 93).

prophets: individuals called by God to speak his word to his people and to the nations. Old Testament prophets often had to deliver a challenging message regarding sin, judgment, and repentance and thus were often met with persecution. In Ephesians, prophets, like apostles, play a foundational role in the Church's life as authorized recipients and spokespersons of divine revelation (2:20; 3:5). Along with evangelists and pastor-teachers, they equip the members of the Church for the work of ministry to build up the body of Christ (4:11–13; see sidebar on p. 88).

pseudonymous (from the Greek for "false name"): published under the name of an important figure, usually from the distant past, for the purpose of linking the work to the life or writing of that figure.

rhetoric: the science and art of persuasive oratory described by Aristotle and his successors (see the introduction).

saints: *see* **holy**.

Semitic: an adjective referring to Semites, thought to be descendants of Noah's son Shem, or to their languages or cultures. The languages include Hebrew, Aramaic, and Arabic; the ethnic groups include Jews and Arabs.

Septuagint: Greek translation of the Hebrew Bible dating from the third or second century BC. The title means "seventy" in Greek, from a tradition that seventy scholars did the translation (the abbreviation is LXX, Latin for "70"). As the Bible used by Greek-speaking Jews and Christians, it is often quoted in the New Testament.

Torah (Hebrew for "law" or "instruction"): the first five books of the Bible, attributed to Moses and thus also called the law of Moses, the books of Moses, or the Pentateuch. Torah is also used more broadly to refer to all God's teachings on how to live an upright life in covenant relationship with him.

type: a person, place, institution, or event in an earlier stage of salvation history that foreshadows God's action at a later stage in Christ, the Church, the sacraments, or the future kingdom.

undisputed letters: seven New Testament letters attributed to Paul that scholars almost universally agree were authored by the Apostle: Romans, 1 and 2 Corinthians, Galatians, Philippians, 1 Thessalonians, and Philemon. *See also* **disputed letters**.

walk: *see* **live**.

world (Greek *kosmos*): (1) creation or the universe and all it contains (1:4); (2) all human beings; (3) human society insofar as it is opposed to God and under the sway of the devil (2:2; 1 John 5:19).

wrath: (1) God's uncompromising opposition to evil expressed in his just punishment of wrongdoing in the present and at the end of history (5:6; Col 3:6); (2) excessive or unrelenting human anger (4:31; Col 3:8).

YHWH: God's holy name, revealed to Moses at the burning bush (Exod 3:14). According to ancient custom, Jews refrain from pronouncing the divine name out of reverence; when reading the Scriptures aloud they substitute the title "the LORD" (Hebrew *Adonai*) for the divine name. The form YHWH (called the Tetragrammaton) is used to reflect the four letters of the Hebrew script, which has no vowels; the word "Yahweh" is sometimes used to approximate the original pronunciation. *See* also **LORD**.

Index of Pastoral Topics

This index indicates where Ephesians mentions various topics that may be useful for evangelization, catechesis, apologetics, and other forms of pastoral ministry.

Index of Sidebars

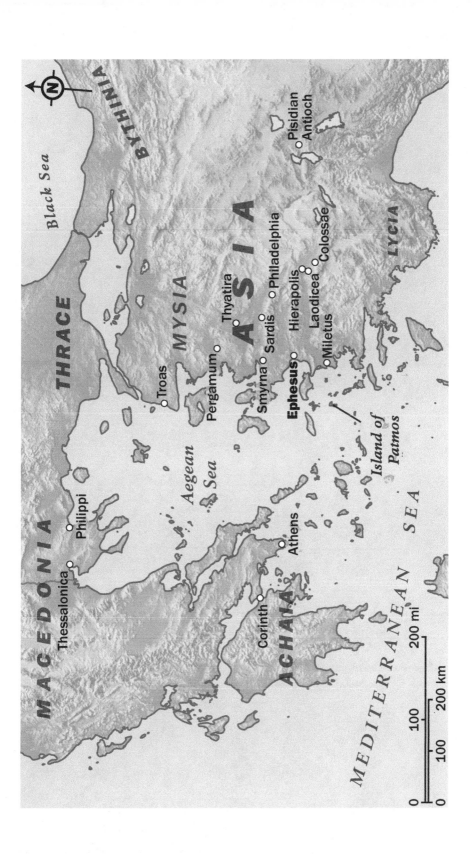